VisiCalc®

HOME AND OFFICE
COMPANION

VisiCalc®

HOME AND OFFICE
COMPANION

By David M. Castlewitz
and Lawrence J. Chisausky
with Patricia Kronberg

Illustrations by
L.D. Chukman

Disclaimer of Warranties and Limitation of Liabilities. The authors have taken due care in preparing this book and the programs in it, including research, development, and testing to ascertain their effectiveness. The authors and the publishers make no expressed or implied warranty of any kind with regard to these programs nor the supplementary documentation in this book. In no event shall the authors or the publishers be liable for incidental or consequential damages in connection with or arising out of the furnishing, performance, or use of any of these programs.

VisiCalc is a registered trademark of VisiCorp. *VisiCalc: Home and Office Companion* is not sponsored or approved by or connected with VisiCorp. All references to VisiCalc in the text of this book are to the trademark of VisiCorp.

Apple is a registered trademark of Apple Computer Inc.
SuperCalc is a trademark of Sorcim Corporation.
TRS-80 is a trademark of Tandy Corportation.
PET is a registered trademark and CBM is a trademark of
 Commodore Business Machines.

The model In Stock Position was contributed by Mary Borchers, Osborne/McGraw-Hill.

The model Professional Services Fee Analysis is based on a method developed by Howard L. Shenson at the seminar "How to Build and Maintain Your Own Part-Time/Full-Time Consulting Seminar," copyright © 1982, Howard L. Shenson, Inc., 20121 Ventura Blvd., Woodland Hills, CA. Used with permission.

Published by
OSBORNE/McGraw-Hill
630 Bancroft Way
Berkeley, California 94710
U.S.A

For information on other Osborne books, translations and distributors outside of the U.S.A., please write Osborne/McGraw-Hill at the above address.

VISICALC®: HOME AND OFFICE COMPANION

ISBN 0-931988-50-0

2 3 4 5 6 7 8 9 0 DLDL 89098765432

Cover illustration by Gaynelle Grover.

"As a general rule, the most successful man in life is the man who has the best information."

Benjamin Disraeli

CONTENTS

INTRODUCTION

VisiCalc®, a program distributed by VisiCorp™ (formerly Personal Software Inc.), was written by Dan Bricklin and Bob Frankston of Software Arts, Inc. Simply stated, VisiCalc is an "electronic spread sheet" program that makes working with pencils, paper, and a calculator old-fashioned. With VisiCalc, the paper is your computer display, the pencils, your cursor and keyboard, and the calculator is your personal computer.

Fast, efficient, and an ideal tool, the VisiCalc program has become extremely popular among users of personal computers. This book presents 50 VisiCalc models; some have been designed for home uses, and others for business applications. Each model is an actual working sample and can be used as it is presented in this book. However, these models cannot represent the gamut of the VisiCalc program's usefulness, and many of the models can be expanded to meet your individual needs. In addition, the algorithms and VisiCalc modeling techniques presented here, combined with your own needs and imagination, may help you design many new and useful models.

All the models in this book were created with the Apple® version of the VisiCalc program, but they should perform well on other machines, including the IBM® Personal Computer, the Radio Shack TRS-80™, and the Commodore PET® and CBM™. The models have been tested for accuracy by the authors on versions 3.2 and 3.3 of the VisiCalc program. The printouts and listings were produced on an Epson MX-80 dot matrix printer using condensed type (16.5 characters per inch) for the sample printout, and regular type (10 characers per inch) for the coordinate listings.

SuperCalc™ users can enhance these models to take advantage of additional SuperCalc™ features.

How to Use This Book

If your computer can run the VisiCalc program, you can enter and use any of these 50 models

immediately. In most cases, you will merely enter your own data in place of the sample data or substitute a label or list of entries to make a model more meaningful. The descriptive narrative for each model will suggest ways to customize each sample model.

A printout and listing are included for each model. The sample printout will show you the organization of the model and will indicate both the data you are required to input and the computations performed by the model itself. The shaded areas on the sample report represent the values you must provide; the values in the unshaded areas are calculated as part of your VisiCalc model.

The listings show exactly how each model was keyed in to produce the printout shown. You can key in these listings just as you would key in a program printed in BASIC or Pascal. Entries are provided by grid location, with each grid location referenced by its VisiCalc coordinates. The greater than symbol (>) marks the beginning of each grid entry; it is followed by the coordinates of that grid and a colon. You should key into each grid location only those characters which follow the colon.

One of the features that makes the VisiCalc program neat and easy to use is its ability to format data. If any grid location requires a formatted entry, the format command is included in the listing. For example, entering the /FL characters creates a left-justified entry. Grid entries without format controls default to the general or global format that has been set for that model. Global formats are printed at the end of each listing; the common VisiCalc defaults, /W1 and /GC9 (one window, nine characters per column), need not be entered into a specific model.

When you want to use one of these models, enter it exactly as it is shown in the listing. Use the same data, formulas, and labels. Check your results against the sample printout, and, if the answers match, the model has been entered correctly. You can then change the data and labels and expand the model to serve your particular needs. Don't forget to save the model on disk for future use.

When you are loading any model from a disk you may see an ERROR message print for many calculations. This message is caused by the model's forward and backward referencing of data. Not all the equations can be solved during the first pass through the model. Pressing the exclamation point (!) recalculation command over those grid locations should correct the ERROR message.

Parameters required to print each sample printout are given for each model. In printing your model, keep in mind the line length limit of your printer. Some models may spread farther across than your printer can print; when this happens, you must print your model on two pages. However, if your printer can condense print, you may not have to print on two pages. Some parts of some models, such as lookup tables and calculation areas, need not be printed.

Some Special VisiCalc Features

This book does not teach you how to use the VisiCalc program; refer to the VisiCalc manual by VisiCorp for those instructions. This book and its models give you practical experience with many VisiCalc program features. In combination with the VisiCorp manual and reference card, this may be the best way to learn to use the VisiCalc program.

One feature that you will find incorporated into some models is the @LOOKUP table which permits you to define values based on a variable. Events Scheduling, for instance, uses the @LOOKUP table to establish clock time based on elapsed minutes as events are completed. In that model, the table consists of two adjacent columns, but @LOOKUP can be used with adjacent rows as well.

Two common, global format commands are /G$ and /GRM. The G$ format command creates a dollar-and-cents entry, while the GRM format command suppresses the VisiCalc program's automatic recalculation feature and allows recalculation only when you request it (use the exclamation point). This recalculation feature is useful when there is a lot of data to enter because you are not required to wait between entries while equations are recalculated.

The replicate command, /R, is a timesaving feature that can be used when a series of the same calculation is performed or a running total is kept. Unfortunately, the listings cannot show the use of the /R command, because each formula, although replicated, is listed in its entirety and the /R command is not part of the grid formula.

You can decide when to use the replicate command. For example, look at the Personal Finance and Budget Plan listing. The formulas at grid locations E83 through E93 could easily be entered using the replicate command. You would first enter the formula at E83, then replicate it from E84 through E93, indicating the first variable (E79) as no change (N), and the second variable (C83) as relative (R).

One of the most useful features of the VisiCalc program, and certainly its greatest advantages over pencil and paper, is its ability to perform "what if" calculations. When you have a model running on your computer, you can change any value, and the VisiCalc program will recalculate the entire model based on the value you have entered. This makes it easy to test data for business and personal planning.

Many other features and functions are used in the models in this book, and you will undoubtedly find ways to enhance them further by applying your own knowledge of the VisiCalc program.

* * *

If you find any errors in the models presented here, the authors would appreciate your writing a brief description of the error and its correction, if known. Suggestions for improvements to the models are also welcome. Please write to the authors, in care of the publisher, at the following address:

David Castlewitz, et al.
c/o OSBORNE/McGraw-Hill
630 Bancroft Way
Berkeley, CA 94710

LOANS AND INVESTMENTS

BOND PORTFOLIO

Calculating costs and value of your holdings is an excellent application for the VisiCalc program. This model is for a bond portfolio. The calculations shown here represent a sample of bond market characteristics you may wish to follow. In preparing your own model, you can add or delete any items you prefer to calculate.

The number of columns needed for this model totaled more than 132 print characters, so the printout is on two pages. If you find that confusing, you can horizontally change the axis by putting the bond names across the top, with the data and calculating fields along the left-hand side (Column A). Regardless of how it is organized, the calculations are basically the same. Simply substitute coordinates for the variables expressed in the formulas.

As daily prices change, key them into the model for an up-to-date bottom line on your holdings.

PRINT A1...L12, Page 1
M1...S12, Page 2

Model Run

BOND PORTFOLIO

BOND	INTEREST RATE	YEARS TO MATURITY	PAR VALUE	# HELD	VALUE OF INVESTMNT	COMM PAID	PURCH PRICE	COST PER BOND	NET COST	TOTAL COST	DAY'S HIGH
ABC 6S 92	.06	12	1000.00	3	3000.00	15.00	0.90	900.00	2700.00	2715.00	0.98
CDE 7S 85	.07	4	1000.00	2	2000.00	15.00	0.95	950.00	1900.00	1915.00	0.95
EF 7.5 87	.075	6	1000.00	1	1000.00	15.00	1.05	1050.00	1050.00	1065.00	0.96
MNX 8 90	.08	10	1000.00	5	5000.00	25.00	1.01	1010.00	5050.00	5075.00	1.03
TOTALS			4000.00	11	11000.00	70.00		3910.00	10700.00	10770.00	
AVERAGES			1000.00	2.75	2750.00	17.50	0.98	977.50	2675.00	2692.50	

Page 1

DAY'S LOW	CURR PRICE	HIGH VALUE	LOW VALUE	CURRENT VALUE	ANNUAL INTEREST	YIELD TO MATURITY
0.90	0.97	2940.00	2700.00	2910.00	60.00	.0719298
0.94	0.95	1900.00	1880.00	1900.00	70.00	.0846154
0.92	0.94	960.00	920.00	940.00	75.00	.0650407
0.98	0.99	5150.00	4900.00	4950.00	80.00	.0786070
		10950.00	10400.00	10700.00	285.00	0.30
		2737.50	2600.00	2675.00	71.25	0.08

Page 2

Listing

```
>A  5:"BOND                          >F12:@AVERAGE(F6...F9)
>A  6:"ABC 6S 92
>A  7:"CDE 7S 85                     >G  4:/FR"COMM
>A  8:"EF 7.5 87                     >G  5:/FR"PAID
>A  9:"MNX 8 90                      >G  6:15
>A10:/--                             >G  7:15
>A11:"TOTALS                         >G  8:15
>A12:"AVERAGES                       >G  9:25
                                     >G10:/--
>B  4:"INTEREST                      >G11:@SUM(G6...G9)
>B  5:"RATE                          >G12:@AVERAGE(G6...G9)
>B  6:/FL.06
>B  7:/FL.07                         >H  4:/FR"PURCH
>B  8:/FL.075                        >H  5:/FR"PRICE
>B  9:/FL.08                         >H  6:.9
>B10:/--                             >H  7:.95
                                     >H  8:1.05
>C  4:"YEARS TO                      >H  9:1.01
>C  5:"MATURITY                      >H10:/--
>C  6:/FL12                          >H12:@AVERAGE(H6...H9)
>C  7:/FL4
>C  8:/FL6                           >I  3:/FR"COST
>C  9:/FL10                          >I  4:/FR"PER
>C10:/--                             >I  5:/FR"BOND
                                     >I  6:+H6*D6
>D  5:"PAR VALUE                     >I  7:+H7*D7
>D  6:/F$1000                        >I  8:+H8*D8
>D  7:1000                           >I  9:+H9*D9
>D  8:1000                           >I10:/--
>D  9:1000                           >I11:@SUM(I6...I9)
>D10:/--                             >I12:@AVERAGE(I6...I9)
>D11:@SUM(D6...D9)
>D12:@AVERAGE(D6...D9)               >J  4:/FR"NET
                                     >J  5:/FR"COST
>E  1:"BOND PORT                     >J  6:+H6*F6
>E  5:"  # HELD                      >J  7:+H7*F7
>E  6:/FL3                           >J  8:+H8*F8
>E  7:/FL2                           >J  9:+H9*F9
>E  8:/FL1                           >J10:/--
>E  9:/FL5                           >J11:@SUM(J6...J9)
>E10:/--                             >J12:@AVERAGE(J6...J9)
>E11:/FL@SUM(E6...E9)
>E12:/FL@AVERAGE(E6...E9)            >K  4:/FR"TOTAL
                                     >K  5:/FR"COST
>F  1:"FOLIO                         >K  6:+G6+J6
>F  4:"VALUE OF                      >K  7:+G7+J7
>F  5:"INVESTMNT                     >K  8:+G8+J8
>F  6:+D6*E6                         >K  9:+G9+J9
>F  7:+D7*E7                         >K10:/--
>F  8:+D8*E8                         >K11:@SUM(K6...K9)
>F  9:+D9*E9                         >K12:@AVERAGE(K6...K9)
>F10:/--
>F11:@SUM(F6...F9)                   >L  4:/FR"DAY'S
```

```
>L  5:/FR"HIGH
>L  6:.98
>L  7:.95
>L  8:.96
>L  9:1.03
>L10:/--

>M  4:/FR"DAY'S
>M  5:/FR"LOW
>M  6:.9
>M  7:.94
>M  8:.92
>M  9:.98
>M10:/--

>N  4:/FR"CURR
>N  5:/FR"PRICE
>N  6:.97
>N  7:.95
>N  8:.94
>N  9:.99
>N10:/--

>O  4:/FR"HIGH
>O  5:/FR"VALUE
>O  6:+L6*F6
>O  7:+L7*F7
>O  8:+L8*F8
>O  9:+L9*F9
>O10:/--
>O11:@SUM(O6...O9)
>O12:@AVERAGE(O6...O9)

>P  4:/FR"LOW
>P  5:/FR"VALUE
>P  6:+M6*F6
>P  7:+M7*F7
>P  8:+M8*F8
>P  9:+M9*F9
```

```
>P10:/--
>P11:@SUM(P6...P9)
>P12:@AVERAGE(P6...P9)

>Q  4:/FR"CURRENT
>Q  5:/FR"VALUE
>Q  6:+N6*F6
>Q  7:+N7*F7
>Q  8:+N8*F8
>Q  9:+N9*F9
>Q10:/--
>Q11:@SUM(Q6...Q9)
>Q12:@AVERAGE(Q6...Q9)

>R  4:/FR"ANNUAL
>R  5:/FR"INTEREST
>R  6:+D6*B6
>R  7:+D7*B7
>R  8:+D8*B8
>R  9:+D9*B9
>R10:/--
>R11:@SUM(R6...R9)
>R12:@AVERAGE(R6...R9)

>S  4:/FR"YIELD TO
>S  5:/FR"MATURITY
>S  6:/FR+R6+(D6-I6/C6)/((I6+D6)/2)
>S  7:/FR+R7+(D7-I7/C7)/((I7+D7)/2)
>S  8:/FR+R8+(D8-I8/C8)/((I8+D8)/2)
>S  9:/FR+R9+(D9-I9/C9)/((I9+D9)/2)
>S10:/--
>S11:@SUM(S6...S9)
>S12:@AVERAGE(S6...S9)

/GC9
/GF$
/GOC
/GRA
/W1
```

STOCK PORTFOLIO

The VisiCalc program is a perfect tool for quickly analyzing a stock portfolio. As your portfolio grows, you can easily add the new purchases by adding rows to the model. You can also add columns for additional calculations you want to perform on each stock. Everything you want to know about a stock can be kept on your VisiCalc file.

One addition that can be made is to list separately your purchases for the same stock and keep an aggregate average price on file to use in calculating your gain or loss. You could also incorporate the *Dow Jones Industrial Average* index at the time of purchase and keep a plus (+) or minus (−) figure to reflect the stock's relative performance.

PRINT A1...H13

Model Run

```
              STOCK PORTFOLIO


   NAME OF   TICKER   NUMBER OF   PURCH    CURR    GAIN/    DIV PER    YIELD
   STOCK     SYMBOL   SHARES      PRICE    PRICE   LOSS     SHARE


   INT'L TEL   ITT    1000.00     34.50    33.00  -1500.00   0.00      0.00
   BALLY       BLY    1500.00     24.50    23.13  -2062.50   0.30      1.30
   BENDIX      BX     2000.00     59.75    66.50  13500.00   0.88      1.32
   MCDONALDS   MCD    1000.00     60.00    61.13   1130.00   0.99      1.62
                      ---------                  ---------           ---------
              TOTALS  5500.00                    11067.50              4.24
```

Listing

```
>A 5:"NAME OF
>A 6:"STOCK
>A 8:"INT'L TEL
>A 9:"BALLY
>A10:"BENDIX
>A11:"MCDONALDS

>B 5:"TICKER
>B 6:"SYMBOL
>B 8:"   ITT
>B 9:"   BLY
>B10:"    BX
>B11:"   MCD
>B13:"TOTALS

>C 1:"STOCK POR

>C 5:"NUMBER OF
>C 6:"SHARES
>C 8:1000
>C 9:1500
>C10:2000
>C11:1000
>C12:/--
>C13:@SUM(C8...C12)

>D 1:"TFOLIO
>D 5:/FR"PURCH
>D 6:/FR"PRICE
>D 8:34.5
>D 9:24.5
>D10:59.75
>D11:60
```

```
>E  5:/FR"CURR
>E  6:/FR"PRICE
>E  8:33
>E  9:23.125
>E10:66.5
>E11:61.13

>F  5:/FR"GAIN/
>F  6:/FR"LOSS
>F  8:(C8*E8)-(C8*D8)
>F  9:(C9*E9)-(C9*D9)
>F10:(C10*E10)-(C10*D10)
>F11:(C11*E11)-(C11*D11)
>F12:/--
>F13:@SUM(F8...F12)

>G  5:/FR"DIV PER
>G  6:/FR"SHARE
```

```
>G  8:.22
>G  9:.3
>G10:.88
>G11:.99

>H  5:/FR"YIELD
>H  8:(G8/E8)*100
>H  9:(G9/E9)*100
>H10:(G10/E10)*100
>H11:(G11/E11)*100
>H12:/--
>H13:@SUM(H8...H12)

/GC9
/GF$
/GOC
/GRA
/W1
```

PROMISSORY NOTES

The amount of money people owe you in personal or business notes represents an important asset. Banks and other lending institutions put a certain amount of value on such information when considering home mortgages or other loans, and the more organized your financial records are, the more impressive they will be to someone else.

The model presented here shows the disbursement of monies lent by Samson Enterprises to private individuals. Each note has principal, an annual interest rate, and a time factor expressed in days. The VisiCalc program has calculated the total interest due and the maturity value of each note.
PRINT A1...G16

Model Run

```
                    PROMISSORY NOTES

PAYEE:    SAMSON ENTERPRISES

BORROWER                  INTEREST        INTEREST MATURITY
(MARKER)        PRINCIPAL   RATE    DAYS    DUE     VALUE
========        =========   ====    ====    ===    =====
M. SMITH          400.00      6      60     4.00   404.00
D. JONES         1000.00     6.5     90    16.25  1016.25
H. MCDEY         1500.00     10      60    25.00  1525.00
R. SERIT          800.00      8     120    21.33   821.33
J. FRANKS         750.00     7.5     60     9.37   759.37
O. MANN           250.00      6      30     1.25   251.25
                ----------------------------------------
TOTALS:          4700.00                   77.21  4777.21
AVERAGES          783.33     7.33    70    12.87   796.20
```

Listing

```
>A  3:"PAYEE:                >C  1:"PROMISSOR
>A  5:"BORROWER              >C  3:"TERPRISES
>A  6:" (MARKER)             >C  6:"PRINCIPAL
>A  7:"========              >C  7:"=========
>A  8:"M. SMITH              >C  8:400
>A  9:"D. JONES              >C  9:1000
>A10:"H. MCDEY               >C10:1500
>A11:"R. SERIT               >C11:800
>A12:"J. FRANKS              >C12:750
>A13:"O. MANN                >C13:250
>A15:"TOTALS:                >C14:/--
>A16:"AVERAGES               >C15:/F$@SUM(C8...C13)
                             >C16:/F$@AVERAGE(C8...C13)
>B  3:"SAMSON EN
```

```
>D  1:"Y NOTES                      >F  8:+C8*(D8/100)*(E8/360)
>D  5:/FR"INTEREST                  >F  9:+C9*(D9/100)*(E9/360)
>D  6:/FR"RATE                      >F10:+C10*(D10/100)*(E10/360)
>D  7:"      ====                   >F11:+C11*(D11/100)*(E11/360)
>D  8:/FR6                          >F12:+C12*(D12/100)*(E12/360)
>D  9:/FR6.5                        >F13:+C13*(D13/100)*(E13/360)
>D10:/FR10                          >F14:/--
>D11:/FR8                           >F15:@SUM(F8...F13)
>D12:/FR7.5                         >F16:/F$@AVERAGE(F8...F13)
>D13:/FR6
>D14:/--                            >G  5:/FR"MATURITY
>D16:/F$@AVERAGE(D8...D13)          >G  6:/FR"VALUE
                                    >G  7:"      =====
>E  6:/FR"DAYS                      >G  8:+C8+F8
>E  7:"      ====                   >G  9:+C9+F9
>E  8:/FI60                         >G10:+C10+F10
>E  9:/FI90                         >G11:+C11+F11
>E10:/FI60                          >G12:+C12+F12
>E11:/FI120                         >G13:+C13+F13
>E12:/FI60                          >G14:/--
>E13:/FI30                          >G15:@SUM(G8...G13)
>E14:/--                            >G16:/F$@AVERAGE(G8...G13)
>E15:/FR
>E16:/FI@AVERAGE(E8...E13)          /GC9
                                    /GF$
>F  5:/FR"INTEREST                  /GOC
>F  6:/FR"DUE                       /GRA
>F  7:"        ===                  /W1
```

MAXIMUM LOAN AMOUNT

This VisiCalc model can help you assess the affordability of a loan, based on your monthly income, the term and interest of the loan, the percentage of your income toward repayment, and the percentage of the loan payment that is applied to taxes, insurance, and assessments.

Once the basic model is in memory, you can experiment with different interest rates, terms, and down payments to generate a maximum loan amount that fits your budget.

The formula used to find the principal on the maximum loan amount is

$$P = R*N*(1-1/(1+I/N)*N*Y)/I$$

where R = the regular payment amount,
  N = the number of payments per year,
  I = the annual interest rate, and
  Y = the number of years (or term of the loan).

To make this calculation work properly, it has been broken into four parts, labeled CALC 1 through CALC 4. They appear in the area surrounded by asterisks in the printout. The result of CALC 4 is the maximum loan amount, which is repeated at the top of the report next to its title.

PRINT A1...G23

Model Run

```
                MAXIMUM LOAN AMOUNT


MONTHLY INCOME:       3500.00      MAXIMUM LOAN AMT:  62375.53
% OF INCOME TOWARDS REPAY:  30
PERCENTAGE OF LOAN PAYMNT           DOWN PAYMENT % :   10
TOWARDS TAX,INS,ASSMNTS  :  35      AFFORDABLE HOUSE:  69306.14

                                    DOWN PAYMENT DUE:   6930.61

TERM OF THE LOAN IN YEARS:  29
INTEREST ON THE LOAN     :  14.75
DECIMAL EQUIVALENT INTRST:  .1475

MAXIMUM MONTHLY PAYMNT   :  1050.00
MAXIMUM LOAN PAYMNT/MONTH:   777.78
PAYMENTS PER YEAR        :  12
TOTAL # OF PAYMENTS DUE  :  348


*********************
* CALC 1: 9333.333 *
* CALC 2: .0142439 *
* CALC 3: .9857561 *
* CALC 4: 62375.53 *
*********************
```

Listing

```
>A  3:"MONTHLY I
>A  4:"% OF INCO
>A  5:"PERCENTAG
>A  6:"TOWARDS T
>A  9:"TERM OF T
>A10:"INTEREST
>A11:"DECIMAL E
>A13:"MAXIMUM M
>A14:"MAXIMUM L
>A15:"PAYMENTS
>A16:"TOTAL # O
>A18:/-*
>A19:"* CALC 1:
>A20:"* CALC 2:
>A21:"* CALC 3:
>A22:"* CALC 4:
>A23:/-*

>B  3:"NCOME:
>B  4:"ME TOWARD
>B  5:"E OF LOAN
>B  6:"AX,INS,AS
>B  9:"HE LOAN I
>B10:"ON THE LO
>B11:"QUIVALENT
>B13:"ONTHLY PA
>B14:"OAN PAYMN
>B15:"PER YEAR
>B16:"F PAYMENT
>B18:/-*
>B19:+D14*D15
>B20:1/(D11/D15+1)^D16
>B21:1-B20
>B22:(B19/D11)*B21
>B23:/-*

>C  1:"MAXIMUM L
>C  3:/F$3500
>C  4:"S REPAY:
>C  5:" PAYMNT
>C  6:"SMNTS  :
>C  9:"N YEARS:
>C10:"AN     :
```

```
>C11:"  INTRST:
>C13:"YMNT   :
>C14:"T/MONTH:
>C15:/FR"          :
>C16:"S DUE  :
>C18:"**
>C19:"  *
>C20:"  *
>C21:"  *
>C22:"  *
>C23:"**

>D  1:"OAN AMOUN
>D  4:/FL30
>D  6:/FL35
>D  9:/FL29
>D10:/FL14.75
>D11:/FL+D10/100
>D13:/F$+C3*(D4/100)
>D14:/F$(D13/(100+D6)*100
>D15:/FL12
>D16:/FL+D15*D9

>E  1:"T
>E  3:"MAXIMUM L
>E  5:"DOWN PAYM
>E  6:"AFFORDABL
>E  8:"DOWN PAYM

>F  3:"OAN AMT:
>F  5:"ENT %  :
>F  6:"E HOUSE:
>F  8:"ENT DUE:

>G  3:/F$1*B22
>G  5:/FL10
>G  6:/F$(G3/(100-G5))*100
>G  8:/F$+G6*(G5/100)

/GC9
/GOC
/GRA
/W1
```

REBATE DUE

If you decide to pay off a loan before its term expires, you have to know how much interest will be rebated in order to calculate the actual amount due.

This model will perform the necessary calculations based on the terms of your loan and the number of regular payments made before the expected final payment. This sample solves the problem for just one loan, but if you have several outstanding debts, they could be incorporated into an expanded version of this model by simply replicating the formulas. Using the model in that fashion can help decide which loan offers the best rebate, and which is the most beneficial and affordable to pay off.

PRINT A1...D18

Model Run

```
                        REBATE DUE




AMOUNT OF LOAN   :   1500.00
ANNUAL INT RATE  :     12.67
LIFE OF LOAN (MO):        24
PAYMENTS/MONTH   :         1
REGULAR PAYMNT $ :     71.58
LAST PAY # MADE  :        19


COST OF LOAN     =    380.10
TOTAL # OF PYMNTS=        24


INTEREST REBATE  =     25.56
TOTAL $ DUE      =    357.90


PAYOFF AMOUNT    =    332.34
```

Listing

```
>A  5:"AMOUNT OF
>A  6:"ANNUAL IN
>A  7:"LIFE OF L
>A  8:"PAYMENTS/
>A  9:"REGULAR P
>A10:"LAST PAY
>A12:"COST OF L
>A13:"TOTAL # O
>A15:"INTEREST
>A16:"TOTAL $ D
>A18:"PAYOFF AM

>B  5:" LOAN    :
>B  6:"T RATE   :
>B  7:"OAN (MO):
>B  8:"MONTH    :
>B  9:"AYMNT $  :
>B10:"# MADE   :
>B12:"OAN      =
>B13:"F PYMNTS=
>B15:"REBATE   =
>B16:"UE       =
>B18:"OUNT     =

>C  1:"REBATE DU
>C  5:1500
>C  6:12.67
>C  7:/FI24
>C  8:/FI1
>C  9:71.58
>C10:/FI19
>C12:(C6/12)*C7*C5/100
>C13:/FI+C8*C7
>C15:(C13-C10+1)*(C13-C10)/C13^2+C13
>C16:+C9*(C13-C10)
>C18:+C16-C15

>D  1:"E

/GC9
/GF$
/GOC
/GRA
/W1
```

RENTAL PROPERTY

If you own rental property, you know that the expenses of upkeep and repairs can greatly affect your profit. This model is designed to help organize the necessary records of a rental property.

In this example there are four units. Each pays a monthly rent which changes during the year because of new leases and rent increases. When entering rents, you need only enter the amount for January or any fluctuation when it occurs. Afterward, when each rent is entered, it duplicates the previous month's rent by multiplying it by one. In this way, any change to the rental fee is carried from wherever it is entered to the end of the year without affecting preceding months.

Expenses and repairs are listed and entered for each month. Standard amounts for insurance and taxes can be replicated across the grid to minimize entry. At the beginning of the year, other expenses could be estimated and repeated the same as rents, with true figures entered as they become available.

PRINT A1...M55

Listing

```
>A  3: "CONVERTED
>A  4: "410 S. 9T
>A  5: "NO. OF UN
>A  7: "MONTHLY R
>A  8: /-=
>A10: "UNIT #
>A11: /FL1
>A12: /FL2
>A13: /FL3
>A14: /FL4
>A15: /---
>A16: "TOTAL
>A19: "EXPENSES
>A20: /-=
>A22: "INSURANCE
>A23: "CLEANING
>A24: "LEGAL
>A25: "UTILITIES
>A26: "TELEPHONE
>A27: "SUPPLIES
>A28: "MAINT'CE
>A29: "CLERICAL
>A30: "TAXES
>A33: "REPAIRS
>A34: /-=
>A36: "PLUMBING
>A37: "WINDOW
>A38: "PAINTING
>A39: "RUG
>A40: "HALLWAY
>A41: "LIGHT FIX
>A42: "STAIRS
```

```
>A44: /-=
>A47: "TOTAL
>A48: "EXPENSES
>A51: "CASH GAIN
>A53: "ANNUAL EX
>A54: "ANNUAL RE
>A55: "ANNUAL CA

>B  3: "  BROWNSTO
>B  4: "H STREET
>B  5: "ITS : 4
>B  7: "ENTALS
>B  8: "======
>B10: /FR"JAN
>B11: 430
>B12: 440
>B13: 420
>B14: 410
>B15: /---
>B16: @SUM(B11...B14)
>B22: 25
>B23: 35
>B24: 50
>B25: 80
>B26: 45
>B27: 30
>B28: 200
>B29: 500
>B30: 210
>B36: 250
>B38: 150
>B44: /-=
```

Model Run

```
                 RENTAL PROPERTY

CONVERTED BROWNSTONE
410 S. 9TH STREET
NO. OF UNITS : 4

MONTHLY RENTALS
===============
```

UNIT #	JAN	FEB	MAR	APR	MAY	JUNE	JULY	AUG	SEPT	OCT	NOV	DEC
1	430.00	430.00	430.00	430.00	430.00	430.00	430.00	450.00	450.00	450.00	450.00	450.00
2	440.00	440.00	440.00	440.00	440.00	475.00	475.00	475.00	475.00	475.00	475.00	475.00
3	420.00	420.00	420.00	440.00	440.00	440.00	440.00	440.00	440.00	440.00	440.00	440.00
4	410.00	410.00	410.00	410.00	410.00	410.00	410.00	430.00	430.00	430.00	430.00	430.00
TOTAL	1700.00	1700.00	1700.00	1720.00	1720.00	1755.00	1755.00	1795.00	1795.00	1795.00	1795.00	1795.00

```
EXPENSES
========
```

	JAN	FEB	MAR	APR	MAY	JUNE	JULY	AUG	SEPT	OCT	NOV	DEC
INSURANCE	25.00	25.00	25.00	25.00	25.00	25.00	25.00	25.00	25.00	25.00	25.00	25.00
CLEANING	35.00	35.00	35.00	35.00	35.00	45.00	45.00	55.00	35.00	35.00	35.00	35.00
LEGAL	50.00	50.00	50.00	50.00	50.00	50.00	50.00	50.00	50.00	50.00	50.00	50.00
UTILITIES	80.00	80.00	80.00	75.00	75.00	75.00	75.00	75.00	75.00	75.00	75.00	75.00
TELEPHONE	45.00	45.00	45.00	45.00	45.00	45.00	45.00	45.00	45.00	45.00	45.00	45.00
SUPPLIES	30.00	30.00	30.00	30.00	30.00	30.00	30.00	30.00	30.00	30.00	30.00	30.00
MAINT'CE	200.00	200.00	200.00	200.00	200.00	200.00	200.00	200.00	200.00	200.00	200.00	200.00
CLERICAL	500.00	500.00	500.00	500.00	500.00	500.00	500.00	500.00	500.00	500.00	500.00	500.00
TAXES	210.00	210.00	210.00	210.00	210.00	210.00	210.00	210.00	210.00	210.00	210.00	210.00

```
REPAIRS
=========
```

	JAN	FEB	MAR	APR	MAY	JUNE	JULY	AUG	SEPT	OCT	NOV	DEC
PLUMBING	250.00											
WINDOW		45.00			60.00		50.00					
PAINTING	150.00								300.00		250.00	
RUG		200.00				300.00			500.00		250.00	
HALLWAY				35.00		50.00			45.00		55.00	
LIGHT FIX			25.00		20.00					17.50		
STAIRS							250.00					

```
===============================================================================
```

	JAN	FEB	MAR	APR	MAY	JUNE	JULY	AUG	SEPT	OCT	NOV	DEC
TOTAL EXPENSES	1575.00	1420.00	1200.00	1205.00	1250.00	1530.00	1480.00	1235.00	1970.00	1187.50	1725.00	1170.00
CASH GAIN	125.00	280.00	500.00	495.00	450.00	170.00	220.00	465.00	-270.00	512.50	-25.00	530.00

```
ANNUAL EXPENSES:  16947.50
ANNUAL RENT    :  21025.00
ANNUAL CASH GAIN:  3452.50
```

```
>B48:@SUM(B22...B42)              >E11:1*D11
>B51:+B16-B48                     >E12:1*D12
>B53:"PENSES:                     >E13:440
>B54:"NT      :                   >E14:1*D14
>B55:"SH GAIN:                    >E15:/--
                                  >E16:@SUM(E11...E14)
>C 1:"RENTAL PR                   >E22:25
>C 3:"NE                          >E23:35
>C10:/FR"FEB                      >E24:50
>C11:1*B11                        >E25:75
>C12:1*B12                        >E26:45
>C13:1*B13                        >E27:30
>C14:1*B14                        >E28:200
>C15:/--                          >E29:500
>C16:@SUM(C11...C14)              >E30:210
>C22:25                           >E40:35
>C23:35                           >E44:/-=
>C24:50                           >E48:@SUM(E22...E42)
>C25:80                           >E51:+B16-E48
>C26:45
>C27:30                           >F10:/FR"MAY
>C28:200                          >F11:1*E11
>C29:500                          >F12:1*E12
>C30:210                          >F13:1*E13
>C37:45                           >F14:1*E14
>C39:200                          >F15:/--
>C44:/-=                          >F16:@SUM(F11...F14)
>C48:@SUM(C22...C42)              >F22:25
>C51:+B16-C48                     >F23:35
>C53:@SUM(B48...M48)              >F24:50
>C54:@SUM(B16...M16)              >F25:75
>C55:@SUM(B51...M51)              >F26:45
                                  >F27:30
>D 1:"OPERTY                      >F28:200
>D10:/FR"MAR                      >F29:500
>D11:1*C11                        >F30:210
>D12:1*C12                        >F37:60
>D13:1*C13                        >F41:20
>D14:1*C14                        >F44:/-=
>D15:/--                          >F48:@SUM(F22...F42)
>D16:@SUM(D11...D14)              >F51:+B16-F48
>D22:25
>D23:35                           >G10:/FR"JUNE
>D24:50                           >G11:1*F11
>D25:80                           >G12:475
>D26:45                           >G13:1*F13
>D27:30                           >G14:1*F14
>D28:200                          >G15:/--
>D29:500                          >G16:@SUM(G11...G14)
>D30:210                          >G22:25
>D41:25                           >G23:45
>D44:/-=                          >G24:50
>D48:@SUM(D22...D42)              >G25:75
>D51:+B16-D48                     >G26:45
>E10:/FR"APR                      >G27:30
```

```
>G28:200
>G29:500
>G30:210
>G39:300
>G40:50
>G44:/-=
>G48:@SUM(G22...G42)
>G51:+B16-G48

>H10:/FR"JULY
>H11:1*G11
>H12:1*G12
>H13:1*G13
>H14:1*G14
>H15:/--
>H16:@SUM(H11...H14)
>H22:25
>H23:45
>H24:50
>H25:75
>H26:45
>H27:30
>H28:200
>H29:500
>H30:210
>H37:50
>H42:250
>H44:/-=
>H48:@SUM(H22...H42)
>H51:+B16-H48

>I10:/FR"AUG
>I11:450
>I12:1*H12
>I13:1*H13
>I14:430
>I15:/--
>I16:@SUM(I11...I14)
>I22:25
>I23:55
>I24:50
>I25:75
>I26:45
>I27:30
>I28:200
>I29:500
>I30:210
>I40:45
>I44:/-=
>I48:@SUM(I22...I42)
>I51:+B16-I48

>J10:/FR"SEPT
>J11:1*I11
>J12:1*I12
```

```
>J13:1*I13
>J14:1*I14
>J15:/--
>J16:@SUM(J11...J14)
>J22:25
>J23:35
>J24:50
>J25:75
>J26:45
>J27:30
>J28:200
>J29:500
>J30:210
>J38:300
>J39:500
>J44:/-=
>J48:@SUM(J22...J42)
>J51:+B16-J48

>K10:/FR"OCT
>K11:1*J11
>K12:1*J12
>K13:1*J13
>K14:1*J14
>K15:/--
>K16:@SUM(K11...K14)
>K22:25
>K23:35
>K24:50
>K25:75
>K26:45
>K27:30
>K28:200
>K29:500
>K30:210
>K41:17.5
>K44:/-=
>K48:@SUM(K22...K42)
>K51:+B16-K48

>L10:/FR"NOV
>L11:1*K11
>L12:1*K12
>L13:1*K13
>L14:1*K14
>L15:/--
>L16:@SUM(L11...L14)
>L22:25
>L23:35
>L24:50
>L25:75
>L26:45
>L27:30
>L28:200
>L29:500
```

```
>L30:210                              >M24:50
>L38:250                              >M25:75
>L39:250                              >M26:45
>L40:55                               >M27:30
>L44:/-=                              >M28:200
>L48:@SUM(L22...L42)                  >M29:500
>L51:+B16-L48                         >M30:210
                                      >M44:/-=
>M10:/FR"DEC                          >M48:@SUM(M22...M42)
>M11:1*L11                            >M51:+B16-M48
>M12:1*L12
>M13:1*L13                            /GC9
>M14:1*L14                            /GF$
>M15:/--                              /GOC
>M16:@SUM(M11...M14)                  /GRA
>M22:25                               /W1
>M23:35
```

MOVING AVERAGE CALCULATOR

The moving average is a strong indicator of the value of a particular commodity, since it reduces the effect of seasonal variations, irregular movement, and market cycles. In this model, the time period used is 24 months, and the prices are retail pork prices during that period. The moving average starts at month number 12 and continues to month number 24.

Any time period can be used. Some commodities are best averaged over 5- or 8-day cycles. In order to start the calculation, be sure to enter as many lead-in figures as moving averages you want calculated.

By examining this model, you'll see that the method used was @AVERAGING at the end of the first 12 months, then replicating the formula to the end of the list, making each month relative to the previous. In this way, the first of the 12 was dropped off and the next of the 12 was added to the calculation.

As new prices become available, you can add them by simply duplicating the formula. You can create a model for each commodity being studied, or combine several commodities into one electronic spread sheet.

PRINT A1...E30

Listing

```
>A  6:"PERIOD
>A  7:"JAN
>A  8:"FEB
>A  9:"MAR
>A10:"APR
>A11:"MAY
>A12:"JUNE
>A13:"JULY
>A14:"AUG
>A15:"SEP
>A16:"OCT
>A17:"NOV
>A18:"DEC
>A19:"JAN
>A20:"FEB
>A21:"MAR
>A22:"APR
>A23:"MAY
>A24:"JUNE
>A25:"JULY
>A26:"AUG
>A27:"SEP
>A28:"OCT
>A29:"NOV
>A30:"DEC

>B  4:/FR"AVERAGE
>B  5:/FR"PRICE
>B  6:/FR"PER POUND
>B  7:/F$76.55
```

```
>B  8:/F$76.57
>B  9:/F$76.4
>B10:/F$76.32
>B11:/F$76.2
>B12:/F$76.5
>B13:/F$76.77
>B14:/F$78.09
>B15:/F$78.1
>B16:/F$75.3
>B17:/F$75.01
>B18:/F$74.98
>B19:/F$74.9
>B20:/F$74.5
>B21:/F$75.1
>B22:/F$75.2
>B23:/F$75.7
>B24:/F$75.8
>B25:/F$75.6
>B26:/F$75.51
>B27:/F$75.55
>B28:/F$75.4
>B29:/F$75.3
>B30:/F$75.22
>B31:/F$

>C  1:"MOVING AV

>D  5:/FR"MOVING
>D  6:/FR"AVERAGE
>D18:@SUM(B7...B18)/@COUNT(B7...B18)
```

```
>D  1:"ERAGE CAL
>D19:@SUM(B8...B19)/@COUNT(B8...B19)
>D20:@SUM(B9...B20)/@COUNT(B9...B20)
>D21:@SUM(B10...B21)/@COUNT(B10...B21)
>D22:@SUM(B11...B22)/@COUNT(B11...B22)
>D23:@SUM(B12...B23)/@COUNT(B12...B23)
>D24:@SUM(B13...B24)/@COUNT(B13...B24)
>D25:@SUM(B14...B25)/@COUNT(B14...B25)
>D26:@SUM(B15...B26)/@COUNT(B15...B26)
>D27:@SUM(B16...B27)/@COUNT(B16...B27)
>D28:@SUM(B17...B28)/@COUNT(B17...B28)
>D29:@SUM(B18...B29)/@COUNT(B18...B29)
>D30:@SUM(B19...B30)/@COUNT(B19...B30)

>E  1:"CULATOR

/GC9
/GOC
/GRA
/W1
```

Model Run

MOVING AVERAGE CALCULATOR

PERIOD	AVERAGE PRICE PER POUND	MOVING AVERAGE
JAN	76.55	
FEB	76.57	
MAR	76.40	
APR	76.32	
MAY	76.20	
JUNE	76.50	
JULY	76.77	
AUG	78.09	
SEP	78.10	
OCT	75.30	
NOV	75.01	
DEC	74.98	76.39917
JAN	74.90	76.26167
FEB	74.50	76.08917
MAR	75.10	75.98083
APR	75.20	75.8875
MAY	75.70	75.84583
JUNE	75.80	75.7875
JULY	75.60	75.69
AUG	75.51	75.475
SEP	75.55	75.2625
OCT	75.40	75.27083
NOV	75.30	75.295
DEC	75.22	75.315

GENERAL
BUSINESS

BREAK-EVEN POINT

If you're involved in manufacturing, whether for a local crafts fair or an international market, knowing your break-even point is vital to successful management. This model uses a manufacturer who produces three products. But your model can be increased or decreased to fit your needs, since the calculations are based on a composite figure that is based on the sales ratio of one product to another. In the model shown, the ratios are 5, 3, 2 for Products A, B, C, respectively. This means that out of 10 units sold, 5 are type A, 3 are type B, and 2 are type C.

In calculating the break-even point, a contribution margin for the composite is calculated by subtracting the total extended variable cost from the selling price. Then, the total overhead is divided by the composite contribution margin. This figure then tells you how many composite units must be sold to break even. To calculate the break-even point for the individual products, multiply the composite figure by that product's sales ratio.

By including current sales for each unit, a safety margin can be determined, that is, you can calculate how far sales can decrease before losses are incurred. Because of the VisiCalc program's special features, "what if" scenarios can simulate a product's performance in the marketplace. For example, if the sales ratio for Product A were to decrease, what would happen? With this model,

you can change any or all of the figures and the result will be calculated automatically. You could use yearly, weekly, or even daily figures for your particular analysis.

In addition, you can itemize fixed costs in greater detail than shown here. To calculate break-even point for a small shop, you could list employees and their monthly gross salaries, or all the supplies used in producing your products. The "what if" scenarios you devise could then include the effects that taxes or salary increases would have on your margin of safety if sales remained the same.

PRINT A1...K31

Listing

```
>A 1:"    <<<<
>A 3:"COMPANY N
>A 4:"SUBMITTED
>A 5:"DATE
>A 7:"MONTHLY F
>A 9:"RENT
>A10:"ELECTRIC
>A11:"HEAT
>A12:"WAGES
>A13:"TAXES
>A14:"MISC
>A16:"TOTAL
>A21:"PRODUCT
```

```
>A23:"PROD A
>A24:"PROD B
>A25:"PROD C
>A30:/FR"CONTRIBUT
>A31:"BREAK-EVE
>A41:"<<<< PROF
>A43:"MONTHLY S
>A45:"PROFIT =

>B 1:"BREAK-EVE
>B 3:"AME
>B 4:" BY:
>B 7:"IXED COST
```

Model Run

```
         <<<<  BREAK-EVEN POINT ANALYSIS  >>>

    COMPANY NAME
    SUBMITTED BY:
    DATE

    MONTHLY FIXED COST  (OVERHEAD)


    RENT       15000.00
    ELECTRIC     890.00
    HEAT        2250.00
    WAGES      23500.00
    TAXES        800.00
    MISC        2500.00
               ---------
    TOTAL      44940.00
```

		UNIT SELLING PRICE	EXTENDED SELLING PRICE	VARIABLE UNIT COST	EXTENDED VARIABLE COST	BREAK- EVEN- POINT	CURRENT UNITS SALES	CURRENT SALES DOLLARS	MARGIN OF SAFETY
PRODUCT	SALES RATIO								
PROD A	5	6.67	33.35	1.23	6.15	4685	5000	33350	6.30 %
PROD B	3	7.54	22.62	2.34	7.02	2811	3500	26390	19.68 %
PROD C	2	4.55	9.10	1.97	3.94	1874	2200	10010	14.82 %
		-------	-------	-------	-------	-------	-------	-------	-------
TOTALS:		65.07	5.54	17.11	9370	10700	69750		
MEAN :		21.69	1.85	5.70	3123	3567	23250	13.60 %	

```
    CONTRIBUTION MARGIN PER COMPOSITE UNIT =      47.96
    BREAK-EVEN POINT FOR COMPOSITE UNITS    =       937
```

```
>B 9:/F$15000                    >B43:"ALES VOL:
>B10:/F$890                      >B45:/F$(B29-B20)*(C43-@ERROR)
>B11:/F$2250
>B12:/F$23500                    >C 1:"N POINT A
>B13:/F$800                      >C 7:"  (OVERHE
>B14:/F$2500                     >C19:/FR"UNIT
>B15:/--                         >C20:/FR"SELLING
>B16:/F$@SUM(B9...B14)           >C21:/FR"PRICE
>B20:/F$"SALES                   >C23:/F$6.67
>B21:"RATIO                      >C24:/F$7.54
>B23:/FL5                        >C25:/F$4.55
>B24:/FL3                        >C27:"TOTALS:
>B25:/FL2                        >C28:"MEAN  :
>B29:/F$                         >C30:"N PER COM
>B30:"ION MARGI                  >C31:"OR COMPOS
>B31:"N POINT F                  >C41:"IS  >>>>
>B41:"IT ANALYS                  >C43:3000
```

```
>D 1:"NALYSIS              >G25:/FI+B25*F31
>D 7:"AD)                  >G26:/--
>D19:/FR"EXTENDED          >G27:/FI@SUM(G23...G25)
>D20:/FR"SELLING           >G28:/FI@AVERAGE(G23...G25)
>D21:/FR"PRICE
>D23:/F$+C23*B23           >H19:/FR"CURRENT
>D24:/F$+C24*B24           >H20:/FR"UNITS
>D25:/F$+C25*B25           >H21:/FR"SALES
>D26:/--                   >H23:5000
>D27:/F$@SUM(D23...D25)    >H24:3500
>D28:/F$@AVERAGE(D23...D25) >H25:2200
>D30:"POSITE UN            >H26:/--
>D31:"ITE UNITS            >H27:@SUM(H23...H25)
                           >H28:/FI@AVERAGE(H23...H25)
>E 1:">>>
>E19:/FR"VARIABLE          >I19:/FR"CURRENT
>E20:/FR"UNIT              >I20:/FR"SALES
>E21:/FR"COST              >I21:/FR"DOLLARS
>E23:/F$1.23               >I23:+C23*H23
>E24:/F$2.34               >I24:+C24*H24
>E25:/F$1.97               >I25:+C25*H25
>E26:/--                   >I26:/--
>E27:@SUM(E23...E25)       >I27:@SUM(I23...I25)
>E28:/F$@AVERAGE(E23...E25) >I28:/FI@AVERAGE(I23...I25)
>E30:"IT =
>E31:"    =                >J19:/FR"MARGIN
                           >J20:/FR"OF
>F19:/FR"EXTENDED          >J21:/FR"SAFETY
>F20:/FR"VARIABLE          >J23:/F$((I23-(G23*C23))/I23)*100
>F21:/FR"COST              >J24:/F$((I24-(G24*C24))/I24)*100
>F23:/F$+E23*B23           >J25:/F$((I25-(G25*C25))/I25)*100
>F24:/F$+E24*B24           >J26:/--
>F25:/F$+E25*B25           >J28:/F$@AVERAGE(J23...J25)
>F26:/--
>F27:/F$@SUM(F23...F25)    >K23:" %
>F28:/F$@AVERAGE(F23...F25) >K24:" %
>F30:/F$+D27-F27           >K25:" %
>F31:/FI+B16/F30           >K28:" %

>G19:/FR"BREAK-            /GC9
>G20:/FR"EVEN-             /GOC
>G21:/FR"POINT             /GRA
>G23:/FI+B23*F31           /W1
>G24:/FI+B24*F31
```

CASH FLOW ANALYSIS

This model addresses the problem of keeping track of your cash. Broken into two parts — Cash Flow In and Cash Flow Out — it reports both a monthly and current cash position. Any business, large or small, could benefit from cash flow analysis.

Each figure entered here is an accumulated monthly total, but this model can be revised for detailed entries that reflect exactly where the money is going to or coming from.

PRINT A1...K50

Listing

```
>A11:/--
>A12:"  - CASH
>A13:"        (S
>A14:/--
>A15:"CONSULTIN
>A16:"    FROM R
>A18:"HARDWARE
>A19:"    FROM S
>A22:"TOTAL CAS
>A25:/--
>A26:"  - CASH
>A27:"       (BY
>A28:/--
>A29:"TO: SUPPLI
>A30:"    (H/W R
>A32:"    MONTHL
>A33:"    (FROM
>A35:"MISC/OTHE
>A36:"   >SELF I
>A39:"TOTAL CAS
>A41:"    MONTHL
>A44:/FR"CA
>A45:"    (WORKI
>A49:"NOTE1:

>B11:/--
>B12:"FLOW IN -
>B13:"OURCE)
>B14:/--
>B15:"G
>B16:"EVENUE PR
>B18:"RESALE (S
>B19:"ALES FORE
>B22:"H IN >>>>
>B25:/--
>B26:" FLOW OUT
>B27:"FUNCTION)
>B28:/--
>B29:"IER
```

```
>B30:"ESALE)
>B32:"Y EXPENSE
>B33:"FIN. STMT
>B35:"R CASH OU
>B36:"NSURANCE<
>B39:"H OUT >>>
>B41:"Y CASH PO
>B44:"SH POSITI
>B45:"NG CAPITA
>B49:"THESE NUM
>B50:"THE RETAI

>C 4:"ACME MODE
>C 5:"881 WEST
>C 7:"(312) 555
>C 9:"         -
>C10:"        (
>C11:/--
>C14:"----------
>C16:"OJECTIONS
>C18:"EE NOTE1)
>C19:"CAST
>C22:">>>>>
>C25:/--
>C26:" -
>C28:/--
>C32:"S
>C33:")
>C35:"T
>C39:">>>>>
>C41:"SITION
>C44:"ON
>C45:"L)
>C49:"BERS ARE
>C50:"L SALES P

>D 4:"RN BUSINES
>D 5:"5TH. PL.,
>D 7:"-9099
```

Model Run

```
              ACME MODERN BUSINESS MACHINES        FEIN# 36-90000001
              881 WEST 5TH. PL.,WESTTON, IL 60988 27   ROT#  47908111
                                                   SSN # 336-70-0001
                (312) 555-9099

                      - CASH FLOW ANALYSIS -      DATE:5/15/81
                      (6 MONTH PROJECTION)
        ---------------------------------------------------------------    **********
          - CASH FLOW IN -    (30 DA) (60 DA) (90 DA) (120 DA) (150 DA) (180 DA)   <TTL>
            (SOURCE)                                                              6 MONTHS
        ---------------------------------------------------------------    **********
        CONSULTING
          FROM REVENUE PROJECTIONS  2700.00 3100.00 3700.00 3725.00 3925.00 4250.00   21400.00

        HARDWARE RESALE (SEE NOTE1)
          FROM SALES FORECAST       9475.00 1000.00 3050.00 3580.00    0.00    0.00   17105.00
                                    -------- -------- -------- -------- -------- --------
        TOTAL CASH IN >>>>>>>>>     12175.00 4100.00 6750.00 7305.00 3925.00 4250.00   38505.00
                                    ================================================   =========


        ---------------------------
          - CASH FLOW OUT -
            (BY FUNCTION)
        ---------------------------
        TO: SUPPLIER                          10325.00 1530.00 3250.00 3630.00   18735.00
            (H/W RESALE)

          MONTHLY EXPENSES          1710.00 1710.00 1710.00 1710.00 1710.00 1710.00   10260.00
            (FROM FIN. STMT)

        MISC/OTHER CASH OUT
          >SELF INSURANCE<           120.00  120.00  120.00  120.00  120.00  120.00     720.00
                                    ================================================   =========
        TOTAL CASH OUT >>>>>>>>      1830.00 1830.00 12155.00 3360.00 5080.00 5460.00   29715.00
                                    -------- -------- -------- -------- -------- --------
          MONTHLY CASH POSITION     10345.00 2270.00 -5405.00 3945.00 -1155.00 -1210.00  8790.00
                                    ======== ======== ======== ======== ======== ========  **********

              CASH POSITION         10345.00 12615.00 7210.00 11155.00 10000.00 8790.00
            (WORKING CAPITAL)       -------- -------- -------- -------- -------- --------


        NOTE1:   THESE NUMBERS ARE BASED ON
                 THE RETAIL SALES PRICE.
```

```
>D 9:"CASH FLOW               >F23:/-=
>D10:"6 MONTH P               >F29:10325
>D11:/--                      >F32:1710
>D12:" (30 DA)                >F36:120
>D14:"----------              >F38:/-=
>D16:2700                     >F39:@SUM(F29...F37)
>D19:/F$9475                  >F40:" ----------
>D21:" ----------             >F41:+F22-F39
>D22:@SUM(D16...D20)          >F42:" ========
>D23:/-=                      >F44:+E44+F41
>D32:1710                     >F45:" ----------
>D36:120
>D38:/-=                      >G 5:"27
>D39:@SUM(D29...D37)          >G 9:"DATE:5/15
>D40:" ----------             >G11:/--
>D41:+D22-D39                 >G12:" (120 DA)
>D42:" ========              >G14:"----------
>D44:0+D41                    >G16:3725
>D45:" ----------             >G19:3580
>D49:"BASED ON                >G21:" ----------
>D50:"RICE.                   >G22:@SUM(G15...G20)
                              >G23:/-=
>E 4:"SS MACHIN               >G29:1530
>E 5:"WESTTON,                >G32:1710
>E 9:" ANALYSIS               >G36:120
>E10:"ROJECTION               >G38:/-=
>E11:/--                      >G39:@SUM(G29...G37)
>E12:" (60 DA)                >G40:" ----------
>E14:"----------              >G41:+G22-G39
>E16:3100                     >G42:" ========
>E19:1000                     >G44:+F44+G41
>E21:" ----------             >G45:" ----------
>E22:@SUM(E15...E20)
>E23:/-=                      >H 4:"FEIN# 36-
>E32:1710                     >H 5:"ROT#  479
>E36:120                      >H 6:"SSN # 336
>E38:/-=                      >H 9:"/81
>E39:@SUM(E29...E37)          >H11:/--
>E40:" ----------             >H12:" (150 DA)
>E41:+E22-E39                 >H14:"----------
>E42:" ========              >H16:3925
>E44:+D44+E41                 >H19:0
>E45:" ----------             >H21:" ----------
                              >H22:@SUM(H15...H20)
>F 4:"ES                      >H23:/-=
>F 5:"IL 60988                >H29:3250
>F 9:" -                      >H32:1710
>F10:")                       >H36:120
>F11:/--                      >H38:/-=
>F12:" (90 DA)                >H39:@SUM(H29...H37)
>F14:"----------              >H40:" ----------
>F16:3700                     >H41:+H22-H39
>F19:3050                     >H42:" ========
>F21:" ----------             >H44:+G44+H41
>F22:@SUM(F15...F20)          >H45:" ----------
```

```
>I  4:"90000001          >K12:"  <TTL>
>I  5:"08111             >K13:"  6 MONTHS
>I  6:"-70-0001          >K14:/-*
>I11:/--                 >K16:ƏSUM(D16...I16)
>I12:"  (180 DA)         >K19:ƏSUM(D19...I19)
>I14:"---------          >K22:ƏSUM(D22...I22)
>I16:4250                >K23:/-=
>I19:0                   >K29:ƏSUM(F29...I29)
>I21:"  ---------        >K32:ƏSUM(D32...I32)
>I22:ƏSUM(I15...I20)     >K36:ƏSUM(D36...I36)
>I23:/-=                 >K38:/-=
>I29:3630                >K39:ƏSUM(D39...I39)
>I32:1710                >K40:"  ---------
>I36:120                 >K41:+K22-K39
>I38:/-=                 >K42:"*********
>I39:ƏSUM(I29...I37)
>I40:"  ---------        /GC9
>I41:+I22-I39            /GF$
>I42:"  ========        /GOC
>I44:+H44+I41            /GRA
>I45:"  ---------        /W1

>K11:/-*
```

PLANNED EXPENSE ANALYSIS

This model analyzes planned and actual expenses on a monthly basis. It calculates the difference between each month's planned and actual expenses and the dollar and percentage change in actual expenses from month to month.

Since each department set-up is exactly like the other, you can create one department model, and then duplicate it for as many departments as you need. To do this, enter and save one department model on disk. Then, with the one model on your screen, insert (/I) 23 lines (enough lines to hold one model) at the beginning of your file (before the first department model). Now, load the model from the disk back onto the screen. You

should now have two department models on one screen. Insert another 23 lines at the beginning of the file, load the original model on disk onto your screen again, and you should have three department model set-ups for one report. Repeat this procedure — insert and load — until you have enough department models in your report.

When you have enough department models, enter the final formula to total all departments (lines 66 and 67). Then enter the correct department names and all the department data.

PRINT A1...F45, Page 1
A46...F67, Page 2

Listing

```
>A  5:"DEPARTMENT  A
>A  8:"MONTH
>A  9:"JANUARY
>A10:"FEBRUARY
>A11:"MARCH
>A12:"APRIL
>A13:"MAY
>A14:"JUNE
>A15:"JULY
>A16:"AUGUST
>A17:"SEPTEMBER
>A18:"OCTOBER
>A19:"NOVEMBER
>A20:"DECEMBER
>A21:/--
>A22:"TOTALS
>A26:"DEPARTMENT  B
>A29:"MONTH
>A30:"JANUARY
>A31:"FEBRUARY
>A32:"MARCH
>A33:"APRIL
>A34:"MAY
>A35:"JUNE
>A36:"JULY
>A37:"AUGUST
>A38:"SEPTEMBER
>A39:"OCTOBER
>A40:"NOVEMBER
>A41:"DECEMBER
>A42:/--
```

```
>A43:"TOTALS
>A46:"DEPARTMENT  C
>A49:"MONTH
>A50:"JANUARY
>A51:"FEBRUARY
>A52:"MARCH
>A53:"APRIL
>A54:"MAY
>A55:"JUNE
>A56:"JULY
>A57:"AUGUST
>A58:"SEPTEMBER
>A59:"OCTOBER
>A60:"NOVEMBER
>A61:"DECEMBER
>A62:/--
>A63:"TOTALS
>A66:"ALL  DEPTS
>A67:"FOR  THE  YEAR

>B  5:"  EXPENSE  COD
>B  8:/FR"PLANNED
>B  9:4500
>B10:4500
>B11:4000
>B12:4000
>B13:4000
>B14:4000
>B15:5000
>B16:5000
>B17:5500
```

Model Run

```
                        PLANNED EXPENSE ANALYSIS
                           <BY DEPARTMENT>


        DEPARTMENT A EXPENSE CODE 6710


                                                    <FROM PREV MONTH>
        MONTH        PLANNED      ACTUAL  DIFFERENCE    $ CHG      % CHG
        JANUARY       4500.00    4000.00    500.00
        FEBRUARY      4500.00    4350.00    150.00     350.00      8.05
        MARCH         4000.00    3950.00     50.00    -400.00    -10.13
        APRIL         4000.00    4100.00   -100.00     150.00      3.66
        MAY           4000.00    4200.00   -200.00     100.00      2.38
        JUNE          4000.00    4150.00   -150.00     -50.00     -1.20
        JULY          5000.00    4750.00    250.00     600.00     12.63
        AUGUST        5000.00    4900.00    100.00     150.00      3.06
        SEPTEMBER     5500.00    5700.00   -200.00     800.00     14.04
        OCTOBER       5500.00    5200.00    300.00    -500.00     -9.62
        NOVEMBER      5500.00    5000.00    500.00    -200.00     -4.00
        DECEMBER      6000.00    5750.00    250.00     750.00     13.04
        -----------------------------------------------------------------
        TOTALS       57500.00   56050.00   1450.00    1750.00



        DEPARTMENT B EXPENSE CODE 6720


                                                    <FROM PREV MONTH>
        MONTH        PLANNED      ACTUAL  DIFFERENCE    $ CHG      % CHG
        JANUARY       3000.00    3000.00
        FEBRUARY      3000.00    3100.00   -100.00     100.00      3.23
        MARCH         3000.00    3000.00      0.00    -100.00     -3.33
        APRIL         3000.00    3000.00      0.00       0.00      0.00
        MAY           3000.00    2900.00    100.00    -100.00     -3.45
        JUNE          3000.00    2950.00     50.00      50.00      1.69
        JULY          3000.00    3000.00      0.00      50.00      1.67
        AUGUST        3000.00    3050.00    -50.00      50.00      1.64
        SEPTEMBER     3000.00    3200.00   -200.00     150.00      4.69
        OCTOBER       3000.00    3300.00   -300.00     100.00      3.03
        NOVEMBER      3000.00    3100.00   -100.00    -200.00     -6.45
        DECEMBER      3500.00    3050.00    450.00     -50.00     -1.64
        -----------------------------------------------------------------
        TOTALS       36500.00   36650.00   -150.00      50.00
```

```
>B18:5500                                >B30:3000
>B19:5500                                >B31:3000
>B20:6000                                >B32:3000
>B21:/--                                 >B33:3000
>B22:@SUM(B9...B20)                       >B34:3000
>B26:" EXPENSE COD                        >B35:3000
>B29:/FR"PLANNED                          >B36:3000
```

```
DEPARTMENT C  EXPENSE CODE 6730
```

				<FROM PREV MONTH>	
MONTH	PLANNED	ACTUAL	DIFFERENCE	$ CHG	% CHG
JANUARY	2000.00	1900.00	100.00		
FEBRUARY	2000.00	1850.00	150.00	-50.00	-2.70
MARCH	2000.00	1950.00	50.00	100.00	5.13
APRIL	2500.00	2300.00	200.00	350.00	15.22
MAY	2500.00	2300.00	200.00	0.00	0.00
JUNE	2500.00	2350.00	150.00	50.00	2.13
JULY	2500.00	2550.00	-50.00	200.00	7.84
AUGUST	2500.00	2700.00	-200.00	150.00	5.56
SEPTEMBER	2000.00	2200.00	-200.00	-500.00	-22.73
OCTOBER	2000.00	2100.00	-100.00	-100.00	-4.76
NOVEMBER	2000.00	1950.00	50.00	-150.00	-7.69
DECEMBER	2000.00	2050.00	-50.00	100.00	4.88
--------	--------	--------	--------	--------	--------
TOTALS	26500.00	26200.00	300.00	150.00	
ALL DEPTS					
FOR THE YEAR	120500.00	118900.00	1600.00	1950.00	

Page 2

```
>B37:3000
>B38:3000
>B39:3000
>B40:3000
>B41:3500
>B42:/--
>B43:@SUM(B30...B41)
>B46:"   EXPENSE CO
>B49:/FR"PLANNED
>B50:2000
>B51:2000
>B52:2000
>B53:2500
>B54:2500
>B55:2500
>B56:2500
>B57:2500
>B58:2000
>B59:2000
>B60:2000
>B61:2000
>B62:/--
>B63:@SUM(B50...B61)
>B67:+B22+B43+B63

>C 1:"PLANNED EXPE
>C 2:"   <BY DEPAR
>C 5:"E 6710
>C 8:/FR"ACTUAL
>C 9:4000
```

```
>C10:4350
>C11:3950
>C12:4100
>C13:4200
>C14:4150
>C15:4750
>C16:4900
>C17:5700
>C18:5200
>C19:5000
>C20:5750
>C21:/--
>C22:@SUM(C9...C20)
>C26:"E 6720
>C29:/FR"ACTUAL
>C30:3000
>C31:3100
>C32:3000
>C33:3000
>C34:2900
>C35:2950
>C36:3000
>C37:3050
>C38:3200
>C39:3300
>C40:3100
>C41:3050
>C42:/--
>C43:@SUM(C30...C41)
>C46:"DE 6730
```

```
>C49:/FR"ACTUAL                        >D56:+B56-C56
>C50:1900                              >D57:+B57-C57
>C51:1850                              >D58:+B58-C58
>C52:1950                              >D59:+B59-C59
>C53:2300                              >D60:+B60-C60
>C54:2300                              >D61:+B61-C61
>C55:2350                              >D62:/--
>C56:2550                              >D63:@SUM(D50...D61)
>C57:2700                              >D67:+D22+D43+D63
>C58:2200
>C59:2100                              >E 7:/FR"    <FROM
>C60:1950                              >E 8:/FR"  $ CHG
>C61:2050                              >E10:+C10-C9
>C62:/--                               >E11:+C11-C10
>C63:@SUM(C50...C61)                   >E12:+C12-C11
>C67:+C22+C43+C63                      >E13:+C13-C12
                                       >E14:+C14-C13
                                       >E15:+C15-C14
>D 1:"NSE ANALYSIS                     >E16:+C16-C15
>D 2:"TMENT>                           >E17:+C17-C16
>D 8:/FR"DIFFERENCE                    >E18:+C18-C17
>D 9:+B9-C9                            >E19:+C19-C18
>D10:+B10-C10                          >E20:+C20-C19
>D11:+B11-C11                          >E21:/--
>D12:+B12-C12                          >E22:@SUM(E9...E20)
>D13:+B13-C13                          >E28:/FR"<FROM
>D14:+B14-C14                          >E29:/FR"  $ CHG
>D15:+B15-C15                          >E31:+C31-C30
>D16:+B16-C16                          >E32:+C32-C31
>D17:+B17-C17                          >E33:+C33-C32
>D18:+B18-C18                          >E34:+C34-C33
>D19:+B19-C19                          >E35:+C35-C34
>D20:+B20-C20                          >E36:+C36-C35
>D21:/--                               >E37:+C37-C36
>D22:@SUM(D9...D20)                    >E38:+C38-C37
>D29:/FR"DIFFERENCE                    >E39:+C39-C38
>D31:+B31-C31                          >E40:+C40-C39
>D32:+B32-C32                          >E41:+C41-C40
>D33:+B33-C33                          >E42:/--
>D34:+B34-C34                          >E43:@SUM(E30...E41)
>D35:+B35-C35                          >E48:/FR"    <FROM
>D36:+B36-C36                          >E49:/FR"  $ CHG
>D37:+B37-C37                          >E51:+C51-C50
>D38:+B38-C38                          >E52:+C52-C51
>D39:+B39-C39                          >E53:+C53-C52
>D40:+B40-C40                          >E54:+C54-C53
>D41:+B41-C41                          >E55:+C55-C54
>D42:/--                               >E56:+C56-C55
>D43:@SUM(D30...D41)                   >E57:+C57-C56
>D49:/FR"DIFFERENCE                    >E58:+C58-C57
>D50:+B50-C50                          >E59:+C59-C58
>D51:+B51-C51                          >E60:+C60-C59
>D52:+B52-C52                          >E61:+C61-C60
>D53:+B53-C53                          >E62:/--
>D54:+B54-C54                          >E63:@SUM(E51...E61)
>D55:+B55-C55                          >E67:+E22+E43+E63
```

```
>F 7:" PREV MONTH>           >F39:(E39/C39)*100
>F 8:/FR"  % CHG             >F40:(E40/C40)*100
>F10:(E10/C10)*100           >F41:(E41/C41)*100
>F11:(E11/C11)*100           >F42:/--
>F12:(E12/C12)*100           >F48:" PREV MONTH>
>F13:(E13/C13)*100           >F49:/FR"  % CHG
>F14:(E14/C14)*100           >F51:(E51/C51)*100
>F15:(E15/C15)*100           >F52:(E52/C52)*100
>F16:(E16/C16)*100           >F53:(E53/C53)*100
>F17:(E17/C17)*100           >F54:(E54/C54)*100
>F18:(E18/C18)*100           >F55:(E55/C55)*100
>F19:(E19/C19)*100           >F56:(E56/C56)*100
>F20:(E20/C20)*100           >F57:(E57/C57)*100
>F21:/--                     >F58:(E58/C58)*100
>F28:" PREV MONTH>           >F59:(E59/C59)*100
>F29:/FR"  % CHG             >F60:(E60/C60)*100
>F31:(E31/C31)*100           >F61:(E61/C61)*100
>F32:(E32/C32)*100           >F62:/--
>F33:(E33/C33)*100
>F34:(E34/C34)*100           /GC12
>F35:(E35/C35)*100           /GF$
>F36:(E36/C36)*100           /GOC
>F37:(E37/C37)*100           /GRM
>F38:(E38/C38)*100           /W1
```

DEPRECIATION SCHEDULE

There are several methods for computing depreciation on equipment. This model uses the declining balance method, which provides for large depreciation claims early in the life of the equipment, to calculate annual depreciation. It also reports the cumulative total of depreciation claimed, which should help to avoid exceeding the total allowable depreciation.

The example shown is for a stamp press that costs $4500.00, has a life of seven years, and has a salvage value at the end of that period of $750.00. Thus, total annual depreciation is $3750.00. The declining balance is twice straight-line depreciation, which generates a factor of 29%. In year 1, $1285.71 may be claimed. By year 6, $86.70 is all that can be claimed without exceeding the cost minus the salvage value.

PRINT A1...F24

Model Run

```
DEPRECIATION SCHEDULE: DECLINING BALANCE


ITEM:     STAMP PRESS
COST:      4500.00
LIFE:            7
SALV VAL:   750.00

TOTL DEPR
ALLOWED :  3750.00

STR LN X:        2
D/B FACTR    29 %

          DEPRECTN CUMULTV   MAX    AMT TO
YEAR       CALC'D   TOTAL  ALLOWED  CLAIM

1         1285.71 1285.71 3750.00 1285.71
2          918.37 2204.08 2464.29  918.37
3          655.98 2860.06 1545.92  655.98
4          468.55 3328.61  889.94  468.55
5          334.68 3663.30  421.39  334.68
6          239.06 3902.35   86.70   86.70
7          170.76 4073.11 -152.35 -152.35
```

Listing

```
>A  4:"ITEM:
>A  5:"COST:
>A  6:"LIFE:
>A  7:"SALV VAL:
>A  9:"TOTL DEPR
>A10:"ALLOWED :
>A12:"STR LN X:
>A13:"D/B FACTR
>A16:"YEAR
>A18:/FL1+A16
>A19:/FL1+A18
>A20:/FL1+A19
>A21:/FL1+A20
>A22:/FL1+A21
>A23:/FL1+A22
>A24:/FL1+A23

>B  1:"DEPRECIAT
>B  4:"STAMP PRE
>B  5:4500
>B  6:/FI7
>B  7:750
>B10:+B5-B7
>B12:/FI2
>B13:/FI(100/B6)*B12
>B15:/FR"DEPRECTN
>B16:/FR"CALC'D
>B18:(B5-C16)*(B13/100)
>B19:(B5-C18)*(B13/100)
>B20:(B5-C19)*(B13/100)
>B21:(B5-C20)*(B13/100)
>B22:(B5-C21)*(B13/100)
>B23:(B5-C22)*(B13/100)
>B24:(B5-C23)*(B13/100)

>C  1:"ION SCHED
>C  4:"SS
>C13:" %
>C15:/FR"CUMULTV
>C16:/FR"TOTAL
>C18:+C16+B18
>C19:+C18+B19
>C20:+C19+B20
>C21:+C20+B21
>C22:+C21+B22
>C23:+C22+B23
>C24:+C23+B24
```

```
>D  1:"ULE:  DECL
>D15:/FR"MAX
>D16:/FR"ALLOWED
>D18:+B10-C16
>D19:+B10-C18
>D20:+B10-C19
>D21:+B10-C20
>D22:+B10-C21
>D23:+B10-C22
>D24:+B10-C23


>E  1:"INING BAL
>E15:/FR"AMT TO
>E16:/FR"CLAIM
>E18:@MIN(B18...D18)
```

```
>E19:@MIN(B19...D19)
>E20:@MIN(B20...D20)
>E21:@MIN(B21...D21)
>E22:@MIN(B22...D22)
>E23:@MIN(B23...D23)
>E24:@MIN(B24...D24)


>F  1:"ANCE

/GC9
/GF$
/GOR
/GRA
/W1
```

MINI ACCOUNTS RECEIVABLE

The VisiCalc model used here organizes and reports a small accounts receivable. For each invoice, you must enter the invoice number, the date, the sales amount, and freight charges. Tax is also included in the total amount due; it is calculated from a single tax rate. Aging is reported in days and calculated from the invoice date.

The model is broken into four sections: Aged Trial Balance, Invoice Calculation, Day Table, and Customer Calculations. The Aged Trial Balance will report the status of a customer's invoice based on input in other working areas of the model. Total accounts receivable is reported at the end of the Aged Trial Balance. The remaining three report sections are work and calculation areas.

Enter your invoice data in the Invoice Calculation area. The invoice date must be entered in the *mmddyy* (month, day, year) format. The Invoice Calculation area also contains aging formulas, which you will use for the life of the invoice. When you have entered all new invoices in this area, you can move them into customer groups in the Aged Trial Balance and Customer Calculations areas. Notice that the Customer Calculations area includes the last five columns of the Invoice Calculation report. (This

part of the report is not normally found in a Trial Balance report.) As any invoice is paid, you merely delete it from the customer Trial Balance.

As lines are moved from the Invoice Calculation area, it decreases in size. When there is only one line left, you can insert a number of lines and replicate the formulas throughout the blank lines. This will save you from having to replicate formulas with each invoice you enter.

Aging is performed by comparing the invoice date with Today's Date. It's important that you enter the current date whenever you enter new invoices or print a Trial Balance report. Today's date must also be entered in the *mmddyy* format. To calculate aging, the Day Table is used to compare month, day, and year figures in the two dates. Aging is reported in days in the final column of the Trial Balance report.

Each customer's total accounts receivable is repeated in the final column of the Customer Calculations area; this enables a total accounts receivable to be calculated by @SUMming that final column.

PRINT A20...G50, Aged Trial Balance
A1...L19, Invoice Calculation
Q14...AD19, Day Table
H24...N47, Customer Calculations

Listing

```
>A 4:"INVOICE #
>A 5:/FI1105
>A 6:/FI1117
>A 7:/FI1125
>A 8:/FI1127
>A 9:/FI1140
>A10:/FI
>A11:/FI
>A12:/FI
>A13:/FI
>A14:/-=
>A15:/-=
>A16:"TODAY'S
>A19:/-=
>A22:"CUSTOMER
>A24:"INVOICE #
>A25:/FI123
```

```
>A26:/FI456
>A27:/FI666
>A28:/--
>A31:"CUSTOMER
>A33:"INVOICE #
>A34:/FI757
>A35:/FI915
>A36:/FI1088
>A37:/--
>A40:"CUSTOMER
>A42:"INVOICE #
>A43:/FI901
>A44:/FI1071
>A45:/FI1090
>A46:/--
>A50:"TOTAL A/R
```

Model Run

```
                    AGED TRIAL BALANCE MM/DD/YY

CUSTOMER NAME

INVOICE # INV DATE SALE AMT    TAX  FREIGHT TOTL DUE    AGING
     123    70781   100.00    7.00    8.00   115.00      164
     456    80181   200.00   14.00    7.55   221.55      139
     666    90281   250.00   17.50    9.85   277.35      107
          -----------------------------------------------
                    550.00   38.50   25.40   613.90

CUSTOMER NAME

INVOICE # INV DATE SALE AMT    TAX  FREIGHT TOTL DUE    AGING
     757    90881   150.00   10.50   15.00   175.50      101
     915   101481   325.67   22.80   23.45   371.92       65
    1088   101881   105.00    7.35    1.98   114.33       61
          -----------------------------------------------
                    580.67   40.65   40.43   661.75

CUSTOMER NAME

INVOICE # INV DATE SALE AMT    TAX  FREIGHT TOTL DUE    AGING
     901   101181   650.00   45.50   55.75   751.25       68
    1071   101581   455.00   31.85   12.45   499.30       64
    1090   102181   110.00    7.70    2.35   120.05       58
          -----------------------------------------------
                   1215.00   85.05   70.55  1370.60


TOTAL A/R  2646.25
```

Aged Trial Balance

```
            MINI A/R

            (INVOICE CALCULATION AREA)
INVOICE # INV DATE SALE AMT    TAX  FREIGHT TOTL DUE  AGING  MO CODE DAY CODE  YEAR CD   DY YR DYS PR YR
    1105   113081   120.00    8.40    5.55   133.95    18      11      30        81       334      0
    1117   120181   135.00    9.45   17.00   161.45    17      12       1        81       335      0
    1125   120781   180.00   12.60    8.97   201.57    11      12       7        81       341      0
    1127   120781   176.55   12.36    2.35   191.26    11      12       7        81       341      0
    1140   120881   180.00   12.60    4.55   197.15    10      12       8        81       342      0
                      0.00            0.00     0.00    NA       0       0         0        NA     730
                      0.00            0.00     0.00    NA       0       0         0        NA     730
                      0.00            0.00     0.00    NA       0       0         0        NA     730
                      0.00            0.00     0.00    NA       0       0         0        NA     730
==================================================================================================
==================================================================================================
TODAY'S DATE:    121881  MONTH CD: 12      DAY #:   352    CURR SALES TAX % = .07
                         DAY  : 18
                         YEAR : 81
==================================================================================================
```

Invoice Calculation

DAYS	0	31	28	31	30	31	30	31	31	30	31	30	31
MO	0	1	2	3	4	5	6	7	8	9	10	11	12
YTD DAYS	0	31	59	90	120	151	181	212	243	273	304	334	365
LEAP YR?	0												
YEARS:	0	1	2										
	0	365	730										

Day Table

```
                           DAY OF    DAYS
 MO CODE DAY CODE YEAR CD  THE YR   PRV YR
     7       7       81      198       0
     8       1       81      213       0
     9       2       81      245       0      CUST A/R
-------------------------------------------
                                             613.90


                           DAY OF    DAYS
 MO CODE DAY CODE YEAR CD  THE YR   PRV YR
     9       8       81      251       0
    10      14       81      287       0
    10      18       81      291       0
-------------------------------------------
                                             661.75


                           DAY OF    DAYS
 MO CODE DAY CODE YEAR CD  THE YR   PRV YR
    10      11       81      284       0
    10      15       81      288       0
    10      21       81      294       0
-------------------------------------------
                                            1370.60
```

Customer Calculations

```
>B 4:/FR"INV DATE              >B31:"NAME
>B 5:/FI113081                 >B33:/FR"INV DATE
>B 6:/FI120181                 >B34:/FI90881
>B 7:/FI120781                 >B35:/FI101481
>B 8:/FI120781                 >B36:/FI101881
>B 9:/FI120881                 >B37:/--
>B10:/FI                       >B40:"NAME
>B11:/FI                       >B42:/FR"INV DATE
>B12:/FI                       >B43:/FI101181
>B13:/FI                       >B44:/FI101581
>B14:/-=                       >B45:/FI102181
>B15:/-=                       >B46:/---
>B16:"DATE:                    >B50:@SUM(N29...N47)
>B19:/-=
>B22:"NAME                     >C 1:"MINI A/R
>B24:/FR"INV DATE              >C 3:"(INVOICE
>B25:/FI70781                  >C 4:/FR"SALE AMT
>B26:/FI80181                  >C 5:120
>B27:/FI90281                  >C 6:135
>B28:/---                      >C 7:180
```

```
>C 8:176.55                      >E 3:"ON AREA)
>C 9:180                         >E 4:/FR"FREIGHT
>C14:/-=                         >E 5:5.55
>C15:/-=                         >E 6:17
>C16:/FL121881                   >E 7:8.97
>C19:/-=                         >E 8:2.35
>C24:/FR"SALE AMT                >E 9:4.55
>C25:100                         >E14:/-=
>C26:200                         >E15:/-=
>C27:250                         >E16:/FL@INT(C16*.0001)
>C28:/--                         >E17:/FL@INT(C16*.01)-(E16*100)
>C29:@SUM(C25...C28)             >E18:/FL+C16-((E16*10000)+(E17*100))
>C33:/FR"SALE AMT                >E19:/-=
>C34:150                         >E20:"L BALANCE
>C35:325.67                      >E24:/FR"FREIGHT
>C36:105                         >E25:8
>C37:/--                         >E26:7.55
>C38:@SUM(C34...C37)             >E27:9.85
>C42:/FR"SALE AMT                >E28:/--
>C43:650                         >E29:@SUM(E25...E28)
>C44:455                         >E33:/FR"FREIGHT
>C45:110                         >E34:15
>C46:/--                         >E35:23.45
>C47:@SUM(C43...C46)             >E36:1.98
                                 >E37:/--
                                 >E38:@SUM(E34...E37)
>D 3:"CALCULATI                  >E42:/FR"FREIGHT
>D 4:/FR"TAX                     >E43:55.75
>D 5:+C5*J16                     >E44:12.45
>D 6:+C6*J16                     >E45:2.35
>D 7:+C7*J16                     >E46:/--
>D 8:+C8*J16                     >E47:@SUM(E43...E46)
>D 9:+C9*J16
>D10:+C10*J16                    >F 4:/FR"TOTL DUE
>D11:+C11*J16                    >F 5:@SUM(C5...E5)
>D12:+C12*J16                    >F 6:@SUM(C6...E6)
>D13:+C13*J16                    >F 7:@SUM(C7...E7)
>D14:/-=                         >F 8:@SUM(C8...E8)
>D15:/-=                         >F 9:@SUM(C9...E9)
>D16:"MONTH CD:                  >F10:@SUM(C10...E10)
>D17:"DAY      :                 >F11:@SUM(C11...E11)
>D18:"YEAR     :                 >F12:@SUM(C12...E12)
>D19:/-=                         >F13:@SUM(C13...E13)
>D20:"AGED TRIA                  >F14:/-=
>D24:/FR"TAX                     >F15:/-=
>D25:+C25*J16                    >F16:"DAY #:
>D26:+C26*J16                    >F19:/-=
>D27:+C27*J16                    >F20:/FR"MM/DD/YY
>D28:/--                         >F24:/FR"TOTL DUE
>D29:@SUM(D25...D28)             >F25:@SUM(C25...E25)
>D33:/FR"TAX                     >F26:@SUM(C26...E26)
>D34:+C34*J16                    >F27:@SUM(C27...E27)
>D35:+C35*J16                    >F28:/--
>D36:+C36*J16                    >F29:@SUM(F25...F28)
>D37:/--                         >F33:/FR"TOTL DUE
>D38:@SUM(D34...D37)             >F34:@SUM(C34...E34)
>D42:/FR"TAX                     >F35:@SUM(C35...E35)
>D43:+C43*J16                    >F36:@SUM(C36...E36)
>D44:+C44*J16                    >F37:/--
>D45:+C45*J16                    >F38:@SUM(F34...F37)
>D46:/--                         >F42:/FR"TOTL DUE
>D47:@SUM(D43...D46)
```

```
>F43:@SUM(C43...E43)              >H44:/FI@INT(B44*.0001)
>F44:@SUM(C44...E44)              >H45:/FI@INT(B45*.0001)
>F45:@SUM(C45...E45)              >H46:/--
>F46:/--
>F47:@SUM(F43...F46)              >I 4:/FR"DAY CODE
                                  >I 5:/FI@INT(B5*.01)-(H5*100)
>G 4:/FR"AGING                    >I 6:/FI@INT(B6*.01)-(H6*100)
>G 5:/FI(G16-K5)+L5               >I 7:/FI@INT(B7*.01)-(H7*100)
>G 6:/FI(G16-K6)+L6               >I 8:/FI@INT(B8*.01)-(H8*100)
>G 7:/FI(G16-K7)+L7               >I 9:/FI@INT(B9*.01)-(H9*100)
>G 8:/FI(G16-K8)+L8               >I10:/FI@INT(B10*.01)-(H10*100)
>G 9:/FI(G16-K9)+L9               >I11:/FI@INT(B11*.01)-(H11*100)
>G10:/FI(G16-K10)+L10             >I12:/FI@INT(B12*.01)-(H12*100)
>G11:/FI(G16-K11)+L11             >I13:/FI@INT(B13*.01)-(H13*100)
>G12:/FI(G16-K12)+L12             >I14:/-=
>G13:/FI(G16-K13)+L13             >I15:/-=
>G14:/-=                          >I16:"S TAX % =
>G15:/-=                          >I19:/-=
>G16:/FL@LOOKUP(E16-1,R15...AD15)+E17   >I24:/FR"DAY CODE
>G19:/-=                          >I25:/FI@INT(B25*.01)-(H25*100)
>G24:/FR"AGING                    >I26:/FI@INT(B26*.01)-(H26*100)
>G25:/FI(G16-K25)+L25             >I27:/FI@INT(B27*.01)-(H27*100)
>G26:/FI(G16-K26)+L26             >I28:/--
>G27:/FI(G16-K27)+L27             >I33:/FR"DAY CODE
>G28:/--                          >I34:/FI@INT(B34*.01)-(H34*100)
>G33:/FR"AGING                    >I35:/FI@INT(B35*.01)-(H35*100)
>G34:/FI(G16-K34)+L34             >I36:/FI@INT(B36*.01)-(H36*100)
>G35:/FI(G16-K35)+L35             >I37:/---
>G36:/FI(G16-K36)+L36             >I42:/FR"DAY CODE
>G37:/--                          >I43:/FI@INT(B43*.01)-(H43*100)
>G42:/FR"AGING                    >I44:/FI@INT(B44*.01)-(H44*100)
>G43:/FI(G16-K43)+L43             >I45:/FI@INT(B45*.01)-(H45*100)
>G44:/FI(G16-K44)+L44             >I46:/--
>G45:/FI(G16-K45)+L45
>G46:/--                          >J 4:/FR"YEAR CD
                                  >J 5:/FI+B5-((H5*10000)+(I5*100))
                                  >J 6:/FI+B6-((H6*10000)+(I6*100))
>H 4:/FR"MO CODE                  >J 7:/FI+B7-((H7*10000)+(I7*100))
>H 5:/FI@INT(B5*.0001)            >J 8:/FI+B8-((H8*10000)+(I8*100))
>H 6:/FI@INT(B6*.0001)            >J 9:/FI+B9-((H9*10000)+(I9*100))
>H 7:/FI@INT(B7*.0001)            >J10:/FI+B10-((H10*10000)+(I10*100))
>H 8:/FI@INT(B8*.0001)            >J11:/FI+B11-((H11*10000)+(I11*100))
>H 9:/FI@INT(B9*.0001)            >J12:/FI+B12-((H12*10000)+(I12*100))
>H10:/FI@INT(B10*.0001)           >J13:/FI+B13-((H13*10000)+(I13*100))
>H11:/FI@INT(B11*.0001)           >J14:/-=
>H12:/FI@INT(B12*.0001)           >J15:/-=
>H13:/FI@INT(B13*.0001)           >J16:/FL.07
>H14:/-=                          >J19:/-=
>H15:/-=                          >J24:/FR"YEAR CD
>H16:"CURR SALE                   >J25:/FI+B25-((H25*10000)+(I25*100))
>H19:/-=                          >J26:/FI+B26-((H26*10000)+(I26*100))
>H24:/FR"MO CODE                  >J27:/FI+B27-((H27*10000)+(I27*100))
>H25:/FI@INT(B25*.0001)           >J28:/--
>H26:/FI@INT(B26*.0001)           >J33:/FR"YEAR CD
>H27:/FI@INT(B27*.0001)           >J34:/FI+B34-((H34*10000)+(I34*100))
>H28:/---                         >J35:/FI+B35-((H35*10000)+(I35*100))
>H33:/FR"MO CODE                  >J36:/FI+B36-((H36*10000)+(I36*100))
>H34:/FI@INT(B34*.0001)           >J37:/--
>H35:/FI@INT(B35*.0001)           >J42:/FR"YEAR CD
>H36:/FI@INT(B36*.0001)           >J43:/FI+B43-((H43*10000)+(I43*100))
>H37:/---                         >J44:/FI+B44-((H44*10000)+(I44*100))
>H42:/FR"MO CODE                  >J45:/FI+B45-((H45*10000)+(I45*100))
>H43:/FI@INT(B43*.0001)
```

```
>J46:/--

>K  4:/FR"DY YR
>K  5:/FI@LOOKUP(H5-1,R15...AD15)+I5
>K  6:/FI@LOOKUP(H6-1,R15...AD15)+I6
>K  7:/FI@LOOKUP(H7-1,R15...AD15)+I7
>K  8:/FI@LOOKUP(H8-1,R15...AD15)+I8
>K  9:/FI@LOOKUP(H9-1,R15...AD15)+I9
>K10:/FI@LOOKUP(H10-1,R15...AD15)+I10
>K11:/FI@LOOKUP(H11-1,R15...AD15)+I11
>K12:/FI@LOOKUP(H12-1,R15...AD15)+I12
>K13:/FI@LOOKUP(H13-1,R15...AD15)+I13
>K14:/-=
>K15:/-=
>K19:/-=
>K23:/FR"DAY OF
>K24:/FR"THE YR
>K25:/FI@LOOKUP(H25-1,R15...AD15)+I25
>K26:/FI@LOOKUP(H26-1,R15...AD15)+I26
>K27:/FI@LOOKUP(H27-1,R15...AD15)+I27
>K28:/--
>K32:/FR"DAY OF
>K33:/FR"THE YR
>K34:/FI@LOOKUP(H34-1,R15...AD15)+I34
>K35:/FI@LOOKUP(H35-1,R15...AD15)+I35
>K36:/FI@LOOKUP(H36-1,R15...AD15)+I36
>K37:/--
>K41:/FR"DAY OF
>K42:/FR"THE YR
>K43:/FI@LOOKUP(H43-1,R15...AD15)+I43
>K44:/FI@LOOKUP(H44-1,R15...AD15)+I44
>K45:/FI@LOOKUP(H45-1,R15...AD15)+I45
>K46:/--

>L  4:"DYS PR YR
>L  5:/FI@LOOKUP(E18-J5,R18...T18)
>L  6:/FI@LOOKUP(E18-J6,R18...T18)
>L  7:/FI@LOOKUP(E18-J7,R18...T18)
>L  8:/FI@LOOKUP(E18-J8,R18...T18)
>L  9:/FI@LOOKUP(E18-J9,R18...T18)
>L10:/FI@LOOKUP(E18-J10,R18...T18)
>L11:/FI@LOOKUP(E18-J11,R18...T18)
>L12:/FI@LOOKUP(E18-J12,R18...T18)
>L13:/FI@LOOKUP(E18-J13,R18...T18)
>L14:/-=
>L15:/-=
>L19:/-=
>L23:/FR"DAYS
>L24:/FR"PRV YR
>L25:/FI@LOOKUP(E18-J25,R18...T18)
>L26:/FI@LOOKUP(E18-J26,R18...T18)
>L27:/FI@LOOKUP(E18-J27,R18...T18)
>L28:/--
>L32:/FR"DAYS
>L33:/FR"PRV YR
>L34:/FI@LOOKUP(E18-J34,R18...T18)
>L35:/FI@LOOKUP(E18-J35,R18...T18)
>L36:/FI@LOOKUP(E18-J36,R18...T18)
>L37:/--
>L41:/FR"DAYS
>L42:/FR"PRV YR
>L43:/FI@LOOKUP(E18-J43,R18...T18)
>L44:/FI@LOOKUP(E18-J44,R18...T18)
>L45:/FI@LOOKUP(E18-J45,R18...T18)
>L46:/--

>M17:/FL
>M27:/FR

>N15:/FL
>N25:/FL
>N27:"CUST A/R
>N29:1*F29
>N38:1*F38
>N47:1*F47

>O25:/FL

>P15:/FL
>P25:/FL

>Q14:"DAYS
>Q15:"MO
>Q16:"YTD DAYS
>Q17:"LEAP YR?
>Q18:"YEARS:

>R14:/FIO
>R15:/FIO
>R16:/FIO
>R17:/FIO
>R18:/FIO
>R19:/FIO
>R21:/FI

>S14:/FI31
>S15:/FI1+R15
>S16:/FI+R16+S14
>S18:/FI1
>S19:/FI365

>T14:/FI28
>T15:/FI1+S15
>T16:/FI+S16+T14
>T18:/FI2
>T19:/FI2*S19

>U  1:"<DAYS OF
>U14:/FI31
>U15:/FI1+T15
>U16:/FI+T16+U14

>V  1:"THE YEAR
>V14:/FI30
>V15:/FI1+U15
>V16:/FI+U16+V14

>W  1:"TABLE>
>W14:/FI31
>W15:/FI1+V15
>W16:/FI+V16+W14

>X14:/FI30
>X15:/FI1+W15
```

```
>X16:/FI+W16+X14                          >AB16:/FI+AA16+AB14

>Y14:/FI31                                >AC14:/FI30
>Y15:/FI1+X15                             >AC15:/FI1+AB15
>Y16:/FI+X16+Y14                          >AC16:/FI+AB16+AC14

>Z14:/FI31                                >AD14:/FI31
>Z15:/FI1+Y15                             >AD15:/FI1+AC15
>Z16:/FI+Y16+Z14                          >AD16:/FI+AC16+AD14

>AA14:/FI30                               /GC9
>AA15:/FI1+Z15                            /GF$
>AA16:/FI+Z16+AA14                        /GOC
                                          /GRM
>AB14:/FI31                               /W1
>AB15:/FI1+AA15
```

BUSINESS START-UP WORKSHEET

Any new business requires start-up capital. This worksheet can be used to estimate how much you spend to establish a new business.

There are two parts to the model: recurring monthly expenses and initial costs. To compute recurring monthly expenses, your estimated monthly cost for each item is multiplied by the number of months for start-up (two in this

model). Initial costs are added to this sum to produce a grand total.

In this model, you can add or delete different start-up items, or change the number of start-up months, thereby creating "what if" situations to help you analyze where to place your capital.

PRINT A1...E33

Model Run

```
           BUSINESS START-UP WORKSHEET

NUMBER OF MONTHS
FOR START-UP =      2
---------------------------------------------

DESCRIPTION        MONTHLY  TOTAL $
OF ITEM            ESTIMATE NEEDED

SALARY FOR SELF    1500.00  3000.00
CLERICAL SALARIES  2700.00  5400.00
RENT               2050.00  4100.00
SUPPLIES            500.00  1000.00
PHONE               150.00   300.00
UTILITIES            95.00   190.00
SERVICES             50.00   100.00
MISC EXPENSES       200.00   400.00
                            ---------
                   TOTAL   14490.00

     ONE-TIME COST ESTIMATES

STORE FIXTURES               500.00
EQUIPMENT                    750.00
REDECORATING                1500.00
BEGINNING INVENTORY         3500.00
LICENSE/PERMIT              1200.00
CASH ON HAND               2500.00
MISC DEPOSITS              1000.00
                          ---------
              TOTAL       10950.00

         GRAND TOTAL      25440.00
```

Listing

```
>A  3:"NUMBER OF
>A  4:"FOR START
>A  5:/--
>A  7:"DESCRIPTI
>A  8:"OF ITEM
>A10:"SALARY FO
>A11:"CLERICAL
>A12:"RENT
>A13:"SUPPLIES
>A14:"PHONE
>A15:"UTILITIES
>A16:"SERVICES
>A17:"MISC EXPE
>A21:"  ONE-TIM
>A23:"STORE FIX
>A24:"EQUIPMENT
>A25:"REDECORAT
>A26:"BEGINNING
>A27:"LICENSE/P
>A28:"CASH ON H
>A29:"MISC DEPO

>B  3:"  MONTHS
>B  4:"-UP =
>B  5:/--
>B  7:"ON
>B10:"R SELF
>B11:"SALARIES
>B17:"NSES
>B21:"E COST ES
>B23:"TURES
>B25:"ING
>B26:"  INVENTOR
>B27:"ERMIT
>B28:"AND
```

```
>B29:"SITS
>B33:/FR"GRA

>C 1:"BUSINESS
>C 4:/FL2
>C 5:/--
>C 7:"MONTHLY
>C 8:"ESTIMATE
>C10:1500
>C11:2700
>C12:2050
>C13:500
>C14:150
>C15:95
>C16:50
>C17:200
>C19:/FR"TOTAL
>C21:"TIMATES
>C26:"Y
>C31:/FR"TOTAL
>C33:/FR"ND TOTAL

>D 1:"START-UP
>D 5:/--
>D 7:"TOTAL $
>D 8:"NEEDED
>D10:+C10*C4
>D11:+C11*C4
```

```
>D12:+C12*C4
>D13:+C13*C4
>D14:+C14*C4
>D15:+C15*C4
>D16:+C16*C4
>D17:+C17*C4
>D18:/--
>D19:@SUM(D10...D17)
>D21:"
>D23:500
>D24:750
>D25:1500
>D26:3500
>D27:1200
>D28:2500
>D29:1000
>D30:/--
>D31:@SUM(D23...D29)
>D33:+D19+D31

>E 1:"WORKSHEET
>E 5:/--

/GC9
/GF$
/GOC
/GRA
/W1
```

PROFESSIONAL SERVICES FEE ANALYSIS

Using the VisiCalc program to analyze a daily fee is simply a matter of applying a proven formula to a simple matrix. Once your model is set up, the figures can be changed as often as you like with instantaneous results.

This model shows the fee analysis for a consultant who values his worth at $35,000 a year, has intentions of working 18 days a month, and wants to gain a profit margin of 18%.

All expenses are itemized, then totaled, and divided by the work days to generate a daily overhead amount. By adding in direct labor — daily worth, in effect — and multiplying by the desired profit margin, a daily billing rate is calculated.

To obtain an hourly billing rate this model can be altered to use hours per year or hours per month instead of days per year.

PRINT A1...E31

Listing

```
>A  3:"YEARLY WO
>A  4:"WORK DAYS
>A  5:"WORK DAYS
>A  6:"% PROFIT:
>A10:"EXPENSE
>A11:"CATEGORY
>A12:"OFFICE HE
>A13:"OFFICE RE
>A14:"POSTAGE
>A15:"TELEPHONE
>A16:"CAR
>A17:"HOLIDAYS/
>A18:"SUPPLIES
>A19:"MARKETING
>A20:"LEGAL
>A21:"ACCOUNTIN
>A22:"MISC
>A27:"DAILY OVE
>A28:"DIRECT LA
>A29:"PROFIT:
>A31:"BILLING R

>B  1:"PROFESSIO
>B  3:"RTH :
>B  4:"/MONTH:
>B  5:"/YEAR:
```

```
>B  9:"<OVERHEAD
>B12:"LP
>B13:"NT
>B17:"VACATION
>B21:"G
>B24:/FR"TOTALS:
>B27:"RHEAD:
>B28:"BOR:
>B31:"ATE/DAY:

>C  1:"NAL SERVI
>C  3:35000
>C  4:/FI18
>C  5:/FI12*C4
>C  6:18
>C  9:">
>C11:/FR"MONTHLY
>C12:1200
>C13:1900
>C14:350
>C15:500
>C16:250
>C17:200
>C18:100
>C19:350
>C20:125
```

Model Run

```
          PROFESSIONAL SERVICES: FEE ANALYSIS


    YEARLY WORTH :      35000.00
    WORK DAYS/MONTH:         18
    WORK DAYS/YEAR:         216
    % PROFIT:            18.00



              <OVERHEAD>
    EXPENSE
    CATEGORY          MONTHLY    YEARLY
    OFFICE HELP       1200.00  14400.00
    OFFICE RENT       1900.00  22800.00
    POSTAGE            350.00   4200.00
    TELEPHONE          500.00   6000.00
    CAR                250.00   3000.00
    HOLIDAYS/VACATION  200.00   2400.00
    SUPPLIES           100.00   1200.00
    MARKETING          350.00   4200.00
    LEGAL              125.00   1500.00
    ACCOUNTING         125.00   1500.00
    MISC               100.00   1200.00
                      -------------------
            TOTALS:   5200.00  62400.00


    DAILY OVERHEAD:    288.89
    DIRECT LABOR:      134.10
    PROFIT:             76.14
                      ----------
    BILLING RATE/DAY:  499.13
```

```
>C21:125
>C22:100
>C23:/--
>C24:@SUM(C12...C23)
>C27:/F$+D24/C5
>C28:/F$+C3/261
>C29:/F$(C6*(C27+C28))/100
>C30:/--
>C31:/F$@SUM(C27...C30)

>D 1:"CES: FEE
>D11:/FR"YEARLY
>D12:+C12*12
>D13:+C13*12
>D14:+C14*12
>D15:+C15*12
>D16:+C16*12
>D17:+C17*12
>D18:+C18*12
>D19:+C19*12
>D20:+C20*12
>D21:+C21*12
>D22:+C22*12
>D23:/--
>D24:@SUM(D12...D23)

>E 1:"ANALYSIS

/GC9
/GF$
/GOC
/GRA
/W1
```

CONVENTION SUMMARY

This VisiCalc model summarizes the attendance at a small convention or conference. Attendees' names, entrance fees, and conference bookings are all recorded.

In the sample model, there are three entrance fees tracked by a registration reference number. Attendees pay according to their registration types, and they may also purchase tickets for admission to various functions at the convention. The final entry per registrant is the amount prepaid — and the model will tell you the balance due for each one. If your printer can print lines longer than eight inches, you should be able to print the Registration Report and Attendance

Statement together (PRINT A1...S46), which will put all information for each attendee on one line.

The Calculations for Tickets area multiplies each entry in the Tickets column by the cost per ticket; each row is then added to provide each attendee's amount due for tickets. Each attendee's amount due for registration is found using an @LOOKUP which links the registration fee with the registration code.

PRINT A1...M46, Registration Report
N18...S37, Attendee Statement
T17...AC36, Calculations for Tickets

Listing

```
>A14:"FUNCTION
>A16:"COST/TICK
>A18:"ATTENDEE
>A20:"ADAMS, HE
>A21:"BARRINGTO
>A22:"COLLINS,
>A23:"D'ARLEANE
>A24:"EDWARDS,
>A25:"FARMINGTO
>A26:"HIGGINS,
>A27:"JACOBY, I
>A28:"KELLOGG,
>A29:"LOOMIS, G
>A30:"LOOMIS, H
>A31:"MCASHER,
>A32:"NORMANS,
>A33:"OPPENHEIS
>A34:"ROBERTS,
>A35:"STANISLOF
>A36:/--
>A37:"TOTALS
>A40:"TOTAL TIC
>A41:"TOTAL REG
>A46:"      BAL

>B16:"ET
>B20:"NRY
>B21:"N, G.E.
>B22:"MARK
>B23:", STANLEY
```

```
>B24:"ROBERT
>B25:"N, ESTHER
>B26:"THOMAS
>B27:"SSAC
>B28:"CARL
>B29:"EORGE
>B30:"ELEN
>B31:"JOHN
>B32:"FRANKLIN
>B33:"ER, PAUL
>B34:"GARY
>B35:"ICH, IGMAR
>B36:/--
>B37:"ATTENDEES
>B38:"VALUE OF
>B40:"KET VALUE
>B41:"ISTRATION
>B43:"TOTAL DUE
>B45:"PRE-PAID
>B46:"ANCE DUE

>C 8:/FR"TYPE
>C 9:"LIFE MEMB
>C10:"REGULAR M
>C11:"NON-MEMBE
>C18:"REGISTRN
>C19:"CODE
>C20:/FL1
>C21:/FL2
>C22:/FL3
```

Model Run

```
                    CONVENTION SUMMARY




                    REGISTRATION TYPES
                    ------------------
            TYPE        REF #       FEE
            LIFE MEMBER    1       50.00
            REGULAR MEMBER 2       75.00
            NON-MEMBER     3      100.00
```

FUNCTION		BREAKFAST DAY ONE	LUNCHEON DAY ONE	DINNER DAY ONE	SEMINAR ONE	SEMINAR TWO	SEMINAR THREE	BR'KFAST DAY TWO	LUNCHEON DAY TWO	SEMINAR FOUR	SEMINAR FIVE
COST/TICKET		7.50	13.50	18.00	10.00	10.00	12.50	7.50	13.50	10.00	10.00
ATTENDEE	REGISTRN CODE	TICKETS	TICKETS	TICKETS	TICKETS	TICKETS	TICKETS	TICKETS	TICKETS	TICKETS	TICKETS
ADAMS, HENRY	1	1	1	1	1	1	1	1	1	1	
BARRINGTON, G.E.	2	1	1	1	1		1	1	1		1
COLLINS, MARK	3	1	1	1	1	1	1		1		1
D'ARLEANE, STANLEY	2	1	1	2	1	1		1	1	1	
EDWARDS, ROBERT	1	1	1	1		1		1	1	1	
FARMINGTON, ESTHER	1	1	1	1	1		1	1	1	1	
HIGGINS, THOMAS	2	1	2	1	1	1		1	1		
JACOBY, ISSAC	2	1	1	1	2	1		1	1		
KELLOGG, CARL	3	1	1	1		2	1	1	1		
LOOMIS, GEORGE	3	1	1	1	1	1		1	1	1	
LOOMIS, HELEN	3	1	1	1	1		1	1	1	1	
MCASHER, JOHN	1	1	1	1	2	1		1	1	1	
NORMANS, FRANKLIN	1	1	1	1	1		1	2	1	1	
OPPENHEISER, PAUL	2	1	1	1	1	3		1	1		1
ROBERTS, GARY	3	1	1	1	1	1		1	1		1
STANISLOFICH, IGMAR	1	1	1	1	1	2		1	1		1
TOTALS ATTENDEES 16		16	17	17	16	16	7	15	16	8	5
VALUE OF TICKETS		120.00	229.50	306.00	160.00	160.00	87.50	112.50	216.00	80.00	50.00

```
TOTAL TICKET VALUE   1521.50
TOTAL REGISTRATION   1175.00
                     ---------
        TOTAL DUE    2696.50

         PRE-PAID     950.00
      BALANCE DUE    1746.50
```

DUE FOR TICKETS	DUE FOR REGISTRN	TOTAL DUE	PRE- PAID	BALANCE DUE	
102.50	50.00	152.50	50.00	102.50	!
92.50	75.00	167.50	50.00	117.50	!
95.00	100.00	195.00	100.00	95.00	!
108.00	75.00	183.00	50.00	133.00	!
80.00	50.00	130.00	50.00	80.00	!
92.50	50.00	142.50	50.00	92.50	!
93.50	75.00	168.50	50.00	118.50	!
90.00	75.00	165.00	100.00	65.00	!
92.50	100.00	192.50	100.00	92.50	!
90.00	100.00	190.00	50.00	140.00	!
85.00	100.00	185.00	50.00	135.00	!
100.00	50.00	150.00	50.00	100.00	!
100.00	50.00	150.00	50.00	100.00	!
110.00	75.00	185.00	50.00	135.00	!
90.00	100.00	190.00	50.00	140.00	!
100.00	50.00	150.00	50.00	100.00	!
------	------	------	------	------	
				1746.50	

Attendee Statement

CALCULATIONS FOR TICKETS

7.50	13.50	18.00	10.00	10.00	12.50	7.50	13.50	10.00	0.00
7.50	13.50	18.00	10.00	0.00	12.50	7.50	13.50	0.00	10.00
7.50	13.50	18.00	10.00	10.00	12.50	0.00	13.50	0.00	10.00
7.50	13.50	36.00	10.00	10.00	0.00	7.50	13.50	10.00	0.00
7.50	13.50	18.00	0.00	10.00	0.00	7.50	13.50	10.00	0.00
7.50	13.50	18.00	10.00	0.00	12.50	7.50	13.50	10.00	0.00
7.50	27.00	18.00	10.00	10.00	0.00	7.50	13.50	0.00	0.00
7.50	13.50	18.00	20.00	10.00	0.00	7.50	13.50	0.00	0.00
7.50	13.50	18.00	0.00	20.00	12.50	7.50	13.50	0.00	0.00
7.50	13.50	18.00	10.00	10.00	0.00	7.50	13.50	10.00	0.00
7.50	13.50	18.00	10.00	0.00	12.50	0.00	13.50	10.00	0.00
7.50	13.50	18.00	20.00	10.00	0.00	7.50	13.50	10.00	0.00
7.50	13.50	18.00	10.00	0.00	12.50	15.00	13.50	10.00	0.00
7.50	13.50	18.00	10.00	30.00	0.00	7.50	13.50	0.00	10.00
7.50	13.50	18.00	10.00	10.00	0.00	7.50	13.50	0.00	10.00
7.50	13.50	18.00	10.00	20.00	0.00	7.50	13.50	0.00	10.00

Calculations for Tickets

```
>C23:/FL2
>C24:/FL1
>C25:/FL1
>C26:/FL2
>C27:/FL2
>C28:/FL3
>C29:/FL3
>C30:/FL3
```

```
>C31:/FL1
>C32:/FL1
>C33:/FL2
>C34:/FL3
>C35:/FL1
>C36:/--
>C37:/FL@COUNT(C20...C36)
>C38:"TICKETS
```

>D 1:"CONVENTIO
>D 6:"REGISTRAT
>D 7:/--
>D 9:"ER
>D10:"EMBER
>D11:"R
>D14:"BREAKFAST
>D15:"DAY ONE
>D16:/F$7.5
>D19:/FR"TICKETS
>D20:1
>D21:1
>D22:1
>D23:1
>D24:1
>D25:1
>D26:1
>D27:1
>D28:1
>D29:1
>D30:1
>D31:1
>D32:1
>D33:1
>D34:1
>D35:1
>D36:/--
>D37:@SUM(D20...D36)
>D38:/F$+D37*D16
>D40:/F$@SUM(D38...M38)
>D41:/F$@SUM(O20...O35)
>D42:/--
>D43:/F$+D40+D41
>D45:/F$@SUM(Q20...O35)
>D46:/F$+D43-D45

>E 1:"N SUMMARY
>E 6:"ION TYPES
>E 7:/--
>E 8:"REF #
>E 9:/FL1
>E10:/FL2
>E11:/FL3
>E14:/FR"LUNCHEON
>E15:/FR"DAY ONE
>E16:/F$13.5
>E19:/FR"TICKETS
>E20:1
>E21:1
>E22:1
>E23:1
>E24:1
>E25:1
>E26:2
>E27:1

>E28:1
>E29:1
>E30:1
>E31:1
>E32:1
>E33:1
>E34:1
>E35:1
>E36:/--
>E37:@SUM(E20...E36)
>E38:/F$+E37*E16

>F 8:/FR"FEE
>F 9:/F$50
>F10:/F$75
>F11:/F$100
>F14:/FR"DINNER
>F15:/FR"DAY ONE
>F16:/F$18
>F19:/FR"TICKETS
>F20:1
>F21:1
>F22:1
>F23:2
>F24:1
>F25:1
>F26:1
>F27:1
>F28:1
>F29:1
>F30:1
>F31:1
>F32:1
>F33:1
>F34:1
>F35:1
>F36:/--
>F37:@SUM(F20...F36)
>F38:/F$+F37*F16

>G14:/FR"SEMINAR
>G15:/FR"ONE
>G16:/F$10
>G19:/FR"TICKETS
>G20:1
>G21:1
>G22:1
>G23:1
>G25:1
>G26:1
>G27:2
>G29:1
>G30:1
>G31:2
>G32:1

>G33:1
>G34:1
>G35:1
>G36:/--
>G37:@SUM(G20...G36)
>G38:/F$+G37*G16

>H14:/FR"SEMINAR
>H15:/FR"TWO
>H16:/F$10
>H19:/FR"TICKETS
>H20:1
>H22:1
>H23:1
>H24:1
>H26:1
>H27:1
>H28:2
>H29:1
>H31:1
>H33:3
>H34:1
>H35:2
>H36:/--
>H37:@SUM(H20...H36)
>H38:/F$+H37*H16

>I14:/FR"SEMINAR
>I15:/FR"THREE
>I16:/F$12.5
>I19:/FR"TICKETS
>I20:1
>I21:1
>I22:1
>I25:1
>I28:1
>I30:1
>I32:1
>I36:/--
>I37:@SUM(I20...I36)
>I38:/F$+I37*I16

>J14:/FR"BR'KFAST
>J15:/FR"DAY TWO
>J16:/F$7.5
>J19:/FR"TICKETS
>J20:1
>J21:1
>J23:1
>J24:1
>J25:1
>J26:1
>J27:1
>J28:1
>J29:1

>J31:1
>J32:2
>J33:1
>J34:1
>J35:1
>J36:/--
>J37:@SUM(J20...J36)
>J38:/F$+J37*J16

>K14:/FR"LUNCHEON
>K15:/FR"DAY TWO
>K16:/F$13.5
>K19:/FR"TICKETS
>K20:1
>K21:1
>K22:1
>K23:1
>K24:1
>K25:1
>K26:1
>K27:1
>K28:1
>K29:1
>K30:1
>K31:1
>K32:1
>K33:1
>K34:1
>K35:1
>K36:/--
>K37:@SUM(K20...K36)
>K38:/F$+K37*K16

>L14:/FR"SEMINAR
>L15:/FR"FOUR
>L16:/F$10
>L19:/FR"TICKETS
>L20:1
>L23:1
>L24:1
>L25:1
>L29:1
>L30:1
>L31:1
>L32:1
>L36:/--
>L37:@SUM(L20...L36)
>L38:/F$+L37*L16

>M14:/FR"SEMINAR
>M15:/FR"FIVE
>M16:/F$10
>M19:/FR"TICKETS
>M21:1
>M22:1

```
>M33:1                          >P26:/F$+N26+O26
>M34:1                          >P27:/F$+N27+O27
>M35:1                          >P28:/F$+N28+O28
>M36:/--                        >P29:/F$+N29+O29
>M37:@SUM(M20...M36)            >P30:/F$+N30+O30
>M38:/F$+M37*M16                >P31:/F$+N31+O31
                                >P32:/F$+N32+O32
>N18:/FR"DUE FOR                >P33:/F$+N33+O33
>N19:/FR"TICKETS                >P34:/F$+N34+O34
>N20:/F$@SUM(T20...AC20)        >P35:/F$+N35+O35
>N21:/F$@SUM(T21...AC21)        >P36:/--
>N22:/F$@SUM(T22...AC22)
>N23:/F$@SUM(T23...AC23)        >O18:/FR"PRE-
>N24:/F$@SUM(T24...AC24)        >O19:/FR"PAID
>N25:/F$@SUM(T25...AC25)        >O20:/F$50
>N26:/F$@SUM(T26...AC26)        >O21:/F$50
>N27:/F$@SUM(T27...AC27)        >O22:/F$100
>N28:/F$@SUM(T28...AC28)        >O23:/F$50
>N29:/F$@SUM(T29...AC29)        >O24:/F$50
>N30:/F$@SUM(T30...AC30)        >O25:/F$50
>N31:/F$@SUM(T31...AC31)        >O26:/F$50
>N32:/F$@SUM(T32...AC32)        >O27:/F$100
>N33:/F$@SUM(T33...AC33)        >O28:/F$100
>N34:/F$@SUM(T34...AC34)        >O29:/F$50
>N35:/F$@SUM(T35...AC35)        >O30:/F$50
>N36:/--                        >O31:/F$50
                                >O32:/F$50
>O18:/FR"DUE FOR                >O33:/F$50
>O19:/FR"REGISTRN               >O34:/F$50
>O20:/F$@LOOKUP(C20,E9...E11)   >O35:/F$50
>O21:/F$@LOOKUP(C21,E9...E11)   >O36:/--
>O22:/F$@LOOKUP(C22,E9...E11)
>O23:/F$@LOOKUP(C23,E9...E11)   >R18:/FR"BALANCE
>O24:/F$@LOOKUP(C24,E9...E11)   >R19:/FR"DUE
>O25:/F$@LOOKUP(C25,E9...E11)   >R20:/F$+P20-O20
>O26:/F$@LOOKUP(C26,E9...E11)   >R21:/F$+P21-O21
>O27:/F$@LOOKUP(C27,E9...E11)   >R22:/F$+P22-O22
>O28:/F$@LOOKUP(C28,E9...E11)   >R23:/F$+P23-O23
>O29:/F$@LOOKUP(C29,E9...E11)   >R24:/F$+P24-O24
>O30:/F$@LOOKUP(C30,E9...E11)   >R25:/F$+P25-O25
>O31:/F$@LOOKUP(C31,E9...E11)   >R26:/F$+P26-O26
>O32:/F$@LOOKUP(C32,E9...E11)   >R27:/F$+P27-O27
>O33:/F$@LOOKUP(C33,E9...E11)   >R28:/F$+P28-O28
>O34:/F$@LOOKUP(C34,E9...E11)   >R29:/F$+P29-O29
>O35:/F$@LOOKUP(C35,E9...E11)   >R30:/F$+P30-O30
>O36:/--                        >R31:/F$+P31-O31
                                >R32:/F$+P32-O32
>P18:/FR"TOTAL                  >R33:/F$+P33-O33
>P19:/FR"DUE                    >R34:/F$+P34-O34
>P20:/F$+N20+O20                >R35:/F$+P35-O35
>P21:/F$+N21+O21                >R36:/--
>P22:/F$+N22+O22                >R37:/F$@SUM(R20...R35)
>P23:/F$+N23+O23
>P24:/F$+N24+O24                >S18:/FR
>P25:/F$+N25+O25                >S20:/FR"!
```

```
>S21:/FR"!                          >V21:/F$+F21*F16
>S22:/FR"!                          >V22:/F$+F22*F16
>S23:/FR"!                          >V23:/F$+F23*F16
>S24:/FR"!                          >V24:/F$+F24*F16
>S25:/FR"!                          >V25:/F$+F25*F16
>S26:/FR"!                          >V26:/F$+F26*F16
>S27:/FR"!                          >V27:/F$+F27*F16
>S28:/FR"!                          >V28:/F$+F28*F16
>S29:/FR"!                          >V29:/F$+F29*F16
>S30:/FR"!                          >V30:/F$+F30*F16
>S31:/FR"!                          >V31:/F$+F31*F16
>S32:/FR"!                          >V32:/F$+F32*F16
>S33:/FR"!                          >V33:/F$+F33*F16
>S34:/FR"!                          >V34:/F$+F34*F16
>S35:/FR"!                          >V35:/F$+F35*F16
>S36:/FR/---                        >V36:/---

>T20:/F$+D20*D16                     >W17:"ONS FOR T
>T21:/F$+D21*D16                     >W20:/F$+G20*G16
>T22:/F$+D22*D16                     >W21:/F$+G21*G16
>T23:/F$+D23*D16                     >W22:/F$+G22*G16
>T24:/F$+D24*D16                     >W23:/F$+G23*G16
>T25:/F$+D25*D16                     >W24:/F$+G24*G16
>T26:/F$+D26*D16                     >W25:/F$+G25*G16
>T27:/F$+D27*D16                     >W26:/F$+G26*G16
>T28:/F$+D28*D16                     >W27:/F$+G27*G16
>T29:/F$+D29*D16                     >W28:/F$+G28*G16
>T30:/F$+D30*D16                     >W29:/F$+G29*G16
>T31:/F$+D31*D16                     >W30:/F$+G30*G16
>T32:/F$+D32*D16                     >W31:/F$+G31*G16
>T33:/F$+D33*D16                     >W32:/F$+G32*G16
>T34:/F$+D34*D16                     >W33:/F$+G33*G16
>T35:/F$+D35*D16                     >W34:/F$+G34*G16
>T36:/---                            >W35:/F$+G35*G16
                                     >W36:/---
>U20:/F$+E20*E16
>U21:/F$+E21*E16                     >X17:"ICKETS
>U22:/F$+E22*E16                     >X20:/F$+H20*H16
>U23:/F$+E23*E16                     >X21:/F$+H21*H16
>U24:/F$+E24*E16                     >X22:/F$+H22*H16
>U25:/F$+E25*E16                     >X23:/F$+H23*H16
>U26:/F$+E26*E16                     >X24:/F$+H24*H16
>U27:/F$+E27*E16                     >X25:/F$+H25*H16
>U28:/F$+E28*E16                     >X26:/F$+H26*H16
>U29:/F$+E29*E16                     >X27:/F$+H27*H16
>U30:/F$+E30*E16                     >X28:/F$+H28*H16
>U31:/F$+E31*E16                     >X29:/F$+H29*H16
>U32:/F$+E32*E16                     >X30:/F$+H30*H16
>U33:/F$+E33*E16                     >X31:/F$+H31*H16
>U34:/F$+E34*E16                     >X32:/F$+H32*H16
>U35:/F$+E35*E16                     >X33:/F$+H33*H16
>U36:/---                            >X34:/F$+H34*H16
                                     >X35:/F$+H35*H16
>V17:"CALCULATI                      >X36:/---
>V20:/F$+F20*F16
```

```
>Y20:/F$+I20*I16          >AA33:/F$+K33*K16
>Y21:/F$+I21*I16          >AA34:/F$+K34*K16
>Y22:/F$+I22*I16          >AA35:/F$+K35*K16
>Y23:/F$+I23*I16          >AA36:/--
>Y24:/F$+I24*I16
>Y25:/F$+I25*I16          >AB20:/F$+L20*L16
>Y26:/F$+I26*I16          >AB21:/F$+L21*L16
>Y27:/F$+I27*I16          >AB22:/F$+L22*L16
>Y28:/F$+I28*I16          >AB23:/F$+L23*L16
>Y29:/F$+I29*I16          >AB24:/F$+L24*L16
>Y30:/F$+I30*I16          >AB25:/F$+L25*L16
>Y31:/F$+I31*I16          >AB26:/F$+L26*L16
>Y32:/F$+I32*I16          >AB27:/F$+L27*L16
>Y33:/F$+I33*I16          >AB28:/F$+L28*L16
>Y34:/F$+I34*I16          >AB29:/F$+L29*L16
>Y35:/F$+I35*I16          >AB30:/F$+L30*L16
>Y36:/--                  >AB31:/F$+L31*L16
                          >AB32:/F$+L32*L16
>Z20:/F$+J20*J16          >AB33:/F$+L33*L16
>Z21:/F$+J21*J16          >AB34:/F$+L34*L16
>Z22:/F$+J22*J16          >AB35:/F$+L35*L16
>Z23:/F$+J23*J16          >AB36:/--
>Z24:/F$+J24*J16
>Z25:/F$+J25*J16          >AC20:/F$+M20*M16
>Z26:/F$+J26*J16          >AC21:/F$+M21*M16
>Z27:/F$+J27*J16          >AC22:/F$+M22*M16
>Z28:/F$+J28*J16          >AC23:/F$+M23*M16
>Z29:/F$+J29*J16          >AC24:/F$+M24*M16
>Z30:/F$+J30*J16          >AC25:/F$+M25*M16
>Z31:/F$+J31*J16          >AC26:/F$+M26*M16
>Z32:/F$+J32*J16          >AC27:/F$+M27*M16
>Z33:/F$+J33*J16          >AC28:/F$+M28*M16
>Z34:/F$+J34*J16          >AC29:/F$+M29*M16
>Z35:/F$+J35*J16          >AC30:/F$+M30*M16
>Z36:/--                  >AC31:/F$+M31*M16
                          >AC32:/F$+M32*M16
>AA20:/F$+K20*K16         >AC33:/F$+M33*M16
>AA21:/F$+K21*K16         >AC34:/F$+M34*M16
>AA22:/F$+K22*K16         >AC35:/F$+M35*M16
>AA23:/F$+K23*K16         >AC36:/--
>AA24:/F$+K24*K16
>AA25:/F$+K25*K16         >AD36:/--
>AA26:/F$+K26*K16
>AA27:/F$+K27*K16             /GC9
>AA28:/F$+K28*K16             /GFI
>AA29:/F$+K29*K16             /GOC
>AA30:/F$+K30*K16             /GRM
>AA31:/F$+K31*K16             /W1
>AA32:/F$+K32*K16
```

FINANCIAL SCHEDULES

The following three models prepare schedules that are necessary to support the Income Statement and Balance Sheet models (see next two models). Save the results of these models and input them to your income and balance statements.

Cost of Goods Sold

The statement prepared in this model allocates all manufacturing and service expenses to the appropriate subaccounts in the master chart-of-accounts. It allows detailed allocation of any related expenses incurred in the manufacturing process.

PRINT A1...G53

Listing

```
>A10:"DIRECT MA
>A11:"   MATERI
>A12:"   PURCHA
>A13:"      LES
>A15:"   MATERIAL
>A16:"      LESS
>A18:"       DIR
>A19:"DIRECT LA
>A21:"FACTORY O
>A22:"   INDIRE
>A23:"   SALARI
>A24:"   PAYROLL
>A25:"   POWER
>A26:"   HEAT
>A27:"   LIGHT
>A28:"   FACTOR
>A29:"   DEPREC
>A30:"   DEPREC
>A31:"   REPAIR
>A32:"   PATENT
>A33:"   TOOL &
>A34:"   INSURA
>A35:"   OTHER
>A37:"      TOT
>A39:"TOTAL MAN
>A40:"   ADD WOR
>A43:"   LESS W
>A46:"COST OF G
>A47:"   ADD IN
>A50:"   LESS I
>A52:"COST OF G

>B10:"TERIALS:
>B11:"ALS INVEN
```

```
>B12:"SES
>B13:"S RETURNS
>B15:"ALS AVAIL
>B16:"S MATERIA
>B18:"ECT MATER
>B19:"BOR
>B21:"VERHEAD:
>B22:"CT LABOR
>B23:"ES
>B24:"L TAXES
>B28:"Y SUPPLIE
>B29:"IATION-BU
>B30:"IATION-MA
>B31:"S & MAINT
>B32:" EXPENSES
>B33:" DIE EXPE
>B34:"NCE ON BU
>B35:"OVERHEAD
>B37:"AL FACTOR
>B39:"UFACTURIN
>B40:"RK IN PRO
>B43:"ORK IN PRO
>B46:"OODS MANU
>B47:"VENTORY F
>B50:"NVENTORY
>B52:"OODS SOLD

>C 2:"ANY COMPA
>C 5:"STATEMENT
>C 6:/--
>C 7:"YEAR END:
>C11:"TORY JAN.1
>C13:" & ALLOWA
>C15:"ABLE FOR
```

Model Run

```
                    ANY COMPANY, LARGE AND SMALL


                            SCHEDULE 1
                    STATEMENT OF COST OF GOODS SOLD
                    -------------------------------

                    YEAR END:DECEMBER  31,1980



DIRECT MATERIALS:
    MATERIALS INVENTORY JAN.1 1980   ........$   1572400
    PURCHASES              ........$  8420000
        LESS RETURNS & ALLOWANCES      42000  8378000
                                    ------------------
    MATERIALS AVAILABLE FOR USE . . . . . .$   9950400
        LESS MATERIALS INVENTORY, DEC.31, 1980  1270600
                                              ---------
        DIRECT MATERIALS CONSUMED.....................$   8679800
DIRECT LABOR                                               7346400

FACTORY OVERHEAD:
    INDIRECT LABOR                      $   1329300
    SALARIES                                 972000
    PAYROLL TAXES                            489000
    POWER                                    112000
    HEAT                                      69200
    LIGHT                                     44300
    FACTORY SUPPLIES                          50000
    DEPRECIATION-BUILDINGS                    68300
    DEPRECIATION-MACHINERY                   403000
    REPAIRS & MAINTENANCE                    145800
    PATENT EXPENSES                           33200
    TOOL & DIE EXPENSES                      178600
    INSURANCE ON BUILDING & MACHINERY         21200
    OTHER OVERHEAD                                0
                                            ---------
        TOTAL FACTORY OVERHEAD. . . . . . . . . . .    3915900
                                                       ---------
TOTAL MANUFACTURING COSTS. ........................$ 19942100
    ADD WORK IN PROCESS INVENTORY, JAN 1,1980          2338000
                                                       ---------
                                                     $ 22280100
    LESS WORK IN PROCESS INVENTORY, 12/31/80           1303200
                                                       ---------

COST OF GOODS MANUFACTURED                            20976900
    ADD INVENTORY FINISHED GOODS 1/1/80                 966100
                                                       ---------
                                                      21943000
    LESS INVENTORY FINISHED GOODS 12/31/80              658000
                                                       ---------
COST OF GOODS SOLD.................................$ 21285000
                                                       =========
```

>C16:"LS INVENT
>C18:"IALS CONS
>C28:"S
>C29:"ILDINGS
>C30:"CHINERY
>C31:"ENANCE
>C33:"NSES
>C34:"ILDING &
>C37:"Y OVERHEA
>C39:"G COSTS.
>C40:'CESS INVE
>C43:"OCESS INV
>C46:"FACTURED
>C47:"INISHED G
>C50:"FINISHED
>C52:/-.

>D 2:"NY, LARGE
>D 4:"SCHEDULE
>D 5:" OF COST OF
>D 6:/---
>D 7:"DECEMBER
>D11:"1 1980
>D12:"........$
>D13:"NCES
>D15:"USE . . .
>D16:"ORY, DEC.
>D18:"UMED.....
>D34:"MACHINERY
>D37:"D. . . .
>D39:/-.
>D40:"NTORY, JA
>D43:"ENTORY, 12
>D47:"OODS 1/1/
>D50:"GOODS 12/
>D52:/-.

>E 2:" AND SMAL
>E 4:"1
>E 5:"OF GOODS
>E 6:/---
>E 7:" 31,1980
>E11:"........$
>E12:8420000
>E13:42000
>E14:/---
>E15:" . . . .$
>E16:"31, 1980
>E18:/-.
>E22:" $
>E37:/-.
>E39:/-.
>E40:"N 1,1980
>E43:"2/31/80
>E47:"80
>E50:"31/80

>E52:/-.

>F 2:"L
>F 5:"SOLD
>F 6:"------
>F11:1572400
>F13:+E12-E13
>F14:/---
>F15:+F11+F13
>F16:1270600
>F17:/---
>F18:"........$
>F22:1329300
>F23:972000
>F24:489000
>F25:112000
>F26:69200
>F27:44300
>F28:50000
>F29:68300
>F30:403000
>F31:145800
>F32:33200
>F33:178600
>F34:21200
>F35:0
>F36:/---
>F37:" . . . .
>F39:"........$
>F42:" $
>F52:"........$

>G18:+F15-F16
>G19:7346400
>G37:@SUM(F21...F35)
>G38:/---
>G39:@SUM(G18...G37)
>G40:2338000
>G41:/---
>G42:+G39+G40
>G43:1303200
>G44:/---
>G46:+G42-G43
>G47:966100
>G48:/---
>G49:+G46+G47
>G50:658000
>G51:/---
>G52:+G49-G50
>G53:/-=

/GC9
/GOC
/GRA
/W1

Selling Expenses

This model documents expenses which are attributable to cost of sales. This schedule will assist any marketing and sales manager in allocating expenses to the appropriate selling accounts. You can easily add any ledger accounts and then total the amounts.

PRINT A1...G25

Model Run

```
            ANY COMPANY, LARGE AND SMALL

                    SCHEDULE 2
                  SELLING EXPENSES
                  ----------------

            YEAR END:DECEMBER  31,1980


SALES SALARIES & COMMISSIONS.........................$    330500
TRAVEL EXPENSES                                            43000
PAYROLL TAXES                                             16850
ADVERTISING                                              125000
TELEPHONE & COMMUNICATIONS                               11800
TRAVEL & ENTERTAINMENT                                   21000
DONATIONS & DUES                                          4000
DEPRECIATION-FURNITURE & FIXTURES                        7500
STATIONARY & OFFICE SUPPLIES                             13500
POSTAGE                                                   6850
OTHER SELLING EXPENSES                                      0
                                                     ----------
    TOTAL SELLING EXPENSES. .........................$   580000
                                                     =========
              (THIS TOTAL IS FORWARDED TO
              INCOME STATEMENT)
```

Listing

>A10:"SALES SAL
>A11:"TRAVEL EX
>A12:"PAYROLL T
>A13:"ADVERTISI
>A14:"TELEPHONE
>A15:"TRAVEL & E
>A16:"DONATIONS
>A17:"DEPRECIAT
>A18:"STATIONAR
>A19:"POSTAGE
>A20:"OTHER SEL
>A22:"   TOTAL

>B10:"ARIES & CO
>B11:"PENSES
>B12:"AXES

>B13:"NG
>B14:" & COMMUN
>B15:"ENTERTAINM
>B16:" & DUES
>B17:"ION-FURNITUR
>B18:"Y & OFFICE
>B20:"LING EXPEN
>B22:"SELLING E

>C 2:"ANY COMPA
>C 5:"   SELLIN
>C 6:/---
>C 7:"YEAR END:
>C10:"OMMISSION
>C14:"ICATIONS
>C15:"MENT

```
>C17:"TURE & FIX          >F 2:"L
>C18:"E SUPPLIE           >F10:".........$
>C20:"NSES                >F22:".........$
>C22:"XPENSES.            >F24:"WARDED TO

>D 2:"NY, LARGE           >G10:330500
>D 4:"SCHEDULE            >G11:43000
>D 5:"ING EXPENSES        >G12:16850
>D 6:/--                  >G13:125000
>D 7:"DECEMBER            >G14:11800
>D10:"S........            >G15:21000
>D17:"XTURES              >G16:4000
>D18:"S                   >G17:7500
>D22:/-.                  >G18:13500
>D24:"(THIS TOTAL         >G19:6850
>D25:"INCOME ST           >G20:0
                          >G21:/--
>E 2:" AND SMAL           >G22:@SUM(G10...G20)
>E 4:"2                   >G23:/-=
>E 5:"SES
>E 6:"---                 /GC9
>E 7:" 31,1980            /GOC
>E10:/-.                  /GRA
>E22:/-.                  /W1
>E24:"AL IS FORWA
>E25:"ATEMENT)]
```

General and Administrative Expenses

This schedule allocates all other office and general expenses related to operating any business or department. Again, you can easily add any ledger accounts and then total the amounts.

PRINT A1...G23

Listing

```
>A10:"SALARIES-           >B16:" & COMMUN
>A11:"SALARIES-           >B18:"IONS, DUE
>A12:"TRAVEL EX           >B20:"IN EXPENSE
>A13:"PAYROLL T           >B22:" GENERAL
>A14:"DEPRECIAT
>A15:"STATIONAR           >C 2:"ANY COMPA
>A16:"TELEPHONE           >C 5:"GENERAL &
>A17:"POSTAGE             >C 6:/--
>A18:"SUBSCRIPT           >C 7:"YEAR END:
>A19:"DONATIONS           >C10:"& EXECUTIV
>A20:"OTHER ADMI          >C11:"FFICE EMP
>A22:"    TOTAL           >C14:"TURE & FI
                          >C15:"E SUPPLIES
>B10:"OFFICERS            >C16:"ICATIONS
>B11:"GENERAL O           >C18:"S, & ASSO
>B12:"PENSES              >C20:"ES
>B13:"AXES                >C22:"& ADMIN. E
>B14:"ION-FURNI
>B15:"Y & OFFIC           >D 2:"NY, LARGE
```

Model Run

```
                    ANY COMPANY, LARGE AND SMALL

                           SCHEDULE 3
                   GENERAL & ADMINISTRATIVE EXPENSES
                   ----------------------------------

                   YEAR END:DECEMBER  31,1980



     SALARIES-OFFICERS & EXECUTIVES             $    336200
     SALARIES-GENERAL OFFICE EMPLOYEES               77250
     TRAVEL EXPENSES                                 22450
     PAYROLL TAXES                                   17500
     DEPRECIATION-FURNITURE & FIXTURES               6200
     STATIONARY & OFFICE SUPPLIE                     5450
     TELEPHONE & COMMUNICATIONS                      7800
     POSTAGE                                         3650
     SUBSCRIPTIONS, DUES, & ASSOCIATION ACTIVITIES   4750
     DONATIONS                                       52500
     OTHER ADMIN EXPENSES                               0
                                                  ---------
         TOTAL GENERAL & ADMIN. EXPENSES ...........$   533750
                                                  =========
```

>D 4:"SCHEDULE
>D 5:" ADMINIST
>D 6:/--
>D 7:"DECEMBER
>D10:"VES
>D11:"LOYEES
>D14:"XTURES
>D18:"CIATION A
>D22:"EXPENSES

>E 2:" AND SMAL
>E 4:"3
>E 5:"RATIVE EX
>E 6:/--
>E 7:" 31,1980
>E18:"CTIVITIES
>E22:/-.

>F 2:"L
>F 5:"PENSES
>F 6:"---------
>F10:" $

>F22:".........$

>G10:336200
>G11:77250
>G12:22450
>G13:17500
>G14:6200
>G15:5450
>G16:7800
>G17:3650
>G18:4750
>G19:52500
>G20:0
>G21:/--
>G22:@SUM(G10...G21)
>G23:/-=

/GC9
/GOC
/GRA
/W1

INCOME STATEMENT

The income statement is an important financial report in any business. This model calculates annual net income before and after taxes. The percentage of net sales is also calculated for each expense and profit category.

The cost of goods sold, selling expenses, and general and administrative expense figures can be taken from the bottom lines of the financial schedules you developed in the previous model.

Enter figures for additional income from other sources and deduct other operating expenses to arrive at your net income.

In the sample model, a single tax amount is entered, but you could easily enter a percentage formula to calculate taxes based on your net income and tax rate.

PRINT A1...G37

Listing

```
>A 9:"SALES (#
>A10:"   LESS C
>A13:"GROSS PROFI
>A14:"   LESS OPER
>A15:"     SELL
>A16:"     GEN
>A20:"NET INCOM
>A22:"OTHER INCO
>A23:"   ROYALI
>A24:"   GAIN F
>A25:"   OTHER IN
>A28:"   INTERE
>A33:"NET INCOM
>A34:"   LESS E
>A36:"NET INCOM

>B 9:"UNITS)
>B10:"OST OF GOOD
>B13:"FIT ON SALES
>B14:"PERATING
>B15:"LING EXPENS
>B16:"ERAL & ADMI
>B20:"E FROM OP
>B22:"OME & EXP
>B23:"TIES & DI
>B24:"ROM SALES
>B25:"INCOME IT
>B28:"ST & DEBT
>B30:"NET ADDIT
>B33:"E BEFORE
>B34:"STIMATED
>B36:"E AFTER E

>C 2:"ANY COMPA
>C 6:"YEAR END:
>C 9:/-.
```

```
>C10:"ODS SOLD
>C13:"LES......
>C14:"EXPENSES:
>C15:"NSES (SCH
>C16:"MIN EXPEN
>C17:"(SEE SCHEDU
>C20:"ERATIONS
>C22:"ENSE ITEM
>C23:"VIDENDS..
>C24:" OF FIXED
>C25:"EMS
>C28:" EXPENSES
>C30:"ION .....
>C33:"EST. INCOM
>C34:"INCOME TA
>C36:"STIMATED

>D 2:"NY, LARGE
>D 4:"INCOME ST
>D 5:/--
>D 6:"DECEMBER
>D 9:/-.
>D10:"(SEE SCHE
>D13:/-.
>D15:"EDULE 2)$
>D16:"SE
>D17:"DULE 3)
>D20:/-.
>D22:"S:
>D23:"........$
>D24:" ASSETS
>D30:/-.
>D33:"ME TAXES
>D34:"X
>D36:"TAX PAYMEN
```

Model Run

```
                ANY COMPANY, LARGE AND SMALL

                       INCOME STATEMENT
                       ----------------
                  YEAR END:DECEMBER  31,1980


                                                     %
     SALES (# UNITS)  ..........................$ 24750000   100.00
        LESS COST OF GOODS SOLD (SEE SCHEDULE 1). 21285000    86.00
                                                 ----------------

     GROSS PROFIT ON SALES......................  3465000    14.00
        LESS OPERATING EXPENSES:
             SELLING EXPENSES (SCHEDULE 2)$  580000
             GENERAL & ADMIN EXPENSE
                  (SEE SCHEDULE 3)    533750  1113750     4.50
                                      -------------------------

     NET INCOME FROM OPERATIONS ..................  2351250    9.50

     OTHER INCOME & EXPENSE ITEMS:
         ROYALITIES & DIVIDENDS..........$  167000
         GAIN FROM SALES OF FIXED ASSETS    12000
         OTHER INCOME ITEMS                      0
                                         ---------
                                           179000
         INTEREST & DEBT EXPENSES          129500
                                         ---------
              NET ADDITION ....................   49500    0.20
                                         -------------------

     NET INCOME BEFORE EST. INCOME TAXES ........$ 2400750   9.70
        LESS ESTIMATED INCOME TAX              1064250    4.30
                                              ----------------
     NET INCOME AFTER ESTIMATED TAX PAYMENTS   1336500    5.4
                                              ================
```

```
>E 2:" AND SMAL          >E26:/--
>E 4:"ATEMENT            >E27:@SUM(E23...E25)
>E 5:"--------           >E28:129500
>E 6:" 31,1980           >E29:/---
>E 9:"........$          >E30:/-.
>E10:"DULE 1).           >E33:"........$
>E13:/-.                 >E36:"NTS
>E15:580000
>E17:533750              >F 2:"L
>E18:/---                >F 9:24750000
>E20:/-.                 >F10:21285000
>E23:167000              >F11:/--
>E24:12000               >F13:+F9-F10
>E25:0                   >F17:+E15+E17
```

Income Statement

65

>F18:/---
>F20:+F13-F17
>F30:+E27-E28
>F31:/---
>F33:+F20+F30
>F34:1064250
>F35:/---
 F36:+F33-F34
>F37:/-=

>G 8:"   %
>G 9:/F$100
>G10:/F$+F10/F9*(100)
>G11:/---
>G13:/F$+F13/F9*100

>G17:/F$+F17/F9*100
>G18:/---
>G20:/F$+F20/F9*100
>G30:/F$+F30/F9*100
>G31:/---
>G33:/F$+F33/F9*100
>G34:/F$+F34/F9*100
>G35:/---
>G36:+F36/F9*100
>G37:/-=

/GC9
/GOC
/GRA
/W1

BALANCE SHEET

This model provides a business balance sheet that details assets, liabilities, and stockholder's equity.

If you insert or delete items from any area of this model, be sure to check that total costs balance with total liabilities and stockholder's equity. You may want to isolate such accounts as bad debt reserve or other assets.

PRINT A1...F34, Assets
A35...F63, Liabilities

Listing

```
>A11:"CURRENT A
>A13:"CASH
>A14:"U.S GVMT
>A15:"ACCOUNTS
>A16:"INVENTORI
>A17:"PREPAID INS
>A19:"       TOTA
>A21:"PROPERTY,
>A23:"LAND
>A24:"BUILDINGS
>A25:"MACHINERY
>A28:"     LESS A
>A33:"* TOTAL A
>A37:"CURRENT L
>A39:"ACCOUNTS
>A40:"ACCRUED P
>A41:"ESTIMATED
>A42:"DUE ON LONG
>A44:"       TOTA
>A46:"LONG-TERM
>A47:"OTHER LIA
>A49:"* TOTAL L
>A55:"PREFERRED
>A56:"COMMON ST
>A57:"CONTRIBUT
>A58:"RETAINED
>A60:"TOTAL STO
>A62:"* TOTAL LIAB

>B11:"SSETS:
>B14:"BONDS
>B15:"RECEIVABL
>B16:"ES (MATERIAL
>B17:"NSURANCE,
>B19:"L CURRENT
>B21:" PLANT, &
>B25:" & EQUIPM
>B28:"LLOWANCE
>B29:"      DEPRECI
>B31:"TOTAL PROP
```

```
>B33:"SSETS. . .
>B37:"IABILITIE
>B39:"PAYABLES
>B40:"AYROLL, T
>B41:" INCOME T
>B42:"NG-TERM DEB
>B44:"L CURRENT
>B46:" DEBT(S)
>B47:"BILITIES
>B49:"IABILITIE
>B55:" STOCK
>B56:"OCK
>B57:"ED CAPITA
>B58:"EARNINGS
>B60:"CKHOLDERS
>B62:"IABILITIE

>C 2:"ANY COMPA
>C 6:"YEAR END:
>C15:"E (NET)
>C16:"IALS, WIP
>C17:" TAXES, O
>C19:" ASSETS
>C21:" EQUIPMENT
>C25:"ENT
>C28:"FOR
>C29:"ECIATION
>C31:"PERTY, PL
>C33:/-.
>C37:"S:
>C40:"AXES, INT
>C41:"AXES
>C42:"EBT
>C44:" LIABILIT
>C49:"S........
>C52:"STOCKHOLD
>C53:/--
>C57:"L
>C60:"' EQUITY
>C62:"S & STOCK
```

Model Run

```
                  ANY COMPANY, LARGE AND SMALL

                        BALANCE SHEET
                        -------------
                  YEAR END:DECEMBER  31,1980

                           ASSETS
                           ------


   CURRENT ASSETS:


   CASH                                         2320000
   U.S GVMT BONDS                                820000
   ACCOUNTS RECEIVABLE (NET)                    2661000
   INVENTORIES (MATERIALS, WIP, FIN GDS         3231800
   PREPAID INSURANCE, TAXES, OTHER EXPENSES      220000
                                               ---------
       TOTAL CURRENT ASSETS ...............$  9252800


   PROPERTY, PLANT, & EQUIPMENT


   LAND                              289000
   BUILDINGS                  3406100
   MACHINERY & EQUIPMENT     12529000
                             ---------
                             15935100
   LESS ALLOWANCE FOR
            DEPRECIATION    -8118000  7817100
                           ------------------
       TOTAL PROPERTY, PLANT & EQUIPMENT...  8106100
                                           ---------
   ¢ TOTAL ASSETS. . . . . . . . . . . . .$ 17358900
                                           =========
```

Assets

```
>D  2:"NY, LARGE
>D  4:"BALANCE SHEE
>D  5:/---
>D  6:"DECEMBER
>D  8:"    ASSETS
>D  9:"      ---------
>D16:", FIN GDS
>D17:"THER EXPEN
>D19:/-.
>D21:"T
>D24:3406100
>D25:12529000
>D26:/--
>D27:@SUM(D24...D25)
>D29:-8118000
>D30:/---
```

```
>D31:"ANT & EQUIP
>D33:/- .
>D35:"LIABILITI
>D36:/--
>D40:"EREST, ETC
>D44:"IES . . .
>D49:/-.
>D52:"ERS' EQUI
>D53:/---
>D55:"            $
>D60:/-.
>D62:"HOLDERS'

>E  2:" AND SMAL
>E  4:"HEET
>E  5:"---
>E  6:"  31,1980
>E17:"NSES
>E19:".........$
>E23:289000
>E29:@SUM(D27...D29)
>E30:/---
>E31:"IPMENT...
>E33:".  .  .  .  $
>E35:"ES
>E36:"--
>E40:"C
>E44:"  .  .  .  .$
>E49:".........$
>E52:"TY
>E53:"---
>E55:1126000
>E56:2173000
>E57:2085000
>E58:6870900
>E59:/---
>E60:".........$
>E62:"EQUITY..$

>F  2:"L
>F13:2320000
>F14:820000
>F15:2661000
>F16:3231800
>F17:220000
>F18:/---
>F19:@SUM(F13...F18)
>F31:+E23+E29
>F32:/--
>F33:@SUM(F19...F31)
>F34:/-=
>F39:990800
>F40:1045000
```

```
                        LIABILITIES
                        -----------
      CURRENT LIABILITIES:

      ACCOUNTS PAYABLES                          990800
      ACCRUED PAYROLL, TAXES, INTEREST, ETC     1045000
      ESTIMATED INCOME TAXES                     190700
      DUE ON LONG-TERM DEBT                       200000
                                               ---------
              TOTAL CURRENT LIABILITIES . . . . . . .$  2426500

      LONG-TERM DEBT(S)                         2677500
      OTHER LIABILITIES                              0
                                               ---------
          * TOTAL LIABILITIES........................$  5104000


                     STOCKHOLDERS' EQUITY
                     --------------------

      PREFERRED STOCK                    $    1126000
      COMMON STOCK                           2173000
      CONTRIBUTED CAPITAL                    2085000
      RETAINED EARNINGS                      6870900
                                            ---------
      TOTAL STOCKHOLDERS' EQUITY ................$ 12254900
                                            ---------
          * TOTAL LIABILITIES & STOCKHOLDERS' EQUITY..$ 17358900
                                            =========
```

Liabilities

```
>F41:190700
>F42:200000
>F43:/---
>F44:@SUM(F39...F43)
>F46:2677500
>F47:0
>F48:/---
>F49:@SUM(F44...F47)
>F60:@SUM(E55...E58)
>F61:/---
>F62:+F49+F60
>F63:/-=

/GC9
/GOC
/GRA
/W1
```

INVENTORY CONTROL

ECONOMIC ORDERING QUANTITY

VisiCalc can compute the optimum number of items to order (Economic Ordering Quantity) whenever an order is placed. The formula is:

$$EOQ = \frac{2(F)(S)}{C}$$

where F = the fixed cost of placing and receiving an order,
S = the annual sales in units, and
C = the holding cost per unit.

The formula is based on the assumption that as inventory increases, ordering costs decrease and carrying costs increase.

Economic ordering quantity can be a useful tool for keeping an accurate inventory in large warehouses or small offices.

The worksheet format of the model enables inventory control to create different reports for various costs and sales quantities, and print out any one or all of these reports.

PRINT A1...F10

Model Run

```
#### ECONOMIC ORDERING QUANTITY WORKSHEET ####

   <EST>   <PER UN>  <PER UN> ECONOMIC
 <ANNUAL> <HOLDING>  <FIXED> ORDERING
 <SALES>   <COST>    <COST> QUANTITY


   490000    2.00    300.00    12124 UNITS
   500000    2.50    300.00    10954 UNITS
   550000    3.00    400.00    12111 UNITS
   600000    4.00    400.00    10954 UNITS
```

Listing

```
>A 1:"**** ECON
>A 3:/FL"  <EST>
>A 4:/FL"<ANNUAL>
>A 5:/FL"<SALES>
>A 7:/FR490000
>A 8:/FR500000
>A 9:/FR550000
>A10:600000

>B 1:"OMIC ORDE
>B 3:/FL"<PER UN>
>B 4:/FR"<HOLDING>
>B 5:/FL"  <COST>
>B 7:/F$2
>B 8:/F$2.5
>B 9:/F$3
>B10:/F$4

>C 1:"RING QUAN
>C 3:/FR"<PER UN>
>C 4:/FR"<FIXED>
>C 5:/FR"<COST>
>C 7:/F$300
>C 8:/F$300
>C 9:/F$400
>C10:/F$400

>D 1:"TITY WORK
>D 3:/FR"ECONOMIC
>D 4:/FR"ORDERING
>D 5:/FR"QUANTITY
>D 7:/FI@SQRT((2*C7*A7)/B7)
>D 8:/FI@SQRT((2*C8*A8)/B8)
>D 9:/FI@SQRT((2*C9*A9)/B9)
>D10:@SQRT((2*C10*A10)/B10)

>E 1:"SHEET  **
>E 7:" UNITS
>E 8:" UNITS
>E 9:" UNITS
>E10:" UNITS

>F 1:"**

/GC9
/GFI
/GOC
/GRA
/W1
```

END-OF-YEAR INVENTORY ESTIMATE

This VisiCalc model uses the gross profit method of estimating inventory. This method eliminates the tedious task of counting all merchandise in stock. Retailers can especially benefit from this.

Gross Profit divided by the Sales Volume gives the Percent of Profit. This formula is used to calculate the cost of goods sold, which is then subtracted from the Inventory On Hand to generate the Estimated Closing Inventory. Inventory On Hand is the sum of the Starting Inventory and all purchases. After the inventory is estimated for each department, it is then only a matter of summing up the three calculations for a final figure.

The model presented here exemplifies the method explained above. The example is a store with three departments, labeled A, B, and C. Although this model uses integer figures to represent the dollars, it could be reformatted for dollar notation. The global command would work well here (/GF$).

PRINT A1...F18

Model Run

```
        END-OF-YEAR INVENTORY ESTIMATE

                      DEPT A   DEPT B   DEPT C   TOTALS
        WHOLESALE COST:   24000    14000     5000    43000
        SALES VOLUME:     33000    24500     6500    64000


        GROSS PROFIT:      9000    10500     1500    21000
        % OF PROFIT:        0.27     0.43     0.23     0.33


        STARTING INVENTORY 11500   13400     7500    32400
        PURCHASES          15000    9500     3500    28000
                           ---------
        INVENTORY ON HAND  26500   22900    11000    60400


        ESTIMATED
        CLOSING INVENTORY   2500    8900     6000    17400
```

Listing

```
>A 5:"WHOLESALE
>A 6:"SALES VOL
>A 8:"GROSS PRO
>A 9:"% OF PROF
>A11:"STARTING
>A12:"PURCHASES
>A14:"INVENTORY
>A17:"ESTIMATED
>A18:"CLOSING I

>B 1:/FR"END-OF-YE
>B 5:" COST:
>B 6:"UME:
>B 8:"FIT:
>B 9:"IT:
>B11:"INVENTORY
>B14:" ON HAND
>B18:"NVENTORY

>C 1:"AR INVENT
>C 4:/FR"DEPT A
>C 5:24000
>C 6:33000
>C 8:+C6-C5
>C 9:/F$+C8/C6
>C11:11500
>C12:15000
>C13:/--
>C14:+C11+C12
>C18:+C14-C5
```

```
>D 1:"ORY ESTIM
>D 4:/FR"DEPT B
>D 5:14000
>D 6:24500
>D 8:+D6-D5
>D 9:/F$+D8/D6
>D11:13400
>D12:9500
>D14:+D11+D12
>D18:+D14-D5

>E 1:"ATE
>E 4:/FR"DEPT C
>E 5:5000
>E 6:6500
>E 8:+E6-E5
>E 9:/F$+E8/E6
>E11:7500
>E12:3500
>E14:+E11+E12
>E18:+E14-E5

>F 4:/FR"TOTALS
>F 5:@SUM(C5...E5)
>F 6:@SUM(C6...E6)
>F 8:+F6-F5
>F 9:/F$+F8/F6
>F11:@SUM(C11...E11)
>F12:@SUM(C12...E12)
>F14:+F11+F12
```

```
>F18: +F14-F5

/GC9
/GOC
/GRA
/W1
```

74

VALUE OF INVENTORY

This VisiCalc model calculates an ongoing value of inventory based on a weighted-average cost of all items in stock. You provide the unit cost and quantity of each item added to the inventory and the total number of stock items sold since the last inventory report.

The inventory volume carried forward and the weighted-average cost from the previous quarter must be supplied from the previous report.

The sample model is based on figures for a camera department for the second quarter of the year (April 1-June 30). Throughout the quarter new stock was purchased on various days and at various prices. New stock has a weighted-average unit cost of $35.71. Prior to this quarter, there were 210 units in stock with an average unit cost of $37.12. Averaging the previous average cost per item and the current average cost per item provides a new weighted-average unit cost for the 253 units in stock on June 30, and produces a current weighted value of $9212.78.

PRINT A1...E36

Listing

```
>A  4:"DEPT:
>A  6:"INVENTORY
>A  7:"WEIGHTED
>A12:"PURCHASE
>A13:"DATE
>A14:/FL401
>A15:/FL502
>A16:/FL517
>A17:/FL610
>A18:/FL615
>A19:/FL617
>A20:/FL625
>A25:"WEIGHTED
>A26:"AVERAGE C
>A28:/-*
>A29:"*
>A30:"* INVENTO
>A31:"*   6/30
>A32:"*
>A33:/-*

>B  1:"   VALUE O
>B  4:"CAMERA
>B  6:" CARRIED
>B  7:"AVERAGE F
>B  9:"PURCHASES
>B10:/-=
>B12:/FR"UNIT
>B13:/FR"PRICE
>B14:/F$35
>B15:/F$34.5
>B16:/F$37.75
>B17:/F$36
```

```
>B18:/F$35.25
>B19:/F$38
>B20:/F$37.75
>B22:/FR"TOTAL
>B23:"      SOLD
>B26:"OST THIS
>B28:/-*
>B30:"RY ON
>B31:+C22+E6-C23
>B33:/-*

>C  1:"F INVENTO
>C  4:"INVENTORY
>C  6:"FWD PREV
>C  7:"ROM PREV
>C13:/FR"QUANTITY
>C14:/FR10
>C15:/FR20
>C16:5
>C17:10
>C18:30
>C19:5
>C20:10
>C21:/--
>C22:@SUM(C14...C20)
>C23:47
>C26:"QTR        =
>C28:"**
>C29:" *
>C30:" *
>C31:" *
>C32:" *
>C33:"**
```

```
>D  1:"RY
>D  4:"  FOR END
>D  6:"QTR =
>D  7:"QTR =
>D 12:/FR"TOTAL
>D 13:/FR"PRICE
>D 14:/F$+C14*B14
>D 15:/F$+C15*B15
>D 16:/F$+C16*B16
>D 17:/F$+C17*B17
>D 18:/F$+C18*B18
>D 19:/F$+C19*B19
>D 20:/F$+C20*B20
>D 21:/--
>D 22:/F$@SUM(D14...D20)
```

```
>D26:/F$+D22/C22
>D32:/FR"END OF
>D33:/FR"QUARTER
>D34:/FR"WEIGHTED
>D35:/FR"VALUE
>D36:+B31*(D26+E7/2)

>E  4:"OF QTR #2
>E  6:/FI210
>E  7:/F$37.12

/GC9
/GOC
/GRA
/W1
```

Model Run

```
              VALUE OF INVENTORY


   DEPT:   CAMERA   INVENTORY FOR END OF QTR #2

   INVENTORY CARRIED FWD PREV QTR =      210
   WEIGHTED AVERAGE FROM PREV QTR =     37.12

            PURCHASES
            =========


   PURCHASE     UNIT           TOTAL
   DATE       PRICE QUANTITY   PRICE
    401       35.00      10    350.00
    502       34.50      20    690.00
    517       37.75       5    188.75
    610       36.00      10    360.00
    615       35.25      30   1057.50
    617       38.00       5    190.00
    625       37.75      10    377.50
                        ------------------
            TOTAL       90   3213.75
            SOLD        47


   WEIGHTED
   AVERAGE COST THIS QTR   =    35.71


   *********************
   *                   *
   * INVENTORY ON      *
   *  6/30       253   *
   *                   *     END OF
   *********************    QUARTER
                           WEIGHTED
                             VALUE
                           9212.784
```

IN STOCK POSITION

This model predicts how much time will pass before your current inventory is depleted. You should use it as an indicator of when to reorder inventory, based on your ordering lead-time.

The sample model is for a publishing company, and uses a six-month sales forecast.

To use the publishing model, enter a six-month unit sales forecast for each book and its current inventory count. The VisiCalc model calculates the number of months before each book will be out-of-stock using a monthly average of sales forecasts for the next six months.

If six months does not supply enough advance notice of a potential out-of-stock situation in your business, either extend the sales forecast for an appropriate number of months, or base your forecast on a longer period of time (possibly two-month or quarter periods). Similarly, you may want to reduce the forecast period to better suit your ordering or manufacturing schedules.

You should find this model easier to use if you lock the stock item titles down the left side of your VisiCalc screen, and the forecast month titles across the top of the screen (/TB).

The sample model was run on December 1. To use it on January 1, replace the December sales projections with a June sales forecast; this allows a continuous six-month forecast. Then update the current inventory figures to reflect January 1 stock levels, and the VisiCalc model will report an updated out-of-stock projection.

PRINT A1...K19

Model Run

```
IN STOCK POSITION          DEC 1


   TITLE         FORECAST--------------------------------------------  AVERAGE  CURRENT  MOS. TO
                 DEC     JAN     FEB     MAR     APR     MAY  SALES/MO     INV     O/S   COMMENTS


   BOOK  1       500     500     500     500     500     500     500      422     0.84   ORDERED
   BOOK  2        75      50      75      50      50      50      58     1158    19.85
   BOOK  3       100     120     100     120     100     100     107      538     5.04
   BOOK  4       400     400     400     400     400     400     400     8415    21.04
   BOOK  5      2100    2000    2500    2200    2500    2500    2300     9330     4.06
   BOOK  6       600     500     600     500     500     500     533     3753     7.04   GO O/S
   BOOK  7       500     500     500     500     500     500     500     3993     7.99
   BOOK  8        50      50      50      50      50      50      50      901    18.02
   BOOK  9       900    1200    1500    1200    1200    1200    1200    10046     8.37
   BOOK 10       500     600     500     600     600     600     567     7216    12.73
   BOOK 11       900    1000    1200    1000     900    1200    1033     9103     8.81
   BOOK 12       120     100     150     100      75     150     116      908     7.84
```

Listing

```
>A  1:"IN STOCK
>A  4:"TITLE
>A  8:"BOOK  1
>A  9:"BOOK  2
>A10:"BOOK  3
>A11:"BOOK  4
>A12:"BOOK  5
>A13:"BOOK  6
>A14:"BOOK  7
>A15:"BOOK  8
>A16:"BOOK  9
>A17:"BOOK  10
>A18:"BOOK  11
>A19:"BOOK  12

>B  1:"POSITION
>B  4:"       FORE
>B  5:"       DEC
>B  8:/FI500
>B  9:/FI75
>B10:/FI100
>B11:/FI400
>B12:/FI2100
>B13:/FI600
>B14:500
>B15:/FI50
>B16:/FI900
>B17:/FI500
>B18:/FI900
>B19:/FI120

>C  4:"CAST-----
>C  5:"          JAN
>C  8:/FI500
>C  9:/FI50
>C10:/FI120
>C11:/FI400
>C12:/FI2000
>C13:/FI500
>C14:500
>C15:/FI50
>C16:/FI1200
>C17:/FI600
>C18:/FI1000
>C19:/FI100

>D  1:"DEC 1
>D  4:"----------
>D  5:"          FEB
>D  8:/FI500
>D  9:/FI75
>D10:/FI100
>D11:/FI400
```

```
>D12:/FI2500
>D13:/FI600
>D14:500
>D15:/FI50
>D16:/FI1500
>D17:/FI500
>D18:/FI1200
>D19:/FI150


>E  4:"----------
>E  5:"          MAR
>E  8:/FI500
>E  9:/FI50
>E10:/FI120
>E11:/FI400
>E12:/FI2200
>E13:/FI500
>E14:500
>E15:/FI50
>E16:/FI1200
>E17:/FI600
>E18:/FI1000
>E19:/FI100


>F  4:"----------
>F  5:"          APR
>F  8:/FI500
>F  9:/FI50
>F10:/FI100
>F11:/FI400
>F12:/FI2500
>F13:/FI500
>F14:500
>F15:/FI50
>F16:/FI1200
>F17:/FI600
>F18:/FI900
>F19:/FI75


>G  4:"----------
>G  5:"          MAY
>G  8:/FI500
>G  9:/FI50
>G10:/FI100
>G11:/FI400
>G12:/FI2500
>G13:/FI500
>G14:500
>G15:/FI50
>G16:/FI1200
>G17:/FI600
>G18:/FI1200
>G19:/FI150
```

```
>H  4:"     AVERAGE
>H  5:"  SALES/MO
>H  8:/FI+@SUM(B8...G8)/6
>H  9:/FI+@SUM(B9...G9)/6
>H10:/FI+@SUM(B10...G10)/6
>H11:/FI+@SUM(B11...G11)/6
>H12:/FI+@SUM(B12...G12)/6
>H13:/FI+@SUM(B13...G13)/6
>H14:/FI+@SUM(B14...G14)/6
>H15:/FI+@SUM(B15...G15)/6
>H16:/FI+@SUM(B16...G16)/6
>H17:/FI+@SUM(B17...G17)/6
>H18:/FI+@SUM(B18...G18)/6
>H19:/FI+@SUM(B19...G19)/6

>I  4:"    CURRENT
>I  5:"          INV
>I  8:422
>I  9:1158
>I10:538
>I11:8415
>I12:9330
>I13:3753
>I14:3993
>I15:901
>I16:10046
>I17:7216
>I18:9103
>I19:908

>J  4:"   MOS. TO
>J  5:"          O/S
```

```
>J  8:/F$+I8/H8
>J  9:/F$+I9/H9
>J10:/F$+I10/H10
>J11:/F$+I11/H11
>J12:/F$+I12/H12
>J13:/F$+I13/H13
>J14:/F$+I14/H14
>J15:/F$+I15/H15
>J16:/F$+I16/H16
>J17:/F$+I17/H17
>J18:/F$+I18/H18
>J19:/F$+I19/H19

>K  5:/FR"COMMENTS
>K  8:/FR"ORDERED
>K  9:/FR
>K10:/FR
>K11:/FR
>K12:/FR
>K13:/FR"GO O/S
>K14:/FR
>K15:/FR
>K16:/FR
>K17:/FR
>K18:/FR
>K19:/FR

/GC9
/GFI
/GOC
/GRA
/W1
```

ADVERTISING
AND SALES

SALES vs. OVERHEAD

This VisiCalc model distributes a standard monthly overhead to distinct departments based on each department's monthly percentage of total sales. The model can be used in any business that can departmentalize or categorize its sales. The sample model is for a small hardware store with seven distinct departments.

The formula used to calculate percent of overhead is

$$\frac{\text{total overhead}}{\text{total sales} \times \text{dept. sales} \times 100}$$

The model can be used as a forecasting tool if sales data is entered for months in advance; by entering projections for the coming year and then adjusting your entries as actual sales figures become available, you can calculate the actual percent of overhead.

Since there are calculations made throughout the worksheet, consider setting a global, manual recalculation command. This can save entry time if your application includes many departments. Remember, calculations will be performed only when you type an exclamation mark in the calculation grid.

PRINT A1...J50

Listing

```
>A 4:"MONTHLY O
>A 5:/-=
>A 6:"RENT
>A 7:/F$700
>A13:"SALES
>A14:"OVERHEAD
>A16:"SALES
>A17:"OVERHEAD
>A19:"SALES
>A20:"OVERHEAD
>A22:"SALES
>A23:"OVERHEAD
>A25:"SALES
>A26:"OVERHEAD
>A28:"SALES
>A29:"OVERHEAD
>A31:"SALES
>A32:"OVERHEAD
>A34:"SALES
>A35:"OVERHEAD
>A37:"SALES
>A38:"OVERHEAD
>A40:"SALES
>A41:"OVERHEAD
>A43:"SALES
>A44:"OVERHEAD
>A46:"SALES
>A47:"OVERHEAD
>A49:"Y-T-D SAL
>A50:"Y-T-D OVE
```

```
>B 4:"VERHEAD
>B 5:/-=
>B 6:"ELECTRIC
>B 7:/F$35
>B12:"MONTH
>B13:"JANUARY
>B16:"FEBRUARY
>B19:"MARCH
>B22:"APRIL
>B25:"MAY
>B28:"JUNE
>B31:"JULY
>B34:"AUGUST
>B37:"SEPTEMBER
>B40:"OCTOBER
>B43:"NOVEMBER
>B46:"DECEMBER
>B49:"ES
>B50:"RHEAD

>C 1:"SALES VS.
>C 6:"TELEPHONE
>C 7:/F$150
>C11:"CARPENTRY
>C12:"SUPPLIES
>C13:500
>C14:(G7/J13)*C13
>C16:550
>C17:(G7/J16)*C16
>C19:490
```

Model Run

```
               SALES VS. OVERHEAD


MONTHLY OVERHEAD
==================
RENT    ELECTRIC TELEPHONE   LABOR    HEAT    OTHER   TOTAL
 700.00    35.00   150.00  1200.00   25.00   150.00  2260.00
```

	MONTH	CARPENTRY SUPPLIES	PLUMBING SUPPLIES	HOUSE-WARES	ELECTRIC SUPPLIES	GLASS	FIXTURES	TOOLS	TOTAL SALES
SALES	JANUARY	500.00	600.00	300.00	400.00	250.00	140.00	340.00	2530.00
OVERHEAD		446.64	535.97	267.98	357.31	223.32	125.06	303.72	
SALES	FEBRUARY	550.00	490.00	330.00	500.00	400.00	300.00	410.00	2980.00
OVERHEAD		417.11	371.61	250.27	379.19	303.36	227.52	310.94	
SALES	MARCH	490.00	500.00	400.00	430.00	200.00	300.00	400.00	2720.00
OVERHEAD		407.13	415.44	332.35	357.28	166.18	249.26	332.35	
SALES	APRIL	600.00	500.00	400.00	400.00	300.00	300.00	400.00	2900.00
OVERHEAD		467.59	389.66	311.72	311.72	233.79	233.79	311.72	
SALES	MAY	650.00	550.00	450.00	400.00	300.00	350.00	400.00	3100.00
OVERHEAD		473.87	400.97	328.06	291.61	218.71	255.16	291.61	
SALES	JUNE	650.00	500.00	500.00	500.00	400.00	400.00	400.00	3350.00
OVERHEAD		438.51	337.31	337.31	337.31	269.85	269.85	269.85	
SALES	JULY	750.00	600.00	550.00	550.00	500.00	400.00	400.00	3750.00
OVERHEAD		452.00	361.60	331.47	331.47	301.33	241.07	241.07	
SALES	AUGUST	750.00	600.00	500.00	600.00	550.00	500.00	500.00	4000.00
OVERHEAD		423.75	339.00	282.50	339.00	310.75	282.50	282.50	
SALES	SEPTEMBER	700.00	600.00	500.00	600.00	500.00	500.00	500.00	3900.00
OVERHEAD		405.64	347.69	289.74	347.69	289.74	289.74	289.74	
SALES	OCTOBER	700.00	600.00	500.00	600.00	500.00	500.00	500.00	3900.00
OVERHEAD		405.64	347.69	289.74	347.69	289.74	289.74	289.74	
SALES	NOVEMBER	700.00	600.00	500.00	600.00	500.00	500.00	500.00	3900.00
OVERHEAD		405.64	347.69	289.74	347.69	289.74	289.74	289.74	
SALES	DECEMBER	700.00	600.00	500.00	600.00	500.00	500.00	500.00	3900.00
OVERHEAD		405.64	347.69	289.74	347.69	289.74	289.74	289.74	
		----	----	----	----	----	----	----	----
Y-T-D SALES		7740.00	6740.00	5430.00	6180.00	4900.00	4690.00	5250.00	40930.00
Y-T-D OVERHEAD		5149.17	4542.33	3600.65	4095.67	3186.26	3043.19	3502.74	27120.00

```
>C20: (G7/J19)*C19
>C22:600
>C23: (G7/J22)*C22
>C25:650
>C26: (G7/J25)*C25
>C28:650
>C29: (G7/J28)*C28
>C31:750
>C32: (G7/J31)*C31
>C34:750
>C35: (G7/J34)*C34
>C37:700
>C38: (G7/J37)*C37
>C40:700
>C41: (G7/J40)*C40
>C43:700
>C44: (G7/J43)*C43
>C46:700
>C47: (G7/J46)*C46
>C48:/--
>C49:+C13+C16+C19+C22+C25+C28
        +C31+C34+C37+C40+C43+C46
>C50:+C14+C17+C20+C23+C26+C29
        +C32+C35+C38+C41+C44+C47

>D 1:/FR"OVERHEAD
>D 6:/FR"LABOR
>D 7:/F$1200
>D11:/FR"PLUMBING
>D12:/FR"SUPPLIES
>D13:600
>D14: (G7/J13)*D13
>D16:490
>D17: (G7/J16)*D16
>D19:500
>D20: (G7/J19)*D19
>D22:500
>D23: (G7/J22)*D22
>D25:550
>D26: (G7/J25)*D25
>D28:500
>D29: (G7/J28)*D28
>D31:600
>D32: (G7/J31)*D31
>D34:600
>D35: (G7/J34)*D34
>D37:600
>D38: (G7/J37)*D37
>D40:600
>D41: (G7/J40)*D40
>D43:600
>D44: (G7/J43)*D43
>D46:600
>D47: (G7/J46)*D46
>D48:/--
>D49:+D13+D16+D19+D22+D25+D28
        +D31+D34+D37+D40+D43+D46
>D50:+D14+D17+D20+D23+D26+D29
        +D32+D35+D38+D41+D44+D47

>E 6:/FR"HEAT
>E 7:/F$25
>E11:/FR"HOUSE-
>E12:/FR"WARES
>E13:300
>E14: (G7/J13)*E13
>E16:330
>E17: (G7/J16)*E16
>E19:400
>E20: (G7/J19)*E19
>E22:400
>E23: (G7/J22)*E22
>E25:450
>E26: (G7/J25)*E25
>E28:500
>E29: (G7/J28)*E28
>E31:550
>E32: (G7/J31)*E31
>E34:500
>E35: (G7/J34)*E34
>E37:500
>E38: (G7/J37)*E37
>E40:500
>E41: (G7/J40)*E40
>E43:500
>E44: (G7/J43)*E43
>E46:500
>E47: (G7/J46)*E46
>E48:/--
>E49:+E13+E16+E19+E22+E25+E28
        +E31+E34+E37+E40+E43+E46
>E50:+E14+E17+E20+E23+E26+E29
        +E32+E35+E38+E41+E44+E47

>F 6:/FR"OTHER
>F 7:/F$150
>F11:/FR"ELECTRIC
>F12:/FR"SUPPLIES
>F13:400
>F14: (G7/J13)*F13
>F16:500
>F17: (G7/J16)*F16
>F19:430
>F20: (G7/J19)*F19
>F22:400
>F23: (G7/J22)*F22
>F25:400
>F26: (G7/J25)*F25
>F28:500
```

```
>F29: (G7/J28)*F28                    >H16:300
>F31:550                              >H17: (G7/J16)*H16
>F32: (G7/J31)*F31                    >H19:300
>F34:600                              >H20: (G7/J19)*H19
>F35: (G7/J34)*F34                    >H22:300
>F37:600                              >H23: (G7/J22)*H22
>F38: (G7/J37)*F37                    >H25:350
>F40:600                              >H26: (G7/J25)*H25
>F41: (G7/J40)*F40                    >H28:400
>F43:600                              >H29: (G7/J28)*H28
>F44: (G7/J43)*F43                    >H31:400
>F46:600                              >H32: (G7/J31)*H31
>F47: (G7/J46)*F46                    >H34:500
>F48:/--                              >H35: (G7/J34)*H34
>F49:+F13+F16+F19+F22+F25+F28         >H37:500
      +F31+F34+F37+F40+F43+F46        >H38: (G7/J37)*H37
>F50:+F14+F17+F20+F23+F26+F29         >H40:500
      +F32+F35+F38+F41+F44+F47        >H41: (G7/J40)*H40
                                      >H43:500
                                      >H44: (G7/J43)*H43
>G 6:/FR"TOTAL                        >H46:500
>G 7:/F$@SUM(A7...F7)                 >H47: (G7/J46)*H46
>G12:/FR"GLASS                        >H48:/--
>G13:250                              >H49:+H13+H16+H19+H22+H25+H28
>G14: (G7/J13)*G13                          +H31+H34+H37+H40+H43+H46
>G16:400                              >H50:+H14+H17+H20+H23+H26+H29
>G17: (G7/J16)*G16                          +H32+H35+H38+H41+H44+H47
>G19:200
>G20: (G7/J19)*G19
>G22:300                              >I12:/FR"TOOLS
>G23: (G7/J22)*G22                    >I13:340
>G25:300                              >I14: (G7/J13)*I13
>G26: (G7/J25)*G25                    >I16:410
>G28:400                              >I17: (G7/J16)*I16
>G29: (G7/J28)*G28                    >I19:400
>G31:500                              >I20: (G7/J19)*I19
>G32: (G7/J31)*G31                    >I22:400
>G34:550                              >I23: (G7/J22)*I22
>G35: (G7/J34)*G34                    >I25:400
>G37:500                              >I26: (G7/J25)*I25
>G38: (G7/J37)*G37                    >I28:400
>G40:500                              >I29: (G7/J28)*I28
>G41: (G7/J40)*G40                    >I31:400
>G43:500                              >I32: (G7/J31)*I31
>G44: (G7/J43)*G43                    >I34:500
>G46:500                              >I35: (G7/J34)*I34
>G47: (G7/J46)*G46                    >I37:500
>G48:/--                              >I38: (G7/J37)*I37
>G49:+G13+G16+G19+G22+G25+G28         >I40:500
      +G31+G34+G37+G40+G43+G46        >I41: (G7/J40)*I40
>G50:+G14+G17+G20+G23+G26+G29         >I43:500
      +G32+G35+G38+G41+G44+G47        >I44: (G7/J43)*I43
                                      >I46:500
                                      >I47: (G7/J46)*I46
>H12:/FR"FIXTURES                     >I48:/--
>H13:140
>H14: (G7/J13)*H13
```

```
>I49:+I13+I16+I19+I22+I25+I28          >J34:@SUM(C34...I34)
      +I31+I34+I37+I40+I43+I46         >J37:@SUM(C37...I37)
>I50:+I14+I17+I20+I23+I26+I29          >J40:@SUM(C40...I40)
      +I32+I35+I38+I41+I44+I47         >J43:@SUM(C43...I43)
                                       >J46:@SUM(C46...I46)
>J11:/FR"TOTAL                         >J48:/--
>J12:/FR"SALES                         >J49:@SUM(C49...I49)
>J13:@SUM(C13...I13                    >J50:@SUM(C50...I50)
>J16:@SUM(C16...I16
>J19:@SUM(C19...I19)
>J22:@SUM(C22...I22)                   /GC9
>J25:@SUM(C25...I25)                   /GF$
>J28:@SUM(C28...I28)                   /GOC
>J31:@SUM(C31...I31)                   /GRM
                                       /W1
```

RETAIL MARK-UP

This is a simple model that calculates the retail price of a product based on its unit cost and your desired profit. The desired profit is entered as a percent, and can be different for every product on your list. After each product has been entered, the mark-up percent for your entire list is averaged, and it can be used to monitor your cost-to-profit ratio.

If you enter all your products in this model, you could generate a price list by moving the selling price next to the product name, and printing just those two columns.

PRINT A1...D20

Model Run

```
          <<< RETAIL MARK-UP >>>


                  UNIT  DESIRED  SELLING
    PRODUCT       COST   PROF %    PRICE
    =======       ====   ==== =    =====

    UNIT ONE    523.00      35    804.62
    UNIT TWO    402.00      20    502.50
    UNIT THRE   221.00      40    368.33
    UNIT FOUR   400.00      33    597.01
    UNIT FIVE   123.00      45    223.64
    UNIT SIX     88.00    37.5    140.80



    AVERAGE MARK-UP =  35.08333
```

Listing

```
>A  6:"PRODUCT
>A  7:"=======
>A  9:"UNIT ONE
>A10:"UNIT TWO
>A11:"UNIT THRE
>A12:"UNIT FOUR
>A13:"UNIT FIVE
>A14:"UNIT SIX
>A18:"AVERAGE M

>B  1:"<<<   RETA
>B  5:/FR" UNIT
>B  6:/FR" COST
>B  7:/FR" ====
>B  9:/F$523
>B10:/F$402
>B11:/F$221
>B12:/F$400
>B13:/F$123
>B14:/F$88
>B18:"ARK-UP =

>C  1:"IL MARK-U
>C  5:/FR"DESIRED
>C  6:"  PROF %
>C  7:"  ==== =
>C  9:35
>C10:20
>C11:40
>C12:33
>C13:45
>C14:37.5
>C18:@AVERAGE(C9...C14)

>D  1:"P  >>>
>D  5:/FR"SELLING
>D  6:/FR"PRICE
>D  7:"     =====
>D  9:/F$+B9/(1-(C9/100))
>D10:/F$+B10/(1-(C10/100))
>D11:/F$+B11/(1-(C11/100))
>D12:/F$+B12/(1-(C12/100))
>D13:/F$+B13/(1-(C13/100))
>D14:/F$+B14/(1-(C14/100))

/GC9
/GOC
/GRA
/W1
```

SALES COMMISSIONS REGISTER

This model calculates sales commissions on a sliding scale and, with a few extra steps, keeps a running year-to-date tally on both commissions and draws. Override sales commissions may also be calculated.

The sliding scale is reflected in the Sales Commission Table. Employees who have up to $3000 in sales earn a 35% commission; those whose sales total over $3000 but less than $6000 earn 40% of the difference; over $6000 but less than $10,000 in sales earns them 50% of the difference; and anything over $10,000 earns 50%. For example, if a salesperson sells products or services worth $5000, he or she would be paid 35% of the $3000 plus 40% of $2000. To aid the calculation, the column labeled Plus contains the precalculated commissions on the break-point minus $1.

As an example, $3001 is the first break-point, so the Plus for $3001 is $1050 — 35% of $3000. In calculating a commission, the sales volume is used as an @LOOKUP value applied to the To column (the $1 entry in the table satisfies the less than $6000 in sales requirement). This returns the appropriate percentage, which is used to calculate the total commissions.

The commission to be paid is calculated in three steps:

- Subtracting the Minus amount from the amount of sale, then
- Multiplying the difference by the decimal percentage (%/100), and
- Adding the Plus amount.

In the sample model, salesperson Andersen sold $3500. His commission is calculated as 35% of $3000 plus 40% of $500. The calculation work area shows the numbers of the first three commissions transferred for calculation.

You can also enter override commissions for any salesperson. First, enter the company override percentage rate. Then, if there is an override sale, enter the amount in that column in the model.

In addition to calculating current commissions, this model can also be used as a year-to-date record, although the necessary steps are a little more complicated.

When the model is loaded into memory, it lists the previous period's weekly or monthly calculations, including the current and prior Y-T-D. At this point, the prior Y-T-D should become the current Y-T-D. Thus, you would first copy the figure under current as prior for each salesperson listed. The same should be done for prior Y-T-D draw.

Next, blank out the Amount of Sale (and Override, if applicable). Do the same for Current Draw. When all have been blanked, press the exclamation mark key and the VisiCalc model will recalculate the figures. The end result should be several columns showing NA.

At this point the current period's sales are ready to be entered. Enter new sales amounts or a 0 for any salesperson with no current sales. Recalculate using the exclamation mark, and the NA notations should be replaced with dollar amounts throughout the report. The final result is a new register with updated sales and Y-T-D figures.

Save this register under a new file name. You might want to save it twice, once on your historical data disk as "COMM.REG.mmddyy", and again on your work disk as "CURR.REG". Load CURR.REG the next time commissions are to be figured.

PRINT A1...M29, Sales
Commissions Register
021...Q28, Calculation Work Area

Model Run

```
                SALES COMMISSIONS REGISTER


                   <SALES COMMISSION TABLE >


              TO       PERCENTG     PLUS      MINUS
                  1.00        35       0.00       0.00
               3001.00        40    1050.00    3000.00
               6001.00        45    2250.00    6000.00
              10001.00        50    6750.00   10000.00




           OVERRIDE PERCENTG= 5

   SALES COMMISSION REGISTER FOR PERIOD ENDING: MM/DD/YY
```

SALESMAN	DATE OF SALE	AMT OF SALE	COMM	OVERRIDE SALE	OVERRIDE COMM	PRIOR Y-T-D COMM	CURR Y-T-D COMM	PRIOR Y-T-D DRAW	CURR DRAW	Y-T-D DRAW	SALES LESS DRAW
ANDERSEN	OCT 17	3500.00	1250.00		0.00	2400.00	3650.00	2000.00	500.00	2500.00	1150.00
BARTOK	OCT 15	12000.00	7750.00		0.00	3000.00	10750.00	2500.00	500.00	3000.00	7750.00
HANNING	OCT 7	10000.00	4050.00	2000.00	100.00	1800.00	5950.00	3000.00	500.00	3500.00	2450.00
MCGOWAN	OCT 8	2500.00	875.00		0.00	1000.00	1875.00	3000.00	500.00	3500.00	-1625.00
NELSON	OCT 20	1000.00	350.00	4500.00	225.00	550.00	1125.00	3500.00	500.00	4000.00	-2875.00
TOTALS:		29000.00	14275.00	6500.00	325.00	8750.00	23350.00	14000.00	2500.00	16500.00	6850.00

Sales Commissions Register

```
      CALCULATION WORK AREA
        %     PLUS      MINUS
       40   1050.00    3000.00
       50   6750.00   10000.00
       45   2250.00    6000.00
       35      0.00       0.00
       35      0.00       0.00
      --------------------------
```

Calculation Work Area

Listing

```
>A18:"SALES COM              >A28:/--
>A21:"SALESMAN
>A23:"ANDERSEN              >B18:"MISSION R
>A24:"BARTOK               >B28:/--
>A25:"HANNING
>A26:"MCGOWAN              >C 1:"SALES COM
>A27:"NELSON               >C16:"OVERRIDE
```

```
>C18:"EGISTER F
>C21:/FR"DATE OF
>C22:/FR"SALE
>C23:/FR"OCT 17
>C24:/FR"OCT 15
>C25:/FR"OCT  7
>C26:/FR"OCT  8
>C27:/FR"OCT 20
>C28:/--
>C29:/FR"TOTALS:

>D 1:"MISSIONS
>D 4:"   <SALES
>D 6:/FL"  TO
>D 7:1
>D 8:3001
>D 9:6001
>D10:10001
>D16:"PERCENTG=
>D18:"OR PERIOD
>D21:/FR"AMT OF
>D22:/FR"SALE
>D23:3500
>D24:12000
>D25:10000
>D26:2500
>D27:1000
>D28:/--
>D29:@SUM(D23...D27)

>E 1:"REGISTER
>E 4:" COMMISSI
>E 6:/FR"PERCENTG
>E 7:/FI35
>E 8:/FI40
>E 9:/FI45
>E10:/FI50
>E16:/FL5
>E18:" ENDING:
>E22:/FR"COMM
>E23:(D23-Q23)*(Q23/100)+P23
>E24:(D24-Q24)*(Q24/100)+P24
>E25:(D25-Q25)*(Q25/100)+P25
>E26:(D26-Q26)*(Q26/100)+P26
>E27:(D27-Q27)*(Q27/100)+P27
>E28:/--
>E29:@SUM(E23...E27)

>F 4:"ON TABLE
>F 6:/FR"PLUS
>F 7:0
>F 8:1050
>F 9:2250
>F10:6750
>F18:"MM/DD/YY
```

```
>F21:/FR"OVERRIDE
>F22:/FR"SALE
>F25:2000
>F27:4500
>F28:/--
>F29:@SUM(F23...F27)

>G 4:">
>G 6:/FR"MINUS
>G 7:0
>G 8:3000
>G 9:6000
>G10:10000
>G21:/FR"OVERRIDE
>G22:/FR"COMM
>G23:+F23*(E16/100)
>G24:+F24*(E16/100)
>G25:+F25*(E16/100)
>G26:+F26*(E16/100)
>G27:+F27*(E16/100)
>G28:/--
>G29:@SUM(G23...G27)

>H20:/FR"PRIOR
>H21:/FR"Y-T-D
>H22:/FR"COMM
>H23:2400
>H24:3000
>H25:1800
>H26:1000
>H27:550
>H28:/--
>H29:@SUM(H23...H27)

>I20:/FR"CURR
>I21:/FR"Y-T-D
>I22:/FR"COMM
>I23:+H23+G23+E23
>I24:+H24+G24+E24
>I25:+H25+G25+E25
>I26:+H26+G26+E26
>I27:+H27+G27+E27
>I28:/--
>I29:@SUM(I23...I27)

>J20:/FR"PRIOR
>J21:/FR"Y-T-D
>J22:/FR"DRAW
>J23:2000
>J24:2500
>J25:3000
>J26:3000
>J27:3500
>J28:/--
>J29:@SUM(J23...J27)
```

```
>K20:/FR
>K21:/FR"CURR
>K22:/FR"DRAW
>K23:500
>K24:500
>K25:500
>K26:500
>K27:500
>K28:/--
>K29:@SUM(K23...K27)

>L21:/FR"Y-T-D
>L22:/FR"DRAW
>L23:+J23+K23
>L24:+J24+K24
>L25:+J25+K25
>L26:+J26+K26
>L27:+J27+K27
>L28:/--
>L29:@SUM(L23...L27)

>M20:/FR"SALES
>M21:/FR"LESS
>M22:/FR"DRAW
>M23:+I23-L23
>M24:+I24-L24
>M25:+I25-L25
>M26:+I26-L26
>M27:+I27-L27
>M28:/--
>M29:@SUM(M23...M27)

>O21:/FR"    CALCUL
```

```
>O22:/FR"    %
>O23:/FI@LOOKUP(D23,D7...D10)
>O24:/FI@LOOKUP(D24,D7...D10)
>O25:/FI@LOOKUP(D25,D7...D10)
>O26:/FI@LOOKUP(D26,D7...D10)
>O27:/FI@LOOKUP(D27,D7...D10)
>O28:/--

>P21:"ATION WOR
>P22:/FR"PLUS
>P23:@LOOKUP(O23,E7...E10)
>P24:@LOOKUP(O24,E7...E10)
>P25:@LOOKUP(O25,E7...E10)
>P26:@LOOKUP(O26,E7...E10)
>P27:@LOOKUP(O27,E7...E10)
>P28:/--

>Q21:"K AREA
>Q22:/FR"MINUS
>Q23:@LOOKUP(P23,F7...F10)
>Q24:@LOOKUP(P24,F7...F10)
>Q25:@LOOKUP(P25,F7...F10)
>Q26:@LOOKUP(P26,F7...F10)
>Q27:@LOOKUP(P27,F7...F10)
>Q28:/--

/GC9
/GF$
/GOC
/GRA
/W1
```

RETAIL SALES SUMMARY

This model calculates profit-to-sales, labor-to-sales, and rent-to-sales ratios, as well as stock turnover rates. These ratios are calculated on monthly figures, and then totaled for an annual average.

Like many business models, the Retail Sales Summary report can be used as a forecasting tool. To do so, enter your projected monthly figures, and at the end of any month, enter the actual figures. By the end of the year, you will have an actual annual summary.

PRINT A1...K21

Model Run

```
          RETAIL SALES SUMMARY
```

	MONTHLY RENT	LABOR COSTS	NET SALES	NET PROFIT	PROFIT/ SALES RATIO	LABOR/ SALES RATIO	RENT/ SALES RATIO	UNITS SOLD	AVERAGE STOCK	STOCK TURNOVER
JANUARY	1750.00	3600.00	10500.00	2887.50	27.50	34.29	16.67	658	1500	43.87
FEBUARY	1750.00	3800.00	11000.00	3025.00	27.50	34.55	15.91	690	1450	47.59
MARCH	1750.00	4000.00	10000.00	2750.00	27.50	40.00	17.50	627	1550	40.45
APRIL	1750.00	4000.00	9500.00	2612.00	27.49	42.11	18.42	596	1600	37.25
MAY	1750.00	3750.00	11000.00	3025.00	27.50	34.09	15.91	690	1650	41.82
JUNE	1750.00	4500.00	12000.00	3300.00	27.50	37.50	14.58	752	1650	45.58
JULY	1750.00	5500.00	11050.00	3038.75	27.50	49.77	15.84	693	1700	40.76
AUGUST	1750.00	5250.00	13000.00	3575.00	27.50	40.38	13.46	815	1750	46.57
SEPTEMBER	1750.00	5050.00	12500.00	3437.00	27.50	40.40	14.00	784	1750	44.80
OCTOBER	1750.00	4000.00	11000.00	3025.00	27.50	36.36	15.91	690	1800	38.33
NOVEMBER	1750.00	5500.00	14500.00	3987.00	27.50	37.93	12.07	909	1800	50.50
DECEMBER	1750.00	6500.00	17500.00	4812.50	27.50	37.14	10.00	1097	2000	54.85
ANNUAL	21000.00	55450.00	143550.00	39474.75	27.50	38.71	15.02	750	1683	44.36

Listing

```
>A  8:"JANUARY                >B  5:/FR"MONTHLY
>A  9:"FEBUARY                >B  6:/FR"RENT
>A10:"MARCH                   >B  8:1750
>A11:"APRIL                   >B  9:1750
>A12:"MAY                     >B10:1750
>A13:"JUNE                    >B11:1750
>A14:"JULY                    >B12:1750
>A15:"AUGUST                  >B13:1750
>A16:"SEPTEMBER               >B14:1750
>A17:"OCTOBER                 >B15:1750
>A18:"NOVEMBER                >B16:1750
>A19:"DECEMBER                >B17:1750
>A20:/--                      >B18:1750
>A21:"ANNUAL                  >B19:1750
```

```
>B20:/--
>B21:@SUM(B8...B19)

>C  1:"RETAIL SALES
>C  5:/FR"LABOR
>C  6:/FR"COSTS
>C  8:3600
>C  9:3800
>C10:4000
>C11:4000
>C12:3750
>C13:4500
>C14:5500
>C15:5250
>C16:5050
>C17:4000
>C18:5500
>C19:6500
>C20:/--
>C21:@SUM(C8...C19)

>D  1:"  SUMMARY
>D  5:/FR"NET
>D  6:/FR"SALES
>D  8:10500
>D  9:11000
>D10:10000
>D11:9500
>D12:11000
>D13:12000
>D14:11050
>D15:13000
>D16:12500
>D17:11000
>D18:14500
>D19:17500
>D20:/--
>D21:@SUM(D8...D19)

>E  5:/FR"NET
>E  6:/FR"PROFIT
>E  8:2887.5
>E  9:3025
>E10:2750
>E11:2612
>E12:3025
>E13:3300
>E14:3038.75
>E15:3575
>E16:3437
>E17:3025
>E18:3987
>E19:4812.5
>E20:/--
>E21:@SUM(E8...E19)
```

```
>F  4:/FR"PROFIT/
>F  5:/FR"SALES
>F  6:/FR"RATIO
>F  8:(E8/D8)*100
>F  9:(E9/D9)*100
>F10:(E10/D10)*100
>F11:(E11/D11)*100
>F12:(E12/D12)*100
>F13:(E13/D13)*100
>F14:(E14/D14)*100
>F15:(E15/D15)*100
>F16:(E16/D16)*100
>F17:(E17/D17)*100
>F18:(E18/D18)*100
>F19:(E19/D19)*100
>F20:/--
>F21:@AVERAGE(F8...F19)

>G  4:/FR"LABOR/
>G  5:/FR"SALES
>G  6:/FR"RATIO
>G  8:(C8/D8)*100
>G  9:(C9/D9)*100
>G10:(C10/D10)*100
>G11:(C11/D11)*100
>G12:(C12/D12)*100
>G13:(C13/D13)*100
>G14:(C14/D14)*100
>G15:(C15/D15)*100
>G16:(C16/D16)*100
>G17:(C17/D17)*100
>G18:(C18/D18)*100
>G19:(C19/D19)*100
>G20:/--
>G21:@AVERAGE(G8...G19)

>H  4:/FR"RENT/
>H  5:/FR"SALES
>H  6:/FR"RATIO
>H  8:(B8/D8)*100
>H  9:(B9/D9)*100
>H10:(B10/D10)*100
>H11:(B11/D11)*100
>H12:(B12/D12)*100
>H13:(B13/D13)*100
>H14:(B14/D14)*100
>H15:(B15/D15)*100
>H16:(B16/D16)*100
>H17:(B17/D17)*100
>H18:(B18/D18)*100
>H19:(B19/D19)*100
>H20:/--
>H21:@AVERAGE(H8...H19)

>I  5:/FR"UNITS
```

```
>I  6:/FR"SOLD                        >J18:/FI1800
>I  8:/FI658                          >J19:/FI2000
>I  9:/FI690                          >J20:/--
>I10:/FI627                           >J21:/FI@AVERAGE(J8...J19)
>I11:/FI596
>I12:/FI690                           >K  5:/FR"STOCK
>I13:/FI752                           >K  6:/FR"TURNOVER
>I14:/FI693                           >K  8:(I8/J8)*100
>I15:/FI815                           >K  9:(I9/J9)*100
>I16:/FI784                           >K10:(I10/J10)*100
>I17:/FI690                           >K11:(I11/J11)*100
>I18:/FI909                           >K12:(I12/J12)*100
>I19:/FI1097                          >K13:(I13/J13)*100
>I20:/--                              >K14:(I14/J14)*100
>I21:/FI@AVERAGE(I8...I19)            >K15:(I15/J15)*100
                                      >K16:(I16/J16)*100
>J  5:/FR"AVERAGE                     >K17:(I17/J17)*100
>J  6:/FR"STOCK                       >K18:(I18/J18)*100
>J  8:/FI1500                         >K19:(I19/J19)*100
>J  9:/FI1450                         >K20:/--
>J10:/FI1550                          >K21:@AVERAGE(K8...K19)
>J11:/FI1600
>J12:/FI1650                          /GC12
>J13:/FI1650                          /GF$
>J14:/FI1700                          /GOC
>J15:/FI1750                          /GRM
>J16:/FI1750                          /W1
>J17:/FI1800
```

SEASONAL INDEX

This model uses quarterly sales histories to calculate seasonal indices. These indices can then be used to predict sales. This model will benefit sales managers in those industries which are affected by seasonal sales fluctuations.

Seasonal ratios are calculated for each quarter of sales history by dividing the actual sales by the average quarterly sales for all years. The average of each quarter's ratios over the years produces the seasonal index. The more years of sales history you provide, the more accurate your seasonal index will be.

PRINT A1...G19

Model Run

```
                        SEASONAL INDEX

                                                  AVERAGE
   SALES        YEAR   QTR 1    QTR 2    QTR 3   QTR 4   SALES

                1978    344      357      371     409   370.25
                1979    355      390      383     417   386.25
                1980    388      412      431     488   429.75
                1981    408      429      467     501   451.25



   COMPUTED     1978 .9291020 .9642134 1.002026 1.104659
   RATIOS       1979 .9190939 1.009709 .9915858 1.079612
                1980 .9028505 .9586969 1.002909 1.135544
                1981 .9041551 .9506925 1.034903 1.110249

   SEASONAL          .9138004 .9708279 1.007856 1.107516
   INDICES
```

Listing

```
>A  4:"SALES                    >B15:1980
>A13:"COMPUTED                   >B16:1981
>A14:"RATIOS
>A18:"SEASONAL                   >C  4:/FR"QTR 1
>A19:"INDICES                    >C  6:344
                                 >C  7:355
>B  4:/FR"YEAR                   >C  8:388
>B  6:1978                       >C  9:408
>B  7:1979                       >C13:+C6/G6
>B  8:1980                       >C14:+C7/G7
>B  9:1981                       >C15:+C8/G8
>B13:1978                        >C16:+C9/G9
>B14:1979                        >C18:@AVERAGE(C13...C16)
```

```
>D  1:"SEASONAL                        >F  4:/FR"QTR 4
>D  4:/FR"QTR 2                         >F  6:409
>D  6:357                               >F  7:417
>D  7:390                               >F  8:488
>D  8:412                               >F  9:501
>D  9:429                               >F13:+F6/G6
>D13:+D6/G6                             >F14:+F7/G7
>D14:+D7/G7                             >F15:+F8/G8
>D15:+D8/G8                             >F16:+F9/G9
>D16:+D9/G9                             >F18:@AVERAGE(F13...F16)
>D18:@AVERAGE(D13...D16)
                                        >G  3:/FR"AVERAGE
>E  1:"INDEX                            >G  4:/FR"SALES
>E  4:/FR"QTR 3                         >G  6:@AVERAGE(C6...F6)
>E  6:371                               >G  7:@AVERAGE(C7...F7)
>E  7:383                               >G  8:@AVERAGE(C8...F8)
>E  8:431                               >G  9:@AVERAGE(C9...F9)
>E  9:467
>E13:+E6/G6                             /GC9
>E14:+E7/G7                             /GOC
>E15:+E8/G8                             /GRA
>E16:+E9/G9                             /W1
>E18:@AVERAGE(E13...E16)
```

SINGLE SERVER QUEUING MODEL

This model evaluates how much time customers or clients spend waiting to be served in any single-serve situation, such as a beauty salon or doctor's office. The model assumes customers are served on a first-come, first-served basis.

You must provide two figures: how many customers you can serve in an hour, and the average number of customers that enter your office in an hour.

In the sample model, an eye examiner feels he can complete 15 eye examinations in an hour. The receptionist believes that approximately 11 people enter the office each hour. Given the time it takes to usher patients between the waiting room and the examination area, the model delineates how efficiently time is spent. It can also help evaluate if more examiners or equipment are needed.

PRINT A1...H11

Model Run

```
              SINGLE SERVER
              QUEUING MODEL


   FOR:EYE EXAMINATION
                                                  <IN MINUTES>
                                            TIME  PATIENT   TIME
      <PATIENTS>                            SPENT   TIME    SPENT
      <PER HOUR>    % TIME PATIENTS  AVG #    IN    SPENT   BEING
  MAXIMUM # AVERAGE EXAMINER IN THE PATIENTS  IN   SPENT    BEING
  SERVED   VISTING   BUSY    QUE   WAITING SYSTEM WAITING EXAMINED
     15      11     73.33    2.75    2.02  15.00  11.00    4.00
```

Listing

```
>A  5:/FR"FOR:
>A  7:"          <PA
>A  8:"          <PE
>A  9:"MAXIMUM #
>A10:"SERVED
>A11:15

>B  5:"EYE EXAMI
>B  7:"TIENTS>
>B  8:"R HOUR>
>B  9:/FR"AVERAGE
>B10:/FR"VISTING
>B11:11

>C  1:"SINGLE SE
>C  2:"QUEUING M
>C  5:"NATION
>C  8:/FR"  % TIME
>C  9:/FR"EXAMINER
>C10:/FR"BUSY
>C11:/F$(B11/A11)*100

>D  1:"RVER
>D  2:"ODEL
>D  8:/FR"PATIENTS
>D  9:/FR"IN THE
>D10:/FR"QUE
>D11:/F$+B11/(A11-B11)

>E  8:/FR"AVG #
```

```
>E  9:/FR"PATIENTS
>E10:/FR"WAITING
>E11:/F$+B11^2/(A11*(A11-B11))

>F  7:/FR"TIME
>F  8:/FR"SPENT
>F  9:/FR"IN
>F10:/FR"SYSTEM
>F11:/F$(1/(A11-B11))*60

>G  6:"<IN MINUT
>G  7:/FR"PATIENT
>G  8:/FR"TIME
>G  9:/FR"SPENT
>G10:/FR"WAITING
>G11:/F$(B11/(A11*(A11-B11)))*60

>H  6:"ES>
>H  7:/FR"TIME
>H  8:/FR"SPENT
>H  9:/FR"BEING
>H10:/FR"EXAMINED
>H11:/F$+F11-G11

/GC9
/GOC
/GRA
/W1
```

ADVERTISING COST ANALYSIS

This model summarizes a magazine advertising campaign. Using the circulation figures for each magazine, the size, cost, and number of insertions, and the number of responses per magazine, this model will calculate the cost per response and the cost-to-circulation ratio. You can use either of these last two figures to compare cost effectiveness of your advertising dollars.

Substitute market share for circulation and minutes for ad size to compare radio or television advertising.

PRINT A1...G13.

Model Run

```
                ADVERTISING COST ANALYSIS


                 MERRYVILL CARSON'S  BROWN'S   MODERN    <MAX>
PUBLICATION      GARDEN MO MAGAZINE  FARM MO HOMEST'D  <VALUES>
CIRCULATION         10000     5000     7500      800    10000
AD SIZE <COL INCH>      1        1        2        1        2
COST FOR 1 INSERTN  350.00   275.00   250.00   100.00     350
# OF INSERTIONS         2        3        1        1        3
TOTAL COST          700.00   825.00   250.00   100.00     825
TOTAL RESPONSES        50       40       30       50       50
COST PER RESPONSE    14.00    20.63     8.33     2.00   20.625
COST TO CIRC RATIO    .035     .055  .0333333     .125     .125
```

Listing

```
>A 5:"PUBLICATI          >C 1:"ADVERTISI
>A 6:"CIRCULATI          >C 4:"MERRYVILL
>A 7:"AD SIZE <          >C 5:"GARDEN MO
>A 8:"COST FOR           >C 6:10000
>A 9:"# OF INSE          >C 7:1
>A10:"TOTAL COS          >C 8:/F$350
>A11:"TOTAL RES          >C 9:2
>A12:"COST PER           >C10:/F$+C9*C8
>A13:"COST TO C          >C11:50
                         >C12:/F$+C10/C11
>B 5:"ON                 >C13:+C8/C6
>B 6:"ON
>B 7:"COL INCH>          >D 1:"NG COST A
>B 8:"1 INSERTN          >D 4:/FR"CARSON'S
>B 9:"RTIONS             >D 5:/FR"MAGAZINE
>B10:"T                  >D 6:5000
>B11:"PONSES             >D 7:1
>B12:"RESPONSE           >D 8:/F$275
>B13:"IRC RATIO          >D 9:3
```

```
>D10:/F$+D9*D8          >F 9:1
>D11:40                 >F10:/F$+F9*F8
>D12:/F$+D10/D11        >F11:50
>D13:+D8/D6             >F12:/F$+F10/F11
                        >F13:+F8/F6
>E 1:"NALYSIS
>E 3:/F$                >G 3:/F$
>E 4:/FR"BROWN'S        >G 4:/FR"   <MAX>
>E 5:/FR"FARM MO        >G 5:/FR"<VALUES>
>E 6:7500               >G 6:@MAX(C6...F6)
>E 7:2                  >G 7:@MAX(C7...F7)
>E 8:/F$250             >G 8:@MAX(C8...F8)
>E 9:1                  >G 9:@MAX(C9...F9)
>E10:/F$+E9*E8          >G10:@MAX(C10...F10)
>E11:30                 >G11:@MAX(C11...F11)
>E12:/F$+E10/E11        >G12:@MAX(C12...F12)
>E13:+E8/E6             >G13:@MAX(C13...F13)

>F 4:/FR"MODERN         /GC9
>F 5:/FR"HOMEST'D       /GOC
>F 6:800                /GRA
>F 7:1                  /W1
>F 8:/F$100
```

DIRECT MAIL CAMPAIGN

This model calculates the total cost of a direct mail campaign and analyzes the sales and returns generated by the mailing. It is set up for sales of a single product.

You can begin to use this model while planning the mailing. By entering the postage rate, the number of pieces to be mailed, and other itemized costs required to produce the mailing piece, you can calculate the total cost of the mailing.

The responses to the mailing can be kept on the same worksheet. If you enter the number of responses per week and the number of units sold,

the VisiCalc program will calculate the percentage of total returns, the returns per week, and the cost per return and cost per sale. The VisiCalc program is also set up to track returns per week, so you can evaluate the response time to the mailing. By entering the weekly sales and response figures, you will see profits increase as leads and sales increase.

This model might also be used to track a telephone sales campaign. The net cost of the campaign would be based on the number of calls and the calculated cost per call.

PRINT A1...I51

Listing

```
>A 5:"UNIT RETA
>A 7:"CURRENT P
>A 8:"NUMBER OF
>A 9:"NET COST
>A10:"RETURN PO
>A12:"TOTAL COS
>A15:"LEADS
>A16:"RETURNED
>A17:/FI+D34
>A20:/--
>A39:"  <ITEMIZ
>A41:"SERVICES
>A42:"PAPER
>A43:"TYPSET
>A44:"PRINTING
>A45:"FOLDING
>A46:"MISC
>A47:"ENVELOPES
>A48:"STUFFING
>A49:"POSTAGE
>A51:/FR"TOTAL

>B 4:"UCT
>B 5:"IL PRICE:
>B 7:"OSTAGE RA
>B 8:" PIECES M
>B 9:"OF CAMPAI
>B10:"STAGE
>B12:"T OF CAMP
>B15:/FR" % OF
>B16:/FR"MAILING
```

```
>B17:+F34
>B20:/--
>B39:"ED COSTS>
>B41:3000
>B42:95
>B43:100
>B44:650
>B45:75
>B46:20
>B47:15
>B48:85
>B49:+D7*D8
>B50:/--
>B51:@SUM(B41...B49)

>C 5:125
>C 7:"TE (3RD):
>C 8:"AILED   :
>C 9:"GN      :
>C10:/FR":
>C12:"AIGN     :
>C15:/FR"COST
>C16:/FR"/LEAD
>C17:+D12/A17
>C19:/FR
>C20:/--
>C25:/FR"WEEK
>C26:/FI1
>C27:/FI2
>C28:/FI3
>C29:/FI4
```

Model Run

```
                DIRECT MAIL CAMPAIGN

                   <COST STUDY>
     FOR: PRODUCT
     UNIT RETAIL PRICE:    125.00


     CURRENT POSTAGE RATE (3RD):    .0675
     NUMBER OF PIECES MAILED  :    10000
     NET COST OF CAMPAIGN     :  4715.00
     RETURN POSTAGE           :    26.66
                                ---------
     TOTAL COST OF CAMPAIGN    :  4741.66


                                    COST
     LEADS      % OF     COST      UNITS  PER   TOTAL
     RETURNED  MAILING  /LEAD      SOLD   SALE  SALES $   PROFIT
        395     3.95    12.00        75  63.22  9375.00  4633.34



     ----------------------------------------------------------------


                   <ITEMIZED LEADS>     PERCENT  PERCENT
                                        OF TOTAL OF TOTAL
                   WEEK# RETURNS        MAILING  RETURNS
                     1      50             .5     12.66
                     2      45             .45    11.39
                     3      55             .55    13.92
                     4     180            1.8     45.57
                     5      35             .35     8.86
                     6      20             .2      5.06
                     7      10             .1      2.53
                        ----------      --------------------
                   TOTAL    395            3.95


                             HIGHEST %
                             RETURNS IN ONE WK=     45.57 %

      <ITEMIZED COSTS>


     SERVICES    3000.00
     PAPER         95.00
     TYPSET       100.00
     PRINTING     650.00
     FOLDING       75.00
     MISC          20.00
     ENVELOPES     15.00
     STUFFING      85.00
     POSTAGE      675.00
                ----------
        TOTAL    4715.00
```

```
>C30:/FI5
>C31:/FI6
>C32:/FI7
>C34:/FR"TOTAL

>D 7:/FR.0675
>D 8:/FI10000
>D 9:+B51
>D10:+A17*D7
>D11:/--
>D12:+D9+D10
>D15:/FR
>D16:/FR
>D20:/--
>D23:"<ITEMIZED
>D25:"# RETURNS
>D26:/FI50
>D27:/FI45
>D28:/FI55
>D29:/FI180
>D30:/FI35
>D31:/FI20
>D32:/FI10
>D33:/--
>D34:/FI@SUM(D26...D32)

>E15:/FR"UNITS
>E16:/FR"SOLD
>E17:/FI75
>E20:/--
>E23:" LEADS>

>F14:/FR"COST
>F15:/FR"PER
>F16:/FR"SALE
>F17:+D12/E17
>F20:/--
>F23:/FR"PERCENT
>F24:/FR"OF TOTAL
>F25:/FR"MAILING
```

```
>F26:/FR(D26/D8)*100
>F27:/FR(D27/D8)*100
>F28:/FR(D28/D8)*100
>F29:/FR(D29/D8)*100
>F30:/FR(D30/D8)*100
>F31:/FR(D31/D8)*100
>F32:/FR(D32/D8)*100
>F33:/--
>F34:@SUM(F26...F32)
>F36:"HIGHEST %
>F37:"RETURNS I

>G15:/FR"TOTAL
>G16:/FR"SALES $
>G17:+E17*C5
>G20:/--
>G21:/FR
>G22:/FR
>G23:/FR"PERCENT
>G24:/FR"OF TOTAL
>G25:/FR"RETURNS
>G26:(D26/D34)*100
>G27:(D27/D34)*100
>G28:(D28/D34)*100
>G29:(D29/D34)*100
>G30:(D30/D34)*100
>G31:(D31/D34)*100
>G32:(D32/D34)*100
>G33:/--
>G37:"N ONE WK=

>H16:/FR"PROFIT
>H17:+G17-D12
>H20:/--
>H37:@MAX(G26...G32)

>I37:" %

/GC9
/GF$
```

SALES FORECAST: BASED ON ADVERTISING

This model uses a history of advertising expenditures and sales volumes to estimate sales. An Extended Variable Forecast table, which lists expected sales according to advertising expenditure, is calculated. You can then enter any range of advertising expenditures and compare expected returns.

In the sample model, advertising expenditures and net sales are input for ten months. Based on that data, you can see from the Extended Variable Forecast that an advertising expenditure of $5000, for instance, should result in $494,560 in sales.

The model applies a regression analysis for estimating. The standard error and coefficient of variation are also calculated and printed on the worksheet. Numerous calculations required to solve these formulas are printed on the sample worksheet.

PRINT A1...H59

Listing

```
>A 8:"MONTH
>A10:"JAN
>A11:"FEB
>A12:"MARCH
>A13:"APRIL
>A14:"MAY
>A15:"JUNE
>A16:"JULY
>A17:"AUGUST
>A18:"SEPT
>A19:"OCT
>A20:/--
>A21:"TOTALS
>A22:"MEAN
>A24:"PROJECTED
>A25:"ADVERTISING=
>A27:"SALES
>A28:"FORECAST=
>A30:"STANDARD
>A31:"ERROR =
>A33:"COEFFICIENT
>A34:"OF VARIATN =
>A35:/-=
>A39:"PROJECTED
>A40:"ADVERTISING
>A41:/-=
>A42:.5+A40
>A43:.5+A42
>A44:.5+A43
>A45:.5+A44
>A46:.5+A45
>A47:.5+A46
```

```
>A48:.5+A47
>A49:.5+A48
>A50:.5+A49
>A51:.5+A50
>A52:.5+A51
>A53:.5+A52
>A54:.5+A53
>A55:.5+A54
>A56:.5+A55
>A57:.5+A56
>A58:.5+A57
>A59:.5+A58

>B 5:"(ALL VALUES
>B 7:"ADVERTISING
>B 8:/FR"EXPENDITURES
>B10:4.5
>B11:4.87
>B12:6.22
>B13:5.31
>B14:7.88
>B15:8
>B16:8.1
>B17:3.11
>B18:5.99
>B19:7.12
>B20:/--
>B21:@SUM(B10...B19)
>B22:@AVERAGE(B10...B19)
>B25:5
>B28:(F26*B25)+F27
>B31:@SQRT((H21/(F23-2))
```

Model Run

```
                        SALES FORECAST

                     ( BASED ON ADVERTISING )

               (ALL VALUES IN THOUSANDS OF DOLLARS)

            ADVERTISING       SALES    EXPENDITURES    SALES *   CALCULATED  SALES-PROJ
  MONTH     EXPENDITURES      VOLUME      SQUARED    EXPENDITURES PROJECTION   SQUARED

  JAN          4.50           440.00       20.25      1980.00      444.26      18.19
  FEB          4.87           477.00       23.72      2322.99      481.48      20.07
  MARCH        6.22           650.00       38.69      4043.00      617.26    1071.65
  APRIL        5.31           500.00       28.20      2655.00      525.74     662.31
  MAY          7.88           700.00       62.09      5516.00      784.23    7094.36
  JUNE         8.00           810.00       64.00      6480.00      796.30     187.75
  JULY         8.10           799.00       65.61      6471.90      806.36      54.11
  AUGUST       3.11           301.00        9.67       936.11      304.46      11.95
  SEPT         5.99           588.00       35.88      3522.12      594.13      37.58
  OCT          7.12           797.00       50.69      5674.64      707.79    7959.03
  ---------------------------------       -------------------------------    --------
  TOTALS      61.10          6062.00      398.80     39601.76               17117.00
  MEAN         6.11           606.20

                                         COUNT =          10
  PROJECTED                              NUMERATOR   25629.40
  ADVERTISING=    5.00                   DENOM         254.81
                                         CALC 1 =      100.58
                                         CALC 2 =       -8.35
  SALES
  FORECAST=     494.56

  STANDARD
  ERROR =        46.26

  COEFFICIENT
  OF VARIATN =    7.63
  ============================================================================

                     <EXTENDED VARIABLE FORECASTER>

  PROJECTED          SALES
  ADVERTISING       FORECAST
  ========================
     0.50            41.94
     1.00            92.23
     1.50           142.52
     2.00           192.81
     2.50           243.10
     3.00           293.39
     3.50           343.68
     4.00           393.97
     4.50           444.26
     5.00           494.56
     5.50           544.85
     6.00           595.14
     6.50           645.43
     7.00           695.72
     7.50           746.01
     8.00           796.30
     8.50           846.59
     9.00           896.88
```

```
>B34:(B31/C22)*100
>B35:/-=
>B37:" <EXTENDED V
>B39:/FR"SALES
>B40:/FR"FORECAST
>B41:/-=
>B42:(F26*A42)+F27
>B43:(F26*A43)+F27
>B44:(F26*A44)+F27
>B45:(F26*A45)+F27
>B46:(F26*A46)+F27
>B47:(F26*A47)+F27
>B48:(F26*A48)+F27
>B49:(F26*A49)+F27
>B50:(F26*A50)+F27
>B51:(F26*A51)+F27
>B52:(F26*A52)+F27
>B53:(F26*A53)+F27
>B54:(F26*A54)+F27
>B55:(F26*A55)+F27
>B56:(F26*A56)+F27
>B57:(F26*A57)+F27
>B58:(F26*A58)+F27
>B59:(F26*A59)+F27

>C 1:"  SALES FORE
>C 3:"( BASED ON A
>C 5:"IN THOUSANDS
>C 7:/FR"SALES
>C 8:/FR"VOLUME
>C10:440
>C11:477
>C12:650
>C13:500
>C14:700
>C15:810
>C16:799
>C17:301
>C18:588
>C19:797
>C20:/--
>C21:@SUM(C10...C19)
>C22:@AVERAGE(C10...C19)
>C35:/-=
>C37:"ARIABLE FORE
>C39:/FR
>C40:/FR

>D 1:"CAST
>D 3:"DVERTISING )
>D 5:" OF DOLLARS)
>D35:/-=
>D37:"CASTER>
>D39:/FR
>D40:/FR
```

```
>E 7:"EXPENDITURES
>E 8:"SQUARED
>E10:+B10^2
>E11:+B11^2
>E12:+B12^2
>E13:+B13^2
>E14:+B14^2
>E15:+B15^2
>E16:+B16^2
>E17:+B17^2
>E18:+B18^2
>E19:+B19^2
>E20:/--
>E21:@SUM(E10...E19)
>E23:"COUNT =
>E24:"NUMERATOR
>E25:"DENOM
>E26:"CALC 1 =
>E27:"CALC 2 =
>E35:/-=

>F 7:/FR"SALES *
>F 8:/FR"EXPENDITURES
>F10:+B10*C10
>F11:+B11*C11
>F12:+B12*C12
>F13:+B13*C13
>F14:+B14*C14
>F15:+B15*C15
>F16:+B16*C16
>F17:+B17*C17
>F18:+B18*C18
>F19:+B19*C19
>F20:/--
>F21:@SUM(F10...F19)
>F23:/FI@COUNT(F10...F19)
>F24:(F23*F21)-(B21*C21)
>F25:(F23*E21)-(B21^2)
>F26:+F24/F25
>F27:+C22-(F26*B22)
>F35:/-=

>G 7:/FR"CALCULATED
>G 8:/FR"PROJECTION
>G10:(B10*F26)+F27
>G11:(B11*F26)+F27
>G12:(B12*F26)+F27
>G13:(B13*F26)+F27
>G14:(B14*F26)+F27
>G15:(B15*F26)+F27
>G16:(B16*F26)+F27
>G17:(B17*F26)+F27
>G18:(B18*F26)+F27
>G19:(B19*F26)+F27
>G20:/--
```

```
>H 7:/FR"SALES-PROJ              >H18:(C18-G18)^2
>H 8:/FR"SQUARED                 >H19:(C19-G19)^2
>H10:(C10-G10)^2                 >H20:/---
>H11:(C11-G11)^2                 >H21:@SUM(H10...H19)
>H12:(C12-G12)^2
>H13:(C13-G13)^2                 /GC12
>H14:(C14-G14)^2                 /GF$
>H15:(C15-G15)^2                 /GOC
>H16:(C16-G16)^2                 /GRM
>H17:(C17-G17)^2                 /W1
```

SURVEY RESULTS

This model tabulates the results of any number of questions asked in a survey. They must be entered into the model with a "yes," "no," or multiple-choice response. Statistics such as if the respondent was male or female, married or single, may also be entered.

In the sample survey, one question is asked; its possible responses are "yes," "no," or "maybe." Whatever the response, a "1" is tallied, and a "1" is also entered either under an "M" (for male) or "F" (for female) listing. If the

response to any tabulating column is negative no entry is made. Totals are then calculated according to male, female, and total responses, and percentages are also provided.

It is easy to expand this model to tabulate additional questions asked in a survey. (Remember that the VisiCalc program limits you to a 52 × 254 grid matrix.) For columns that are easy to read, create columns of only three characters (/GC3).

PRINT A1...N49

Listing

```
>A  3:"DAT
>A  4:/--
>A  7:"T
>A  8:"O
>A  9:"T
>A10:"A
>A11:"L
>A12:"S
>A14:"Y=Y
>A15:"N=N
>A16:"MB=
>A18:"RES
>A19:"#
>A20:+A19+1
>A21:+A20+1
>A22:+A21+1
>A23:+A22+1
>A24:+A23+1
>A25:+A24+1
>A26:+A25+1
>A27:+A26+1
>A28:+A27+1
>A29:+A28+1
>A30:+A29+1
>A31:+A30+1
>A32:+A31+1
>A33:+A32+1
>A34:+A33+1
>A35:+A34+1
>A36:+A35+1
>A37:+A36+1
>A38:+A37+1
>A39:+A38+1
```

```
>A40:+A39+1
>A41:+A40+1
>A42:+A41+1
>A43:+A42+1
>A44:+A43+1
>A45:+A44+1
>A46:+A45+1
>A47:+A46+1
>A48:+A47+1

>B  3:"E:
>B  4:/--
>B  8:/FR"M
>B  9:/FR"F
>B14:"ES
>B15:"O
>B16:"MAY

>C  3:"APR
>C  4:/--
>C  7:/FR"Y
>C  8:/FR@SUM(I20...I48)
>C  9:/FR@SUM(L20...L48)
>C10:"--
>C11:/FR+C8+C9
>C16:"BE
>C19:"M
>C20:1
>C21:1
>C23:1
>C24:1
>C25:1
>C28:1
```

Model Run

```
                    SURVEY

DATE: APR 1 QUESTION # 4
------------------------

                    P
T       Y N MB      E  Y  N  MB
O   M   7 6 3 16    R 44 38 19 55
T   F   3 6 4 13    C 23 46 31 45
A       ---------   E ------------
L       10 12 7     N 67 84 50 >>
S                   T


Y=YES       M=MALE
N=NO        F=FEMALE
MB=MAYBE
```

RES #	M	F	Y	N	MB	MY	MN	MMB	FY	FN	FMB
1	1		1			1	0	0	0	0	0
2	1		1			1	0	0	0	0	0
3		1	1			0	0	0	1	0	0
4	1			1		0	1	0	0	0	0
5	1				1	0	0	1	0	0	0
6	1			1		0	1	0	0	0	0
7		1	1			0	0	0	1	0	0
8		1			1	0	0	0	0	0	1
9	1		1			1	0	0	0	0	0
10	1			1		0	1	0	0	0	0
11	1			1		0	1	0	0	0	0
12		1		1		0	0	0	0	1	0
13	1		1			1	0	0	0	0	0
14	1				1	0	0	1	0	0	0
15	1		1			1	0	0	0	0	0
16		1	1			0	0	0	1	0	0
17		1		1		0	0	0	0	1	0
18		1			1	0	0	0	0	0	1
19		1			1	0	0	0	0	0	1
20	1				1	0	0	1	0	0	0
21		1			1	0	0	0	0	0	1
22		1		1		0	0	0	0	1	0
23	1			1		0	1	0	0	0	0
24	1			1		0	1	0	0	0	0
25		1		1		0	0	0	0	1	0
26		1		1		0	0	0	0	1	0
27	1		1			1	0	0	0	0	0
28		1		1		0	0	0	0	1	0
29	1		1			1	0	0	0	0	0

```
>C29:1
>C30:1
>C32:1
>C33:1
>C34:1
>C39:1
>C42:1
>C43:1
>C46:1
>C48:1

>D 3:1
>D 4:/---
>D 7:/FR"N
>D 8:/FR@SUM(J20...J48)
>D 9:/FR@SUM(M20...M48)
>D10:"---
>D11:/FR+D8+D9
>D19:"F
>D22:1
>D26:1
>D27:1
>D31:1
>D35:1
>D36:1
>D37:1
>D38:1
>D40:1
>D41:1
>D44:1
>D45:1
>D47:1

>E 3:"QUE
>E 4:/---
>E 7:/FR"MB
>E 8:/FR@SUM(K20...K48)
>E 9:/FR@SUM(N20...N48)
>E10:"---
>E11:/FR+E8+E9
>E14:"M=M
>E15:"F=F
>E19:"Y
>E20:1
>E21:1
>E22:1
>E26:1
>E28:1
>E32:1
>E34:1
>E35:1
>E46:1
>E48:1
```

```
>F  1:"SUR
>F  3:"STI
>F  4:/--
>F  8:@SUM(C8...E8)
>F  9:@SUM(C9...E9)
>F14:"ALE
>F15:"EMA
>F19:"N
>F23:1
>F25:1
>F29:1
>F30:1
>F31:1
>F36:1
>F41:1
>F42:1
>F43:1
>F44:1
>F45:1
>F47:1

>G  1:"VEY
>G  3:"ON
>G  4:/--
>G  6:/FR"P
>G  7:/FR"E
>G  8:/FR"R
>G  9:/FR"C
>G10:/FR"E
>G11:/FR"N
>G12:/FR"T
>G15:"LE
>G19:"MB
>G24:1
>G27:1
>G33:1
>G37:1
>G38:1
>G39:1
>G40:1

>H  3:"# 4
>H  4:/--
>H  7:/FR"Y
>H  8:(C8/F8)*100
>H  9:(C9/F9)*100
>H10:"  --
>H11:@SUM(H8...H9)

>I  7:/FR"N
>I  8:(D8/F8)*100
>I  9:(D9/F9)*100
>I10:/--
>I11:@SUM(I8...I9)
>I18:"M
```

```
>I19:"Y
>I20:+C20*E20
>I21:+C21*E21
>I22:+C22*E22
>I23:+C23*E23
>I24:+C24*E24
>I25:+C25*E25
>I26:+C26*E26
>I27:+C27*E27
>I28:+C28*E28
>I29:+C29*E29
>I30:+C30*E30
>I31:+C31*E31
>I32:+C32*E32
>I33:+C33*E33
>I34:+C34*E34
>I35:+C35*E35
>I36:+C36*E36
>I37:+C37*E37
>I38:+C38*E38
>I39:+C39*E39
>I40:+C40*E40
>I41:+C41*E41
>I42:+C42*E42
>I43:+C43*E43
>I44:+C44*E44
>I45:+C45*E45
>I46:+C46*E46
>I47:+C47*E47
>I48:+C48*E48

>J  7:/FR"MB
>J  8:(E8/F8)*100
>J  9:(E9/F9)*100
>J10:/--
>J11:@SUM(J8...J9)
>J18:"M
>J19:"N
>J20:+C20*F20
>J21:+C21*F21
>J22:+C22*F22
>J23:+C23*F23
>J24:+C24*F24
>J25:+C25*F25
>J26:+C26*F26
>J27:+C27*F27
>J28:+C28*F28
>J29:+C29*F29
>J30:+C30*F30
>J31:+C31*F31
>J32:+C32*F32
>J33:+C33*F33
>J34:+C34*F34
>J35:+C35*F35
>J36:+C36*F36
```

>J37:+C37*F37
>J38:+C38*F38
>J39:+C39*F39
>J40:+C40*F40
>J41:+C41*F41
>J42:+C42*F42
>J43:+C43*F43
>J44:+C44*F44
>J45:+C45*F45
>J46:+C46*F46
>J47:+C47*F47
>J48:+C48*F48

>K 8:(F8/@SUM(C11...E11))*100
>K 9:(F9/@SUM(C11...E11))*100
>K10:"---
>K11:@SUM(K8...K9)
>K18:"M
>K19:"MB
>K20:+C20*G20
>K21:+C21*G21
>K22:+C22*G22
>K23:+C23*G23
>K24:+C24*G24
>K25:+C25*G25
>K26:+C26*G26
>K27:+C27*G27
>K28:+C28*G28
>K29:+C29*G29
>K30:+C30*G30
>K31:+C31*G31
>K32:+C32*G32
>K33:+C33*G33
>K34:+C34*G34
>K35:+C35*G35
>K36:+C36*G36
>K37:+C37*G37
>K38:+C38*G38
>K39:+C39*G39
>K40:+C40*G40
>K41:+C41*G41
>K42:+C42*G42
>K43:+C43*G43
>K44:+C44*G44
>K45:+C45*G45
>K46:+C46*G46
>K47:+C47*G47
>K48:+C48*G48

>L18:"F
>L19:"Y
>L20:+E20*D20
>L21:+E21*D21
>L22:+E22*D22
>L23:+E23*D23
>L24:+E24*D24
>L25:+E25*D25
>L26:+E26*D26
>L27:+E27*D27
>L28:+E28*D28
>L29:+E29*D29
>L30:+E30*D30
>L31:+E31*D31
>L32:+E32*D32
>L33:+E33*D33
>L34:+E34*D34
>L35:+E35*D35
>L36:+E36*D36
>L37:+E37*D37
>L38:+E38*D38
>L39:+E39*D39
>L40:+E40*D40
>L41:+E41*D41
>L42:+E42*D42
>L43:+E43*D43
>L44:+E44*D44
>L45:+E45*D45
>L46:+E46*D46
>L47:+E47*D47
>L48:+E48*D48

>M18:"F
>M19:"N
>M20:+F20*D20
>M21:+F21*D21
>M22:+F22*D22
>M23:+F23*D23
>M24:+F24*D24
>M25:+F25*D25
>M26:+F26*D26
>M27:+F27*D27
>M28:+F28*D28
>M29:+F29*D29
>M30:+F30*D30
>M31:+F31*D31
>M32:+F32*D32
>M33:+F33*D33
>M34:+F34*D34
>M35:+F35*D35
>M36:+F36*D36
>M37:+F37*D37
>M38:+F38*D38
>M39:+F39*D39
>M40:+F40*D40
>M41:+F41*D41
>M42:+F42*D42
>M43:+F43*D43
>M44:+F44*D44
>M45:+F45*D45
>M46:+F46*D46

```
>M47:+F47*D47          >N35:+G35*D35
>M48:+F48*D48          >N36:+G36*D36
                       >N37:+G37*D37
>N18:"F                >N38:+G38*D38
>N19:"MB               >N39:+G39*D39
>N20:+G20*D20          >N40:+G40*D40
>N21:+G21*D21          >N41:+G41*D41
>N22:+G22*D22          >N42:+G42*D42
>N23:+G23*D23          >N43:+G43*D43
>N24:+G24*D24          >N44:+G44*D44
>N25:+G25*D25          >N45:+G45*D45
>N26:+G26*D26          >N46:+G46*D46
>N27:+G27*D27          >N47:+G47*D47
>N28:+G28*D28          >N48:+G48*D48
>N29:+G29*D29
>N30:+G30*D30          /GC3
>N31:+G31*D31          /GFL
>N32:+G32*D32          /GOC
>N33:+G33*D33          /GRM
>N34:+G34*D34          /W1
```

PERSONNEL
AND
DEPARTMENTS

MINI PAYROLL WORKSHEET

This payroll worksheet will calculate employee income and produce a payroll check register that may be used to produce paychecks.

You must supply the FICA rate, your company's overtime factor, and the number of pay periods per year. The register begins with your entering each employee's hourly rate, marital status, and number of exemptions; then, at the end of each pay period, you enter each employee's hours (regular and overtime). The VisiCalc model will calculate all taxes and gross and net income. If there is a local tax, you should add that into the Payroll Register calculation area.

The federal tax calculation uses a lookup table with information you have entered from Circular E. To accommodate varying pay periods, the annualized method is used and the taxes obtained are then divided by the number of pay periods per year.

To calculate both married and single tax status, this model computes both taxes and multiplies the result by the single and married indicator shown under Employee Records. This causes the married calculation to be zeroed for an employee claiming single status. When the two tax amounts are added, the result reflects only that which

applies to the employee.

The complexity of the @LOOKUPs and calculations in this model necessitates using an FWT Work Area, which you would not normally print. Each column in this section performs a table search and/or calculation that contributes to the final tax amount.

A good way to use this model is to list your employees at the top, with their rate and tax data, and then list them again under the words Payroll Register. Enter the calculations for FICA, Gross, Net, FWT, and State. Be sure to construct your Tax Table and State Tax data, as well as the FWT Work Area for each employee. Save this as a worksheet blank and load it whenever you're ready to calculate your payroll.

As you add employees, insert them in both the Employee Records and Payroll Register areas. Insertions between the first and last names will not require replicating the various formulas, but if you add an employee to the end of the list, be sure to include all the calculations.

PRINT A1...J22, Employee Records and Check Register
A27...L50, Tax Tables
L15...X21, Tax Calculations

Model Run

```
<<< MINI PAYROLL WORKSHEET <<<      OT FACTOR 1.5      FICA RATE 6.1
                                    PAY PERS  52
                EMPLOYEE RECORDS


NAME OF EMPLOYEE             RATE   SINGLE  MARRIED   EXEMPS
ADAMS, JOHN                 5.00      1                  1
BETTMAN, HENRY             10.00               1         2
MCMAHON, ARTHUR            15.00               1         2
OLIVER,MATT                7.50      1                  1
-----------------------------------------------------------------


PAYROLL REGISTER


EMPLOYEE       REG HRS   OT HOURS  TOT HRS    FWT     FICA   STATE    GROSS     NET
ADAMS, JOHN       5.00      0.00     5.00    0.00     1.53    0.14    25.00    23.33
BETTMAN, HENRY   40.00      6.00    46.00   85.99    29.89   11.29   490.00   362.83
MCMAHON, ARTHUR  40.00               40.00  121.38   36.60   14.04   600.00   427.98
OLIVER,MATT      40.00      9.00    49.00   86.00    24.48    9.55   401.25   281.22
-----------------------------------------------------------------------------------
       TOTALS   125.00     15.00   140.00  293.37    92.49   35.02  1516.25  1095.36
```

Employee Records and Check Register

```
==================================================================================
  TAX TABLES      VALUE PER EXEMPTN   1000.00


         SINGLE                                 STATE TAX
RANGE      SUBTRACT  PERCENT     ADD            EXEM VAL    1000.00
   0.00       0.00     0.00     0.00            RATE            .025
1420.00    1420.00     0.15     0.00
3300.00    3300.00     0.18   282.00
6800.00    6800.00     0.21   912.00
10200.00  10200.00     0.26  1626.00
14200.00  14200.00     0.30  2666.00
17200.00  17200.00     0.34  3566.00
22500.00  22500.00     0.39  5368.00


         MARRIED
   0.00       0.00     0.00     0.00
2400.00    2400.00     0.15     0.00
6600.00    6600.00     0.18   630.00
10900.00  10900.00     0.21  1404.00
15000.00  15000.00     0.24  2265.00
19200.00  19200.00     0.28  3273.00
23600.00  23600.00     0.32  4505.00
28900.00  28900.00     0.37  6201.00
```

Tax Table

ANNUAL LESS EX	FWT WORK AREA START AMT	DIFF	SINGLE PERCENT	TAX ON %	TOT TAX	FWT WORK AREA START AMT	DIFF	MARRIED PERCENT	TAX ON %	TOT TAX	FINAL TAX CALC
300.00	0.00	300.00	0.00	0.00	0.00	0.00	300.00	0.00	0.00	0.00	0.00
23480.00	22500.00	980.00	0.39	382.20	5750.20	19200.00	4280.00	0.28	1198.40	4471.40	4471.40
29200.00	22500.00	6700.00	0.39	2613.00	7981.00	28900.00	300.00	0.37	111.00	6312.00	6312.00
19865.00	17200.00	2665.00	0.34	906.10	4472.10	19200.00	665.00	0.28	186.20	3459.20	4472.10

Tax Calculations

Listing

```
>A  1:"<<< MINI
>A  5:"NAME OF E
>A  6:"ADAMS, JO
>A  7:"BETTMAN,
>A  8:"MCMAHON,
>A  9:"OLIVER,MA
>A10:"---------
>A14:"PAYROLL R
>A16:"EMPLOYEE
>A17:"ADAMS, JO
>A18:"BETTMAN,
>A19:"MCMAHON,
>A20:"OLIVER,MA
>A21:"---------
>A27:/-=
>A28:"  TAX TAB
>A31:"RANGE
>A32:0
>A33:1420
>A34:3300
>A35:6800
>A36:10200
>A37:14200
>A38:17200
>A39:22500
>A43:0
>A44:2400
>A45:6600
>A46:10900
>A47:15000
>A48:19200
>A49:23600
>A50:28900

>B  1:"PAYROLL W
>B  5:"MPLOYEE
>B  6:"HN
>B  7:"HENRY
>B  8:"ARTHUR
>B  9:"TT
>B10:"---------
>B14:"EGISTER
>B17:"HN
>B18:"HENRY
>B19:"ARTHUR
>B20:"TT
>B21:"---------
>B22:"TOTALS
>B27:/-=
>B28:"LES
>B30:"SINGLE
>B31:/FR"SUBTRACT
>B32:0
>B33:1420
>B34:3300
>B35:6800
>B36:10200
>B37:14200
>B38:17200
>B39:22500
>B42:"MARRIED
>B43:0
>B44:2400
>B45:6600
>B46:10900
>B47:15000
>B48:19200
>B49:23600
>B50:28900


>C  1:"ORKSHEET
>C  3:"EMPLOYEE
>C10:"---------
>C16:"REG HRS
>C17:5
>C18:40
>C19:40
>C20:40
>C21:"---------
>C22:@SUM(C17...C21)
>C27:/-=
>C28:"VALUE PER
>C31:/FR"PERCENT
>C32:0
>C33:.15
>C34:.18
```

>C35:.21
>C36:.26
>C37:.3
>C38:.34
>C39:.39
>C43:0
>C44:.15
>C45:.18
>C46:.21
>C47:.24
>C48:.28
>C49:.32
>C50:.37

>D 1:"<<<
>D 3:"RECORDS
>D 5:/FR"RATE
>D 6:/F$5
>D 7:/F$10
>D 8:/F$15
>D 9:/F$7.5
>D10:"----------
>D16:/FR"OT HOURS
>D17:0
>D18:6
>D20:9
>D21:"----------
>D22:@SUM(D17...D21)
>D27:/-=
>D28:" EXEMPTN
>D31:/FR"ADD
>D32:0
>D33:0
>D34:282
>D35:912
>D36:1626
>D37:2666
>D38:3566
>D39:5368
>D43:0
>D44:0
>D45:630
>D46:1404
>D47:2265
>D48:3273
>D49:4505
>D50:6201

>E 1:"OT FACTOR
>E 2:"PAY PERS
>E 5:/FR"SINGLE
>E 6:/FI1
>E 7:/FI
>E 8:/FI
>E 9:/FI1

>E10:"----------
>E11:/FR
>E16:/FR"TOT HRS
>E17:+C17+D17
>E18:+C18+D18
>E19:+C19+D19
>E20:+C20+D20
>E21:"----------
>E22:@SUM(E17...E21)
>E27:/-=
>E28:1000

>F 1:/FL1.5
>F 2:/FL52
>F 5:/FR"MARRIED
>F 6:/FI
>F 7:/FI1
>F 8:/FI1
>F 9:/FI
>F10:"----------
>F16:/FR"FWT
>F17:+X17/F2
>F18:+X18/F2
>F19:+X19/F2
>F20:+X20/F2
>F21:"----------
>F22:@SUM(F17...F21)
>F27:/-=

>G 1:"FICA RATE
>G 5:/FR"EXEMPS
>G 6:/FI1
>G 7:/FI2
>G 8:/FI2
>G 9:/FI1
>G10:"----------
>G16:/FR"FICA
>G17:(H1*I17)*.01
>G18:(H1*I18)*.01
>G19:(H1*I19)*.01
>G20:(H1*I20)*.01
>G21:"----------
>G22:@SUM(G17...G21)
>G27:/-=
>G30:"STATE TAX
>G31:"EXEM VAL
>G32:"RATE

>H 1:/FL6.1
>H 5:/FR
>H16:/FR"STATE
>H17:((I17*F2)-(G6*H31)*H32)/F2
>H18:((I18*F2)-(G7*H31)*H32)/F2
>H19:((I19*F2)-(G8*H31)*H32)/F2
>H20:((I20*F2)-(G9*H31)*H32)/F2

```
>H21:"————————
>H22:@SUM(H17...H21)
>H27:/-=
>H31:1000
>H32:/FR.025

>I 5:/FR
>I16:/FR"GROSS
>I17:((D6*F1)*D17)+(D6*C17)
>I18:((D7*F1)*D18)+(D7*C18)
>I19:((D8*F1)*D19)+(D8*C19)
>I20:((D9*F1)*D20)+(D9*C20)
>I21:"————————
>I22:@SUM(I17...I21)
>I27:/-=

>J16:/FR"NET
>J17:+I17-F17-G17-H17
>J18:+I18-F18-G18-H18
>J19:+I19-F19-G19-H19
>J20:+I20-F20-G20-H20
>J21:"————————
>J22:@SUM(J17...J21)
>J27:/-=

>L15:"ANNUAL
>L16:"LESS EX
>L17:(I17*F2)-(G6*E28)
>L18:(I18*F2)-(G7*E28)
>L19:(I19*F2)-(G8*E28)
>L20:(I20*F2)-(G9*E28)
>L21:/--

>M15:"FWT WORK
>M16:"START AMT
>M17:@LOOKUP(L17,A32...A39)
>M18:@LOOKUP(L18,A32...A39)
>M19:@LOOKUP(L19,A32...A39)
>M20:@LOOKUP(L20,A32...A39)
>M21:/--

>N15:"AREA
>N16:/FR"DIFF
>N17:+L17-M17
>N18:+L18-M18
>N19:+L19-M19
>N20:+L20-M20
>N21:/--

>O15:"SINGLE
>O16:/FR"PERCENT
>O17:@LOOKUP(M17,B32...B39)
>O18:@LOOKUP(M18,B32...B39)
>O19:@LOOKUP(M19,B32...B39)
>O20:@LOOKUP(M20,B32...B39)
>O21:/--

>P16:/FR"TAX ON %
>P17:+O17*N17
>P18:+O18*N18
>P19:+O19*N19
>P20:+O20*N20
>P21:/--

>Q16:/FR"TOT TAX
>Q17:@LOOKUP(O17,C32...C39)+P17
>Q18:@LOOKUP(O18,C32...C39)+P18
>Q19:@LOOKUP(O19,C32...C39)+P19
>Q20:@LOOKUP(O20,C32...C39)+P20
>Q21:/--

>R21:/--

>S15:"FWT WORK
>S16:"START AMT
>S17:@LOOKUP(L17,A43...A50)
>S18:@LOOKUP(L18,A43...A50)
>S19:@LOOKUP(L19,A43...A50)
>S20:@LOOKUP(L20,A43...A50)
>S21:/--

>T15:"AREA
>T16:/FR"DIFF
>T17:+L17-S17
>T18:+L18-S18
>T19:+L19-S19
>T20:+L20-S20
>T21:/--

>U15:"MARRIED
>U16:/FR"PERCENT
>U17:@LOOKUP(S17,B43...B50)
>U18:@LOOKUP(S18,B43...B50)
>U19:@LOOKUP(S19,B43...B50)
>U20:@LOOKUP(S20,B43...B50)
>U21:/--

>V16:/FR"TAX ON %
>V17:+U17*T17
>V18:+U18*T18
>V19:+U19*T19
>V20:+U20*T20
>V21:/--

>W16:/FR"TOT TAX
>W17:@LOOKUP(U17,C43...C50)+V17
>W18:@LOOKUP(U18,C43...C50)+V18
>W19:@LOOKUP(U19,C43...C50)+V19
>W20:@LOOKUP(U20,C43...C50)+V20
>W21:/--

>X15:/FR"FINAL
>X16:/FR"TAX CALC
```

```
>X17: (W17*F6)+(Q17*E6)                    /GC9
>X18: (W18*F7)+(Q18*E7)                    /GF$
>X19: (W19*F8)+(Q19*E8)                    /GOC
>X20: (W20*F9)+(Q20*E9)                    /GRA
>X21:/--                                   /W1
```

EEO REPORT

Companies with 100 or more employees are required to file an equal employment opportunity report. By using this VisiCalc model within departments in your company, you can help organize and complete the report.

This type of data organization and calculation can be used to summarize other important information in a large company. It might be used to tally distribution of various office supplies, for instance.

PRINT A1...H39

Listing

```
>A  3:"NAME OF C              >B19:8
>A  4:/FL"ADDRESS             >B20:3
>A  5:/FL"CITY, ST            >B21:2
>A  7:"REPORT PR              >B22:1
>A10:"<WOMEN>                 >B23:/--
>A11:"BLACK                   >B24:@SUM(B19...B22)
>A12:"HISPANIC                >B27:"GE BY DEP
>A13:"ORIENTAL                >B29:(B11+B19)/C39
>A14:"WHITE                   >B30:(B12+B20)/C39
>A15:/--                      >B31:(B13+B21)/C39
>A16:"TOTALS                  >B32:(B14+B22)/C39
>A18:"<MEN>                   >B33:+B24/C39
>A19:"BLACK                   >B34:+B16/C39
>A20:"HISPANIC                >B36:/FL":
>A21:"ORIENTAL                >B37:/FL"EN:
>A22:"WHITE                   >B39:/FL"LOYEES:
>A23:/--
>A24:"TOTALS                  >C  1:"EEO REPOR
>A27:"<PERCENTA               >C  7:": M DONAL
>A29:"BLACK                   >C10:/FR"DEPT B
>A30:"HISPANIC                >C11:/FR5
>A31:"ORIENTAL                >C12:6
>A32:"WHITE                   >C13:5
>A33:"MEN                     >C14:12
>A34:"WOMEN                   >C15:/--
>A36:"TOTAL MEN               >C16:@SUM(C11...C14)
>A37:"TOTAL WOM               >C19:6
>A39:"TOTAL EMP               >C20:5
                              >C21:3
>B  3:/FL"OMPANY              >C22:5
>B  5:/FL" ZIP                >C23:/--
>B  7:"EPARED BY              >C24:@SUM(C19...C22)
>B10:/FR"DEPT A               >C27:/FL"ARTMENT>
>B11:/FR3                     >C29:(C11+C19)/C39
>B12:/FR4                     >C30:(C12+C20)/C39
>B13:/FR5                     >C31:(C13+C21)/C39
>B14:6                        >C32:(C14+C22)/C39
>B15:/--                      >C33:+C24/C39
>B16:@SUM(B11...B14)          >C34:+C16/C39
```

Model Run

```
              EEO REPORT

  NAME OF COMPANY
  ADDRESS
  CITY, ST  ZIP

  REPORT PREPARED BY: M DONALDSEN

                                                    PERCENT
                                                    OF TOTAL
     <WOMEN>  DEPT A  DEPT B  DEPT C  DEPT D  DEPT C  TOTALS  <WOMEN>
      BLACK      3       5       7       4      15      34 .2011834
   HISPANIC      4       6       2       8      22      42 .2485207
   ORIENTAL      5       5       4       5      21      40 .2366864
      WHITE      6      12       6       7      22      53 .3136095
  -----------------------------------------------------------------

     TOTALS     18      28      19      24      80     169

       <MEN>                                                  <MEN>
      BLACK      8       6       8       9      55      86 .2471264
   HISPANIC      3       5      17      15      37      77 .2212644
   ORIENTAL      2       3      31      41      56     133 .3821839
      WHITE      1       5       8      17      21      52 .1494253
  -----------------------------------------------------------------

     TOTALS     14      19      64      82     169     348


  <PERCENTAGE BY DEPARTMENT>

     BLACK .0212766 .0212766 .0290135 .0251451 .1353965
  HISPANIC .0135397 .0212766 .0367505 .0444874 .1141199
  ORIENTAL .0135397 .0154739 .0676983 .0889749 .1489362
     WHITE .0135397 .0328820 .0270793 .0464217 .0831721
       MEN .0270793 .0367505 .1237911 .1586074 .3268859
     WOMEN .0348162 .0541586 .0367505 .0464217 .1547389

  TOTAL MEN:          348 .6731141 %
  TOTAL WOMEN:        169 .3268859 %
                      ---------------
  TOTAL EMPLOYEES:    517     1. %
```

```
>C36:+G24                      >D14:6
>C37:+G16                      >D15:/--
>C38:"     ------              >D16:@SUM(D11...D14)
>C39:+C36+C37                  >D19:8
                               >D20:17
>D 1:/FL"T                     >D21:31
>D 7:/FL"DSEN                  >D22:8
>D10:/FR"DEPT C                >D23:/--
>D11:/FR7                      >D24:@SUM(D19...D22)
>D12:2                         >D29:(D11+D19)/C39
>D13:4                         >D30:(D12+D20)/C39
```

```
>D31:(D13+D21)/C39          >F23:/--
>D32:(D14+D22)/C39          >F24:@SUM(F19...F22)
>D33:+D24/C39               >F29:(F11+F19)/C39
>D34:+D16/C39               >F30:(F12+F20)/C39
>D36:+C36/C39               >F31:(F13+F21)/C39
>D37:+C37/C39               >F32:(F14+F22)/C39
>D38:/--                    >F33:+F24/C39
>D39:+D36+D37               >F34:+F16/C39

>E10:/FR"DEPT D             >G10:/FR"TOTALS
>E11:/FR4                   >G11:/FR@SUM(B11...F11)
>E12:8                      >G12:/FR@SUM(B12...F12)
>E13:5                      >G13:/FR@SUM(B13...F13)
>E14:7                      >G14:/FR@SUM(B14...F14)
>E15:/--                    >G15:/--
>E16:@SUM(E11...E14)        >G16:@SUM(G11...G14)
>E19:9                      >G17:/FR
>E20:15                     >G18:/FR
>E21:41                     >G19:/FR@SUM(B19...F19)
>E22:17                     >G20:/FR@SUM(B20...F20)
>E23:/--                    >G21:/FR@SUM(B21...F21)
>E24:@SUM(E19...E22)        >G22:/FR@SUM(B22...F22)
>E29:(E11+E19)/C39          >G23:/--
>E30:(E12+E20)/C39          >G24:@SUM(G19...G22)
>E31:(E13+E21)/C39
>E32:(E14+E22)/C39          >H 8:"PERCENT
>E33:+E24/C39               >H 9:"OF TOTAL
>E34:+E16/C39               >H10:/FR"<WOMEN>
>E36:/FL" %                 >H11:+G11/G16
>E37:/FL" %                 >H12:+G12/G16
>E39:/FL" %                 >H13:+G13/G16
                            >H14:+G14/G16
>F10:/FR"DEPT C             >H18:"<MEN>
>F11:/FR15                  >H19:+G19/G24
>F12:22                     >H20:+G20/G24
>F13:21                     >H21:+G21/G24
>F14:22                     >H22:+G22/G24
>F15:/--
>F16:@SUM(F11...F14)        /GC9
>F19:55                     /GFR
>F20:37                     /GOC
>F21:56                     /GRA
>F22:21                     /W1
```

PROJECT BOARD

If it sometimes seems like your company has more work than it can handle, the project board model might help you organize the flow of work.

This particular board shows seven projects. Each project has been allocated *x* number of hours a week, and each generates revenue at an average billing rate. There are four workers available to handle these projects. Everything else is calculated on this data.

The board shows how many workers to assign to each project, and, based on the number of available workers, what percentage of them is being kept busy. Naturally, in distributing hours to the project, the idea is to get as close as possible to 100%, thereby obtaining the maximum efforts of everyone involved. When this figure exceeds 100%, more hours have been assigned than there are people to work them. By trimming time from the Hours Per Week column for each project, the percentage calculation can be brought down to a reasonable level.

An additional calculation concerning revenue projections and percentage of total billing helps establish how much time a project should be allotted.

This model could be extended to include the names of individuals assigned to a project, along with their hours of availability. In that case, the Workers Available field would be generated by dividing the sum of the hours available by 40 (with 40 representing one full-time worker a week).

PRINT A1...I19

Model Run

```
                        PROJECT BOARD


    CURRENT          MAN HOURS    % OF         # OF    AVERAGE     PROJ     % OF
    PROJECTS            PER       TOTAL      WORKERS    HOURLY    WEEKLY     PROJ
                       WEEK       HOURS     TO ASSIGN  BILLING   REVENUE   REVENUE
    ADMINISTR STUDY     40        25.16         1       35.00    1400.00  19.35306
    COST ANALYSIS       32        20.13        .8       40.00    1280.00  17.69422
    READER SURVEY       20        12.58        .5       40.00     800.00  11.05889
    MARKET ANALYSIS     17        10.69       .425      40.00     680.00   9.400055
    DIRECT MAIL          8         5.03        .2       35.50     284.00   3.925905
    SALES STRATEGY DEV  10         6.29       .25       55.00     550.00   7.602986
    FINANCIAL SURVEY    32        20.13        .8       70.00    2240.00  30.96489
                      ---------             ---------          -------------------
         TOTALS:       159                    3.975              7234.00    100.

    PROJECTS ON BOARD: 7
    WORKERS AVAILABLE: 4
      % ON PROJECTS:   99.375
```

Listing

```
>A11:"DIRECT MA              >F 6:/FR"TO ASSIGN
>A12:"SALES STR              >F 7:(C7/40)
>A13:"FINANCIAL              >F 8:(C8/40)
>A17:"PROJECTS               >F 9:(C9/40)
>A18:"WORKERS A              >F10:(C10/40)
>A19:" % ON PRO              >F11:(C11/40)
                            >F12:(C12/40)
                            >F13:(C13/40)
>B 7:" STUDY                 >F14:/FI/---
>B 8:"YSIS                   >F15:@SUM(F7...F14)
>B 9:"RVEY
>B10:"ALYSIS                 >G 4:/FR"AVERAGE
>B11:"IL                     >G 5:/FR"HOURLY
>B12:"ATEGY DEV              >G 6:/FR"BILLING
>B13:" SURVEY                >G 7:/F$35
>B15:"TOTALS:                >G 8:/F$40
>B17:"ON BOARD:              >G 9:/F$40
>B18:"VAILABLE:              >G10:/F$40
>B19:"JECTS:                 >G11:/F$35.5
                            >G12:/F$55
                            >G13:/F$70
>C 4:"MAN HOURS
>C 5:"  PER                  >H 4:/FR"  PROJ
>C 6:" WEEK                  >H 5:/FR"WEEKLY
>C 7:/FL40                   >H 6:/FR"REVENUE
>C 8:/FL32                   >H 7:/F$+C7*G7
>C 9:/FL20                   >H 8:/F$+C8*G8
>C10:/FL17                   >H 9:/F$+C9*G9
>C11:/FL8                    >H10:/F$+C10*G10
>C12:/FL10                   >H11:/F$+C11*G11
>C13:/FL32                   >H12:/F$+C12*G12
>C14:"----------            >H13:/F$+C13*G13
>C15:/FL@SUM(C7...C14)       >H14:/---
>C17:/FL@COUNT(C7...C13)     >H15:/F$@SUM(H7...H14)
>C18:/FL4
>C19:/FL+F15/C18*100         >I 4:/FR" % OF
                            >I 5:/FR"PROJ
                            >I 6:/FR"REVENUE
>D 1:"PROJECT B              >I 7:(H7/H15)*100
>D 4:/FR" % OF               >I 8:(H8/H15)*100
>D 5:/FR"TOTAL               >I 9:(H9/H15)*100
>D 6:/FR"HOURS               >I10:(H10/H15)*100
>D 7:/F$(C7/C15)*100         >I11:(H11/H15)*100
>D 8:/F$(C8/C15)*100         >I12:(H12/H15)*100
>D 9:/F$(C9/C15)*100         >I13:(H13/H15)*100
>D10:/F$(C10/C15)*100        >I14:/---
>D11:/F$(C11/C15)*100        >I15:@SUM(I7...I13)
>D12:/F$(C12/C15)*100
>D13:/F$(C13/C15)*100
                            /GC9
                            /GOC
>E 1:"OARD                   /GRA
>E 4:/FR                     /W1
>E 5:/FR

>F 4:"  # OF
>F 5:/FR"WORKERS
```

TIME SHEET

If you're involved in a service or consulting business that bills clients by time or type of service, you can track your hours with this model, and calculate the billing amount at the same time.

You should use one VisiCalc time sheet per client. Merely enter the time spent each day, along with the appropriate rate code. The rate table at the top of the page can be adjusted at any time; by changing a rate in the rate table, a new billing amount will be calculated without having to change any data in the actual time spent area.

By moving the rate table to a non-printing area, you can actually use this report as an invoice for the client.

PRINT A1...F29

Model Run

```
                TIME SHEET

OCT 1 - OCT 31

CONSULTANT'S NAME
NAME OF PROJECT

            <HOURLY RATE CHART>

        #    RATE  SERVICE
        =    ====  =======
        1    20.00  ADMINISTRATIVE
        2    25.00  DESIGN
        3    30.00  CONSULTATION

=========================================================
                                            BILLING
DATE    DESCRIPTION      HOURS  RATE CODE   AMOUNT
----    -----------      -----  ---- ----   ------

OCT 1   SCHEDULE MEETING  1            1      20.00
OCT 2   DESIGN D/R DOCUMNT 3.5         2      87.50
OCT 4   MEETING W/HAYES   2            3      60.00
OCT 6   RE-DESIGN D/R DOC 4            2     100.00
OCT 12  SET-UP DETAIL ANLY 8          2     200.00
OCT 13  DETAIL ANALYSIS   6.5          2     162.50
OCT 15  PROJECT SPECS     3            2      75.00
OCT 20  PROJECT SPECS     3.5          2      87.50
OCT 27  MEETING W/HAYES   3            3      90.00
                         ----------------------------
                TOTALS:  34.5                882.50
```

Listing

```
>A  3:"OCT 1 - O          >C19:"MEETING
>A  5:"CONSULTAN          >C20:"R DOCUMNT
>A  6:"NAME OF P          >C21:"/HAYES
>A10:/FR"#                >C22:" D/R DOC
>A11:/FR"=                >C23:"TAIL ANLY
>A12:1                    >C24:"ALYSIS
>A13:2                    >C25:"PECS
>A14:3                    >C26:"PECS
>A15:/-=                  >C27:"/HAYES
>A17:"DATE                >C29:"TOTALS:
>A18:"----
>A19:"OCT 1               >D  1:"T
>A20:"OCT 2               >D  8:"ART>
>A21:"OCT 4               >D12:"TRATIVE
>A22:"OCT 6               >D14:"ATION
>A23:"OCT 12              >D15:/-=
>A24:"OCT 13              >D17:"HOURS
>A25:"OCT 15              >D18:"-----
>A26:"OCT 20              >D19:/FL1
>A27:"OCT 27              >D20:/FL3.5
                         >D21:/FL2
>B  3:"CT 31              >D22:/FL4
>B  5:"T'S NAME           >D23:/FL8
>B  6:"ROJECT             >D24:/FL6.5
>B  8:"    <HOURL         >D25:/FL3
>B10:/FR"RATE             >D26:/FL3.5
>B11:/FR"====             >D27:/FL3
>B12:/F$20                >D28:/--
>B13:/F$25                >D29:/FL@SUM(D19...D27)
>B14:/F$30
>B15:/-=                  >E15:/-=
>B17:"DESCRIPTI           >E17:"RATE CODE
>B18:"----------          >E18:"---- ----
>B19:"SCHEDULE            >E19:1
>B20:"DESIGN D/           >E20:2
>B21:"MEETING W           >E21:3
>B22:"RE-DESIGN           >E22:2
>B23:"SET-UP DE           >E23:2
>B24:"DETAIL AN           >E24:2
>B25:"PROJECT S           >E25:2
>B26:"PROJECT S           >E26:2
>B27:"MEETING W           >E27:3
                         >E28:/--
>C  1:"TIME SHEE
>C  8:"Y RATE CH          >F15:/-=
>C10:/FR"  SERVICE        >F16:/FR"BILLING
>C11:"  ========          >F17:/FR"AMOUNT
>C12:"  ADMINIS           >F18:"    ------
>C13:"  DESIGN            >F19:/F$@LOOKUP(E19,A12...A14)*D19
>C14:"  CONSULT           >F20:/F$@LOOKUP(E20,A12...A14)*D20
>C15:/-=                  >F21:/F$@LOOKUP(E21,A12...A14)*D21
>C17:"ON                  >F22:/F$@LOOKUP(E22,A12...A14)*D22
>C18:"---                 >F23:/F$@LOOKUP(E23,A12...A14)*D23
```

```
>F24:/F$@LOOKUP(E24,A12...A14)*D24
>F25:/F$@LOOKUP(E25,A12...A14)*D25
>F26:/F$@LOOKUP(E26,A12...A14)*D26
>F27:/F$@LOOKUP(E27,A12...A14)*D27
>F28:/--
>F29:/F$@SUM(F19...F27)

/GC9
/GOC
/GRA
/W1
```

3

GRADE BOOK

This VisiCalc model can easily computerize a teacher's grade book. As each student's test scores are entered during the school year, averages for both the individual students and the class as a whole are automatically updated.

This application is not limited to teachers. It can be used in market surveys for product awareness, or wherever tests are taken and results tabulated.

PRINT A1...K29

Model Run

```
                STUDENTS' GRADE BOOK

                SCORE   SCORE   SCORE   SCORE   SCORE   SCORE   SCORE   SCORE
                FOR TEST FOR TEST FOR TEST FOR TEST FOR TEST FOR TEST FOR TEST FOR TEST
STUDENT NAMES   1       2       3       4       5       6       7       8       AVERAGE
-----------------------------------------------------------------------------------------
AVONDALE,R      98      95      90      89      92      95      94      95      93.5
BETTINGTON,W    82      93      85      80      77      84      90      88      84.875
COLLINS,C       77      60      66      70      73      71      74      75      70.75
CYERSKI,T       99      98      99      95      96      96      95      98      97
EDWARDS,B       70      75      77      76      75      70      79      76      74.75
FARMINGTON,E    50      55      57      61      64      61      67      65      60
HEYDEN,S        80      80      81      80      79      82      84      80      80.75
JAMIESEN,D      90      80      70      75      77      81      85      87      80.625
LAWRENCE,R      77      80      79      81      82      88      71      89      80.875
LOFTEN,A        66      70      74      73      70      67      72      74      70.75
MATHEWS,D       91      90      89      88      90      94      93      91      90.75
NORMANS,V       94      90      85      75      80      83      87      88      85.25
PRICE,L         80      81      80      82      84      82      81      80      81.25
ROBERTSON,F     77      80      85      84      84      85      86      85      83.25
SANDESKI,W      75      81      83      85      85      89      82      79      82.375
SEDGEWICK,J     81      83      80      77      85      88      87      88      83.625
SOUTHBY,V       83      80      76      81      85      88      87      89      83.625
TUTOR,R         90      88      90      92      98      94      95      91      92.25
YOUNG,B         99      91      92      95      97      98      95      99      94.5
ZAMBETIO,L      77      83      85      89      84      87      86      91      85.25


CLASS AVG       81.3    81.65   81.15   81.4    82.85   84.15   84.5    85.4    82.8
```

Listing

```
>A 5:"STUDENT N        >A10:"CYERSKI,T
>A 6:/---              >A11:"EDWARDS,B
>A 7:"AVONDALE,        >A12:"FARMINGTO
>A 8:"BETTINGTO        >A13:"HEYDEN,S
>A 9:"COLLINS,C        >A14:"JAMIESEN,
```

>A15:"LAWRENCE,
>A16:"LOFTEN,A
>A17:"MATHEWS,D
>A18:"NORMANS,V
>A19:"PRICE,L
>A20:"ROBERTSON
>A21:"SANDESKI,
>A22:"SEDGEWICKJ
>A23:"SOUTHBY,V
>A24:"TUTOR,R
>A25:"YOUNG,B
>A26:"ZAMBETIO,
>A29:"CLASS AVG

>B 5:"AMES
>B 6:/--
>B 7:"R
>B 8:"N,W
>B12:"N,E
>B14:"D
>B15:"R
>B20:",F
>B21:"W
>B22:",J
>B26:"L

>C 1:"STUDENTS'
>C 3:"SCORE
>C 4:"FOR TEST
>C 5:/FL1
>C 6:/--
>C 7:98
>C 8:82
>C 9:77
>C10:99
>C11:70
>C12:50
>C13:80
>C14:90
>C15:77
>C16:66
>C17:91
>C18:94
>C19:80
>C20:77
>C21:75
>C22:81
>C23:83
>C24:90
>C25:89
>C26:77
>C29:ƏAVERAGE(C7...C26)

>D 1:" GRADE BO
>D 3:"SCORE

>D 4:"FOR TEST
>D 5:/FL2
>D 6:/--
>D 7:95
>D 8:93
>D 9:60
>D10:98
>D11:75
>D12:55
>D13:80
>D14:80
>D15:80
>D16:70
>D17:90
>D18:90
>D19:81
>D20:80
>D21:81
>D22:83
>D23:80
>D24:88
>D25:91
>D26:83
>D29:ƏAVERAGE(D7...D26)

>E 1:"OK
>E 3:"SCORE
>E 4:"FOR TEST
>E 5:/FL3
>E 6:/---
>E 7:90
>E 8:85
>E 9:66
>E10:99
>E11:77
>E12:57
>E13:81
>E14:70
>E15:79
>E16:74
>E17:89
>E18:85
>E19:80
>E20:85
>E21:83
>E22:80
>E23:76
>E24:90
>E25:92
>E26:85
>E29:ƏAVERAGE(E7...E26)

>F 3:"SCORE
>F 4:"FOR TEST
>F 5:/FL4

>F 6:/--
>F 7:89
>F 8:80
>F 9:70
>F10:95
>F11:76
>F12:61
>F13:80
>F14:75
>F15:81
>F16:73
>F17:88
>F18:75
>F19:82
>F20:84
>F21:85
>F22:77
>F23:81
>F24:92
>F25:95
>F26:89
>F29:ƆAVERAGE(F7...F26)

>G 3:"SCORE
>G 4:"FOR TEST
>G 5:/FL5
>G 6:/--
>G 7:92
>G 8:77
>G 9:73
>G10:96
>G11:75
>G12:64
>G13:79
>G14:77
>G15:82
>G16:70
>G17:90
>G18:80
>G19:84
>G20:84
>G21:85
>G22:85
>G23:85
>G24:98
>G25:97
>G26:84
>G29:ƆAVERAGE(G7...G26)

>H 3:"SCORE
>H 4:"FOR TEST
>H 5:/FL6
>H 6:/--
>H 7:95
>H 8:84

>H 9:71
>H10:96
>H11:70
>H12:61
>H13:82
>H14:81
>H15:88
>H16:67
>H17:94
>H18:83
>H19:82
>H20:85
>H21:89
>H22:88
>H23:88
>H24:94
>H25:98
>H26:87
>H29:ƆAVERAGE(H7...H26)

>I 3:"SCORE
>I 4:"FOR TEST
>I 5:/FL7
>I 6:/--
>I 7:94
>I 8:90
>I 9:74
>I10:95
>I11:79
>I12:67
>I13:84
>I14:85
>I15:71
>I16:72
>I17:93
>I18:87
>I19:81
>I20:86
>I21:82
>I22:87
>I23:87
>I24:95
>I25:95
>I26:86
>I29:ƆAVERAGE(I7...I26)

>J 3:"SCORE
>J 4:"FOR TEST
>J 5:/FL8
>J 6:/--
>J 7:95
>J 8:88
>J 9:75
>J10:98
>J11:76

```
>J12:65                          >K11:@AVERAGE(C11...J11)
>J13:80                          >K12:@AVERAGE(C12...J12)
>J14:87                          >K13:@AVERAGE(C13...J13)
>J15:89                          >K14:@AVERAGE(C14...J14)
>J16:74                          >K15:@AVERAGE(C15...J15)
>J17:91                          >K16:@AVERAGE(C16...J16)
>J18:88                          >K17:@AVERAGE(C17...J17)
>J19:80                          >K18:@AVERAGE(C18...J18)
>J20:85                          >K19:@AVERAGE(C19...J19)
>J21:79                          >K20:@AVERAGE(C20...J20)
>J22:88                          >K21:@AVERAGE(C21...J21)
>J23:89                          >K22:@AVERAGE(C22...J22)
>J24:91                          >K23:@AVERAGE(C23...J23)
>J25:99                          >K24:@AVERAGE(C24...J24)
>J26:91                          >K25:@AVERAGE(C25...J25)
>J29:@AVERAGE(J7...J26)          >K26:@AVERAGE(C26...J26)
                                 >K29:@AVERAGE(K7...K26)
>K 5:"AVERAGE
>K 6:/--                         /GC9
>K 7:@AVERAGE(C7...J7)           /GFL
>K 8:@AVERAGE(C8...J8)           /GOC
>K 9:@AVERAGE(C9...J9)           /GRA
>K10:@AVERAGE(C10...J10)         /W1
```

TRAVEL LOG

This model is suitable for a service representative or consultant who makes regular calls on clients. The miles traveled, as well as notations for gasoline and other authorized purchases for each visit, are entered. During the course of a month, as new calls are added to the list, total miles for the period are increased, along with totals for the year (New Bal). The tax deduction, based on the per mile rate, is also tracked. In addition, the consultant or service representative has documentation for gasoline purchases which shows the average price paid as well as the travel miles to the gallon.

For a service representative, time spent with a client could be incorporated to provide an additional management tool. Figures on total hours at the client's site, the number of calls per day, and averages for the period would help a representative analyze his or her time.

Although this model is designed for quarterly reporting, your models could consist of a year's or month's worth of line entries. If you use the yearly method for tracking your client calls, delete the Bal Fwd columns since they represent the previous period's figures.

PRINT A1. . .H54

Model Run

```
              TRAVEL LOG

DATE:     APR 1 - JUNE 30
CURRENT RATE FOR TAX DEDUCTION:        .15

         <ANALYSIS>

              BAL FWD  CURRENT   NEW BAL
MILES-TO-DATE     630      741      1371
TAX DEDUCTION   94.50   111.15    205.65
COST OF GAS    133.12   153.24    286.36
AVG PRICE PAID   1.35     1.38      2.73
MILES/GALLON     6.65     6.68      6.66
AVG MILES          20    21.17     20.59
```

DATE	CLIENT VISITED	MILES TRAVEL'D	GALLONS OF GAS PURCHASED	PRICE/ GALLON	COST FOR GAS
APR 4	BREN ENTERPRISES	34			0
APR 7	LOCKPORT	14	5.00	1.31	6.55
APR 9	STEMSON PRESS	15	7.00	1.34	9.38
APR 10	BREN	20			0.00
APR 12	KERRY MOTORS	22	15.00	1.44	21.60
APR 13	BRIAR HARDWARE	23			0.00
APR 17	ASHMAN DEALERSHIP	25	5.00	1.39	6.95
APR 21	REYNOLDS FREIGHT	30	3.00	1.40	4.20
APR 23	LITMAN INDUSTRIES	35			0.00
MAY 1	CALMON STEAK HOUSE	40	5.00	1.42	7.10
MAY 2	BREN ENTERPRISES	31	7.00	1.43	10.01
MAY 5	LOCKPORT	12			0.00
MAY 7	LITMAN INDUSTRIES	12	4.00	1.45	5.80
MAY 8	FM STATION	15			0.00
MAY 8	JML	18			0.00
MAY 9	STEWART OFFICE SUPPLIES	22			0.00
MAY 15	BREN	34	5.00	1.41	7.05
MAY 17	LOCKPORT	44	5.00	1.39	6.95
MAY 19	KERRY MOTORS	12	12.00	1.37	16.44
MAY 20	ASHMAN DEALERSHIP	13	9.00	1.36	12.24
MAY 21	SEAMAN SIGNS	17			0.00
MAY 30	JL ELECTRIC	8	6.00	1.34	8.04
JUNE 1	WALD'S BOOKS	9			0.00
JUNE 1	STAN'S CAFE	19	7.00	1.33	9.31
JUNE 3	CALMON STEAK HOUSE	21			0.00
JUNE 7	LOCKPORT	22			0.00
JUNE 5	HARGREN ENGINES	24	8.00	1.34	10.72
JUNE 6	BRAVERN TAVERN	31	3.00	1.35	4.05
JUNE 10	EDGE PAPER	23			0.00
JUNE 12	ROLAN OFFSET	22			0.00
JUNE 14	MARTINS BAKERY	21			0.00
JUNE 20	YOLMAN & FORD	19	5.00	1.37	6.85
JUNE 21	SEAMAN SIGNS	15			0.00
JUNE 22	WEZMAN SPORTS	19			0.00
JUNE 30	EDGE PAPER	18	7.00	1.39	9.73

Listing

>A 3:"DATE:
>A 4:"CURRENT R
>A 9:"MILES-TO-
>A10:"TAX DEDUC
>A11:"COST OF G
>A12:"AVG PRICE
>A13:"MILES/GAL
>A14:"AVG MILES
>A19:"DATE
>A20:"APR 4
>A21:"APR 7
>A22:"APR 9
>A23:"APR 10
>A24:"APR 12
>A25:"APR 13
>A26:"APR 17
>A27:"APR 21
>A28:"APR 23
>A29:"MAY 1
>A30:"MAY 2
>A31:"MAY 5
>A32:"MAY 7
>A33:"MAY 8
>A34:"MAY 8
>A35:"MAY 9
>A36:"MAY 15
>A37:"MAY 17
>A38:"MAY 19
>A39:"MAY 20
>A40:"MAY 21
>A41:"MAY 30
>A42:"JUNE 1
>A43:"JUNE 1
>A44:"JUNE 3
>A45:"JUNE 7
>A46:"JUNE 5
>A47:"JUNE 6
>A48:"JUNE 10
>A49:"JUNE 12
>A50:"JUNE 14
>A51:"JUNE 20
>A52:"JUNE 21
>A53:"JUNE 22
>A54:"JUNE 30

>B 3:"APR 1 - J
>B 4:"ATE FOR T
>B 6:"<ANALYSIS
>B 9:"DATE
>B10:"TION
>B11:"AS
>B12:" PAID
>B13:"LON

>B19:"CLIENT VI
>B20:"BREN ENTER
>B21:"LOCKPORT
>B22:"STEMSON P
>B23:"BREN
>B24:"KERRY MOT
>B25:"BRIAR HAR
>B26:"ASHMAN DE
>B27:"REYNOLDS
>B28:"LITMAN IN
>B29:"CALMON ST
>B30:"BREN ENTE
>B31:"LOCKPORT
>B32:"LITMAN IN
>B33:"FM STATIO
>B34:"JML
>B35:"STEWART O
>B36:"BREN
>B37:"LOCKPORT
>B38:"KERRY MOT
>B39:"ASHMAN DE
>B40:"SEAMAN SI
>B41:"JL ELECTR
>B42:"WALD'S BO
>B43:"STAN'S CA
>B44:"CALMON ST
>B45:"LOCKPORT
>B46:"HARGREN E
>B47:"BRAVERM T
>B48:"EDGE PAPE
>B49:"ROLAN OFF
>B50:"MARTINS B
>B51:"YOLMAN &
>B52:"SEAMAN SI
>B53:"WEZMAN SP
>B54:"EDGE PAPE

>C 1:"TRAVEL LO
>C 3:"UNE 30
>C 4:"AX DEDUCT
>C 6:">
>C 8:"BAL FWD
>C 9:630
>C10:/F$94.5
>C11:133.12
>C12:1.35
>C13:/F$6.65
>C14:20
>C19:"SITED
>C20:"PRISES
>C22:"RESS
>C24:"ORS
>C25:"DWARE

```
>C26:"ALERSHIP              >E28:/FL35
>C27:"FREIGHT               >E29:/FL40
>C28:"DUSTRIES              >E30:/FL31
>C29:"EAK HOUSE             >E31:/FL12
>C30:"RPRISES               >E32:/FL12
>C32:"DUSTRIES              >E33:/FL15
>C33:"N                     >E34:/FL18
>C35:"FFICE SUP             >E35:/FL22
>C38:"ORS                   >E36:/FL34
>C39:"ALERSHIP              >E37:/FL44
>C40:"GNS                   >E38:/FL12
>C41:"IC                    >E39:/FL13
>C42:"OKS                   >E40:/FL17
>C43:"FE                    >E41:/FL8
>C44:"EAK HOUSE             >E42:/FL9
>C46:"NGINES                >E43:/FL19
>C47:"AVERN                 >E44:/FL21
>C48:"R                     >E45:/FL22
>C49:"SET                   >E46:/FL24
>C50:"AKERY                 >E47:/FL31
>C51:"FORD                  >E48:/FL23
>C52:"GNS                   >E49:/FL22
>C53:"ORTS                  >E50:/FL21
>C54:"R                     >E51:/FL19
                            >E52:/FL15
                            >E53:/FL19
>D 1:"G                     >E54:/FL18
>D 4:"ION:                  >E55:/FL
>D 8:"CURRENT
>D 9:@SUM(E20...E53)
>D10:+E4*D9                 >F17:"GALLONS
>D11:@SUM(H21...H53)        >F18:"OF GAS
>D12:/F$@SUM(G21...G53)     >F19:/FR"PURCHASED
     /@COUNT(G21...G53)     >F20:/F$
>D13:/F$+D9/@SUM(F20...F53) >F21:/F$5
>D14:/F$+D9/@COUNT(E20...E54)>F22:/F$7
>D35:"PLIES                 >F23:/F$
                            >F24:/F$15
                            >F25:/F$
>E 4:.15                    >F26:/F$5
>E 8:/FR"NEW BAL            >F27:/F$3
>E 9:+C9+D9                 >F28:/F$
>E10:+C10+D10               >F29:/F$5
>E11:+C11+D11               >F30:/F$7
>E12:/F$+C12+D12            >F31:/F$
>E13:/F$+C13+D13/2          >F32:/F$4
>E14:/F$(C14+D14)/2         >F33:/F$
>E18:"MILES                 >F34:/F$
>E19:"TRAVEL'D              >F35:/F$
>E20:/FL34                  >F36:/F$5
>E21:/FL14                  >F37:/F$5
>E22:/FL15                  >F38:/F$12
>E23:/FL20                  >F39:/F$9
>E24:/FL22                  >F40:/F$
>E25:/FL23                  >F41:/F$6
>E26:/FL25                  >F42:/F$
>E27:/FL30
```

Personnel and Departments

```
>F43:/F$7                           >G52:/F$
>F44:/F$                            >G53:/F$
>F45:/F$                            >G54:/F$1.39
>F46:/F$8                           >G55:/F$
>F47:/F$3
>F48:/F$                            >H17:/FR"COST
>F49:/F$                            >H18:/FR"FOR
>F50:/F$                            >H19:/FR"GAS
>F51:/F$5                           >H20:+F20*G20
>F52:/F$                            >H21:/F$+F21*G21
>F53:/F$                            >H22:/F$+F22*G22
>F54:/F$7                           >H23:/F$+F23*G23
>F55:/F$                            >H24:/F$+F24*G24
                                    >H25:/F$+F25*G25
>G18:/FR"PRICE/                     >H26:/F$+F26*G26
>G19:/FR"GALLON                     >H27:/F$+F27*G27
>G20:/F$                            >H28:/F$+F28*G28
>G21:/F$1.31                        >H29:/F$+F29*G29
>G22:/F$1.34                        >H30:/F$+F30*G30
>G23:/F$                            >H31:/F$+F31*G31
>G24:/F$1.44                        >H32:/F$+F32*G32
>G25:/F$                            >H33:/F$+F33*G33
>G26:/F$1.39                        >H34:/F$+F34*G34
>G27:/F$1.4                         >H35:/F$+F35*G35
>G28:/F$                            >H36:/F$+F36*G36
>G29:/F$1.42                        >H37:/F$+F37*G37
>G30:/F$1.43                        >H38:/F$+F38*G38
>G31:/F$                            >H39:/F$+F39*G39
>G32:/F$1.45                        >H40:/F$+F40*G40
>G33:/F$                            >H41:/F$+F41*G41
>G34:/F$                            >H42:/F$+F42*G42
>G35:/F$                            >H43:/F$+F43*G43
>G36:/F$1.41                        >H44:/F$+F44*G44
>G37:/F$1.39                        >H45:/F$+F45*G45
>G38:/F$1.37                        >H46:/F$+F46*G46
>G39:/F$1.36                        >H47:/F$+F47*G47
>G40:/F$                            >H48:/F$+F48*G48
>G41:/F$1.34                        >H49:/F$+F49*G49
>G42:/F$                            >H50:/F$+F50*G50
>G43:/F$1.33                        >H51:/F$+F51*G51
>G44:/F$                            >H52:/F$+F52*G52
>G45:/F$                            >H53:/F$+F53*G53
>G46:/F$1.34                        >H54:/F$+F54*G54
>G47:/F$1.35
>G48:/F$                            /GC9
>G49:/F$                            /GOC
>G50:/F$                            /GRA
>G51:/F$1.37                        /W1
```

DEPARTMENTAL DISTRIBUTION

This model compares the payroll costs to revenue for individual departments. Each department contributes x amount to total revenue, while generating y amount in payroll costs. With this model, percentages for costs and revenue are obtained.

In the example, Dept. A contributes the lowest percentage of revenue, but its payroll costs are also the lowest. Dept. D, however, costs nearly twice as much as it contributes.

Although the data shown here is limited to payroll, the model can be expanded to include administrative overhead for further comparison.

PRINT A1...F33

Model Run

```
                    DEPARTMENTAL DISTRIBUTION

                    FOR PERIOD ENDING MM/DD/YY

    <REVENUE>

              DEPT A  DEPT B  DEPT C  DEPT D   TOTALS
DIR REV       3400.00 4500.00 9500.00 3500.00 20900.00
% OF TOTL      16.27   21.53   45.45   16.75   100.00


HIGH % OF TOTAL        45.45
LOW % OF TOTAL         16.27


==================================================

    <PAYROLL COSTS>

              DEPT A  DEPT B  DEPT C  DEPT D
# OF EMPS          2       3      10       5       20
REG HOURS         80     120     400     200      800
OT HOURS                   10      35    25.5     70.5
# OF CKS           2       3      10       5       20
GROSS PAY     400.00  980.00 2598.00 1750.00  5728.00
FICA           26.00   63.70  168.87  113.75   372.32
FUT             2.80    6.86   18.19   12.25    40.10
SUT             9.20   22.54   59.75   40.25   131.74
            ------------------------------------------
TOTAL PR      438.00 1073.10 2844.81 1916.25  6272.16
% OF TOTL       6.98   17.11   45.36   30.55   100.00

HIGH % OF TOTAL        45.36
LOW % OF TOTAL          6.98   OT PERCENTAGE    28.37
```

Listing

```
>A 5:"   <REVENU
>A 8:"DIR REV
>A 9:"% OF TOTL
>A11:"HIGH % OF
>A12:" LOW % OF
>A14:/-=
>A17:"   <PAYROL
>A20:"# OF EMPS
>A21:"REG HOURS
>A22:"OT HOURS
>A23:"# OF CKS
>A24:"GROSS PAY
>A25:"FICA
>A26:"FUT
>A27:"SUT
>A29:"TOTAL PR
>A30:"% OF TOTL
>A32:"HIGH % OF
>A33:" LOW % OF

>B 5:"E>
>B 7:/FR"DEPT A
>B 8:/F$3400
>B 9:/F$+B8/F8*100
>B11:/F$" TOTAL
>B12:/F$" TOTAL
>B14:/-=
>B17:"L COSTS>
>B19:/FR"DEPT A
>B20:2
>B21:80
>B23:2
>B24:/F$400
>B25:/F$26
>B26:/F$2.8
```

```
>B27:/F$9.2
>B28:/--
>B29:/F$@SUM(B24...B27)
>B30:/F$(B29/F29)*100
>B32:/F$" TOTAL
>B33:/F$" TOTAL

>C 7:/FR"DEPT B
>C 8:/F$4500
>C 9:/F$+C8/F8*100
>C11:/F$@MAX(B9...E9)
>C12:/F$@MIN(B9...E9)
>C14:/-=
>C19:/FR"DEPT B
>C20:3
>C21:120
>C22:10
>C23:3
>C24:/F$980
>C25:/F$63.7
>C26:/F$6.86
>C27:/F$22.54
>C28:/--
>C29:/F$@SUM(C24...C27)
>C30:/F$(C29/F29)*100
>C32:/F$@MAX(B30...E30)
>C33:/F$@MIN(B30...E30)

>D 1:"DEPARTMEN
>D 3:"FOR PERIO
>D 7:/FR"DEPT C
>D 8:/F$9500
>D 9:/F$+D8/F8*100
>D14:/-=
>D19:/FR"DEPT C
>D20:10
>D21:400
>D22:35
>D23:10
>D24:/F$2598
>D25:/F$168.87
>D26:/F$18.19
>D27:/F$59.75
>D28:/--
>D29:/F$@SUM(D24...D27)
>D30:/F$(D29/F29)*100
```

```
>D33:/FR"OT P

>E 1:"TAL DISTR
>E 3:"D ENDING
>E 7:/FR"DEPT D
>E 8:/F$3500
>E 9:/F$+E8/F8*100
>E14:/-=
>E19:/FR"DEPT D
>E20:5
>E21:200
>E22:25.5
>E23:5
>E24:/F$1750
>E25:/F$113.75
>E26:/F$12.25
>E27:/F$40.25
>E28:/--
>E29:/F$@SUM(E24...E27)
>E30:/F$(E29/F29)*100
>E33:"ERCENTAGE

>F 1:"IBUTION
>F 3:"MM/DD/YY
>F 7:/FR"TOTALS
>F 8:/F$@SUM(B8...E8)
>F 9:/F$+F8/F8*100
>F14:/-=
>F20:@SUM(B20...E20)
>F21:@SUM(B21...E21)
>F22:@SUM(B22...E22)
>F23:@SUM(B23...E23)
>F24:/F$@SUM(B24...E24)
>F25:/F$@SUM(B25...E25)
>F26:/F$@SUM(B26...E26)
>F27:/F$@SUM(B27...E27)
>F28:/--
>F29:/F$@SUM(F24...F27)
>F30:/F$(F29/F29)*100
>F33:/F$(F20/F22)*100

/GC9
/GOC
/GRA
/W1
```

PRODUCTIVITY ANALYSIS

If you can single out criteria for evaluating productivity or performance, you can apply this model to that evaluation.

The sample model gives an analysis of key entry operators working in a large personnel office. It was determined that an operator takes an average of 250 keystrokes to complete one form. This average is used to evaluate the productivity of each key operator.

If you enter the number of hours worked and the number of forms completed, the model will calculate the speed of each key operator, and the percentage of his or her contribution to the total work output. The maximum, minimum, and average totals of keystrokes and documents are reported for comparison purposes.

Mary, for instance, worked on 200 forms in 35 hours. Her total keystrokes were calculated at 500,000, which averages to 11,286 per hour or 238 per minute. She contributed 0.95 documents per minute, or 17% of the forms produced by the five employees that week.

Applying this model to other types of productivity analysis requires no more than replacing the number of keystrokes with the criteria that fit your product.

PRINT A1...H26

Model Run

```
              PRODUCTIVITY ANALYSIS


  DEPT:      KEY ENTRY
  SUBMITTED BY:    R. EMERSEN
  FOR PERIOD:     WK # 33
  DOCUMENT:       PERSONNEL FORM
  KETSTROKES/DOC:    250




  EMPLOYEE   TOTAL      DIRECT   TOTAL KEYSTRKS KEYSTRKS DOCS PER  PERCENT
  NAME     DOCUMENTS   HOURS KEYSTRKS PER HOUR  PER MIN   MINUTE OF TOTAL


  MARY        2000       35   500000 14285.71 238.0952 .9523810 .1714639
  LYNN        1800       32   450000 14062.5  234.375   .9375  .1687848
  HARRIET     2200       30   550000 18333.33 305.5556 1.222222 .2200453
  BETTY       1900       20   475000  23750   395.8333 1.583333 .2850587
  KATHY       1340       26   335000 12884.62 214.7436 .8589744 .1546472


  TOTALS:     9240      143  2310000 83316.16 1388.603 5.554411       1
  MAXIMUMS:   2200       35   550000  23750   395.8333 1.583333 .2850587
  MINIMUMS:   1340       20   335000 12884.62 214.7436 .8589744 .1546472
  AVERAGES:   1848      28.6  462000 16663.23 277.7205 1.110882      .2
```

Listing

```
>A  4:"DEPT:
>A  5:"SUBMITTED
>A  6:"FOR PERIO
>A  7:/FR"DOCUMENT:
>A  8:"KETSTROKE
>A14:"EMPLOYEE
>A15:"NAME
>A17:"MARY
>A18:"LYNN
>A19:"HARRIET
>A20:"BETTY
>A21:"KATHY
>A23:"TOTALS:
>A24:"MAXIMUMS:
>A25:"MINIMUMS:
>A26:"AVERAGES:

>B  4:"KEY ENTRY
>B  5:"  BY:
>B  6:"D:
>B  8:"S/DOC:
>B14:/FR"TOTAL
>B15:"DOCUMENTS
>B17:2000
>B18:1800
>B19:2200
>B20:1900
>B21:1340
>B23:@SUM(B17...B21)
>B24:@MAX(B17...B21)
>B25:@MIN(B17...B21)
>B26:@AVERAGE(B17...B21)

>C  1:"PRODUCTIV
>C  5:"R. EMERSE
>C  6:"WK # 33
>C  7:"PERSONNEL
>C  8:/FL250
>C14:/FR"DIRECT
>C15:/FR"HOURS
>C17:35
>C18:32
>C19:30
>C20:20
>C21:26
>C23:@SUM(C17...C21)
>C24:@MAX(C17...C21)
>C25:@MIN(C17...C21)
>C26:@AVERAGE(C17...C21)

>D  1:"ITY ANALY
>D  5:"N
>D  7:" FORM
```

```
>D14:/FR"TOTAL
>D15:/FR"KEYSTRKS
>D17:+B17*C8
>D18:+B18*C8
>D19:+B19*C8
>D20:+B20*C8
>D21:+B21*C8
>D23:@SUM(D17...D21)
>D24:@MAX(D17...D21)
>D25:@MIN(D17...D21)
>D26:@AVERAGE(D17...D21)

>E  1:"SIS
>E14:/FR"KEYSTRKS
>E15:/FR"PER HOUR
>E17:+D17/C17
>E18:+D18/C18
>E19:+D19/C19
>E20:+D20/C20
>E21:+D21/C21
>E23:@SUM(E17...E21)
>E24:@MAX(E17...E21)
>E25:@MIN(E17...E21)
>E26:@AVERAGE(E17...E21)

>F14:/FR"KEYSTRKS
>F15:/FR"PER MIN
>F17:+E17/60
>F18:+E18/60
>F19:+E19/60
>F20:+E20/60
>F21:+E21/60
>F23:@SUM(F17...F21)
>F24:@MAX(F17...F21)
>F25:@MIN(F17...F21)
>F26:@AVERAGE(F17...F21)

>G14:/FR"DOCS PER
>G15:/FR"MINUTE
>G17:+F17/C8
>G18:+F18/C8
>G19:+F19/C8
>G20:+F20/C8
>G21:+F21/C8
>G23:@SUM(G17...G21)
>G24:@MAX(G17...G21)
>G25:@MIN(G17...G21)
>G26:@AVERAGE(G17...G21)

>H14:/FR"PERCENT
>H15:/FR"OF TOTAL
>H17:+G17/G23
>H18:+G18/G23
```

```
>H19:+G19/G23
>H20:+G20/G23
>H21:+G21/G23
>H23:@SUM(H17...H21)
>H24:@MAX(H17...H21)
>H25:@MIN(H17...H21)
>H26:@AVERAGE(H17...H21)

/GC9
/GOC
/GRA
/W1
```

CLIENT SURVEY

This model tallies a client survey of your own service.

The example is a single-subject questionnaire sent to the clients of a small data processing service bureau. The respondents are asked to rate the customer service department on four points, according to the degree of attention they receive. Each column in the VisiCalc model is numbered, and the total responses for each category are entered in their respective positions.

The model tallies the columns, multiplies each total by the number (1 through 7) at the top of the column, and generates a score. The total score is divided by the total respondents to produce an average rating. Here the average is 5.155, which means that in the overall opinion of the respondents, the customer service department is, on the average, unresponsive, not knowledgeable, discourteous, and ineffective.

PRINT A1...K22

Model Run

```
              CLIENT SURVEY

    DEPARTMENT: CUSTOMER SERVICE

        QUESTION:WHAT ARE YOUR IMPRESSIONS OF
                OUR CUSTOMER SERVICE DEPARTMENT ?

                     1       2       3       4       5       6       7
                  EXTREMELY  VERY  AVERAGE NO OPIN AVERAGE  VERY EXTREMLY

    RESPONSIVE       50      30      33      2       50      20      15   UNRESPONSIVE
    KNOWLEDGABLE     65      35      22      14      40      18      6    NOT KNOWLEDGABLE
    COURTEOUS        63      43      28      8       33      13      12   DISCOURTEOUS
    EFFECTIVE        67      44      31      11      26      14      7    INEFFECTIVE
                   ------------------------------------------------------
            TOTALS   245     152     114     35      149     65      40
    COLUMNAR SCORES  245     304     342     140     745     390     280


    TOTAL RESPONDENTS   200
        TOTAL SCORE     1031
      AVERAGE RATING    5.155
```

Listing

>B11:"E
>B12:"BLE
>B16:"TOTALS
>B17:"SCORES
>B20:"PONDENTS
>B21:"AL SCORE
>B22:"GE RATING

>C 1:"CLIENT SU
>C 3:"ER SERVIC
>C 5:"WHAT ARE
>C 6:"OUR CUSTO
>C 8:1
>C 9:"EXTREMELY
>C11:50
>C12:65
>C13:63
>C14:67
>C15:/--
>C16:@SUM(C11...C14)
>C17:+C16*C8
>C20:@SUM(C11...I11)
>C21:@SUM(C17...F17)
>C22:+C21/C20

>D 1:"RVEY
>D 3:"E
>D 5:"YOUR IMPR
>D 6:"MER SERVI
>D 8:2
>D 9:/FR"VERY
>D11:30
>D12:35
>D13:43
>D14:44
>D15:/--
>D16:@SUM(D11...D14)
>D17:+D16*D8

>E 5:"ESSIONS O
>E 6:"CE DEPART
>E 8:3
>E 9:/FR"AVERAGE
>E11:33
>E12:22
>E13:28
>E14:31
>E15:/--
>E16:@SUM(E11...E14)
>E17:+E16*E8

>F 5:"F
>F 6:"MENT ?
>F 8:4

>F 9:/FR"NOOPIN
>F11:2
>F12:14
>F13:8
>F14:11
>F15:/--
>F16:@SUM(F11...F14)
>F17:+F16*F8

>G 8:5
>G 9:/FR"AVERAGE
>G11:50
>G12:40
>G13:33
>G14:26
>G15:/--
>G16:@SUM(G11...G14)
>G17:+G16*G8

>H 8:6
>H 9:/FR"VERY
>H11:20
>H12:18
>H13:13
>H14:14
>H15:/--
>H16:@SUM(H11...H14)
>H17:+H16*H8

>I 8:7
>I 9:" EXTREMLY
>I11:15
>I12:6
>I13:12
>I14:7
>I15:/--
>I16:@SUM(I11...I14)
>I17:+I16*I8

>J11:" UNRESPO
>J12:" NOT KNO
>J13:" DISCOUR
>J14:" INEFFEC

>K11:"NSIVE
>K12:"WLEDGABLE
>K13:"TEOUS
>K14:"TIVE

/GC9
/GOC
/GRA
/W1

PERSONAL FINANCE

HOME INVENTORY AND PERSONAL POSSESSIONS EVALUATION

This model will assist individuals in itemizing and evaluating their personal possessions. The evaluation is useful for insurance coverage and claims for fire or theft losses.

Each personal possession is evaluated on its original cost, resale value, and replacement cost. The resale value is calculated according to straight-line depreciation, and the replacement cost is based on the local inflation rate.

Possessions might also be evaluated using an accepted price apreciation rate in place of the local inflation rate. The model can also be used to evaluate office or manufacturing equipment.

There is a calculation area shown at the right of the model that need not be printed.

PRINT A1...O66

Listing

```
>A 8:"      CURRE
>A 9:"LOCAL INF
>A13:"   ROOM
>A14:"LOCATION
>A15:/--
>A16:"ATTIC
>A18:"L.R
>A19:"L.R
>A20:"L.R
>A22:"B.R #1
>A23:"B.R #1
>A24:"B.R #1
>A26:"B.R #2
>A28:"KITCHEN
>A29:"KITCHEN
>A31:"BASEMENT
>A32:"BASEMENT
>A33:"BASEMENT
>A34:"BASEMENT
>A35:"BASEMENT
>A37:"GARAGE
>A38:"GARAGE
>A39:"GARAGE
>A40:"GARAGE
>A42:"SAFE DEPO
>A55:/--
>A56:"TOTALS
>A59:"COMPARISI

>B 3:"HOME INVE
>B 4:"PERSONAL
>B 5:"   EVALUATION
```

```
>B 6:/--
>B 8:"NT  YEAR>
>B 9:"LATION %>
>B11:"- I T E M
>B13:"   MAKE &
>B14:"  MODEL  #
>B15:/--
>B16:"OLD STERE
>B18:"DECORATIO
>B19:"FURNITURE
>B20:"NEW STERE
>B22:"FURNITURE
>B23:"HIS-WARDR
>B24:"HERS-WARD
>B26:"OFFICE FU
>B28:"FURNITURE
>B29:"APPLIANCE
>B31:"HOUSEHOLD
>B32:"POOL TABL
>B33:"DEN FURNI
>B34:"DEN COLOR
>B35:"WASHER/DR
>B37:"HIS AUTO
>B38:"HER AUTO
>B39:"GARDEN EQ
>B40:"SPORTS EQU
>B42:"SIT BOX
>B55:/--
>B59:"ON OF ORI
>B62:"WHICH REP

>C 3:"NTORY &
```

Model Run

```
           HOME INVENTORY &        OF NAME:
           PERSONAL POSSESSIONS              -------------------
              EVALUATION          AS OF :MM/DD/YY
           ------------------                 ---------

       CURRENT YEAR>    1981
    LOCAL INFLATION %>   12.5
```

						ESTIMATED		%	CALCULATION AREA	
						CURRENT	REPLACE-	INCREASE		
ROOM	MAKE &	SERIAL	DATE	COST OR	USEFUL	RESALE	MENT	SINCE		
LOCATION	MODEL #	NUMBER	ACQUIRED	BASIS	LIFE-YRS	VALUE	COST	PURCHASE	YRS USED	DEP.RATE
ATTIC	OLD STEREO		1973	4000	9	444	10263	156.58	8	.125
L.R	DECORATIONS		1976	1500	10	750	2703	80.20	5	
L.R	FURNITURE		1975	10000	15	6000	20273	102.73	6	
L.R	NEW STEREO		1977	3500	10	2100	5606	60.18	4	
B.R #1	FURNITURE		1975	1500	15	900	3041	102.73	6	
B.R #1	HIS-WARDROBE		1979	2000	3	667	2531	26.56	2	
B.R #1	HERS-WARDROBE		1978	3500	3	0	4983	42.38	3	
B.R #2	OFFICE FURNITURE		1980	2500	10	2250	2812	12.50	1	
KITCHEN	FURNITURE		1976	895	8	336	1613	80.20	5	
KITCHEN	APPLIANCES		1976	1750	7	500	3154	80.20	5	
BASEMENT	HOUSEHOLD TOOLS		1978	2500	10	1750	3560	42.38	3	
BASEMENT	POOL TABLE		1979	3500	15	3033	4430	26.56	2	
BASEMENT	DEN FURNITURE		1979	2500	12	2083	3164	26.56	2	
BASEMENT	DEN COLOR T.V.		1980	1250	7	1071	1406	12.50	1	
BASEMENT	WASHER/DRYER		1978	1750	10	1225	2492	42.38	3	
GARAGE	HIS AUTO		1977	6500	6	2167	10412	60.18	4	
GARAGE	HER AUTO		1980	7900	6	6583	8887	12.50	1	
GARAGE	GARDEN EQUIPMENT		1977	1250	5	250	2002	60.18	4	
GARAGE	SPORTS EQUIPMENT		1979	1000	3	333	1266	26.56	2	
SAFE DEPOSIT BOX	JEWELS		1980	5000	20	4750	5625	12.50	1	

```
       --------------------------------------------------
TOTALS                         64295         37193  100223
                             ========       ==================


COMPARISION OF ORIGINAL PURCHASE PRICE AND CURRENT REPLACEMENT VALUE DIFERENCE: $    35928
                                                               #########

        WHICH REPRESENTS AN INCREASE OF:      55.88%
               #########
```

```
>C  4:"POSSESSIO            >E35:/FI1978
>C  5:"ATION               >E36:/FI
>C  6:/--                  >E37:/FI1977
>C  8:1981                 >E38:/FI1980
>C  9:/FG12.5              >E39:/FI1977
>C11:" DESCRIPT            >E40:/FI1979
>C14:"#                    >E42:/FI1980
>C15:/--                   >E55:/--
>C16:"O                    >E59:"CE AND CU
>C18:"NS                   >E62:"E OF:
>C20:"O
>C23:"OBE                  >F  4:/--
>C24:"ROBE                 >F  5:"MM/DD/YY
>C26:"RNITURE              >F  6:/--
>C29:"S                    >F13:" COST OR
>C31:" TOOLS               >F14:"   BASIS
>C32:"E                    >F15:/--
>C33:"TURE                 >F16:4000
>C34:" T.V.                >F18:1500
>C35:"YER                  >F19:10000
>C39:"UIPMENT              >F20:3500
>C40:"UIPMENT              >F22:1500
>C42:"JEWELS               >F23:2000
>C55:/--                   >F24:3500
>C59:"GINAL PUR            >F26:2500
>C62:"RESENTS A            >F28:895
                           >F29:1750
>D  4:"NS                  >F31:2500
>D11:"ION    -             >F32:3500
>D13:"  SERIAL             >F33:2500
>D14:" NUMBER              >F34:1250
>D15:/--                   >F35:1750
>D55:/--                   >F37:6500
>D59:"CHASE PRI            >F38:7900
>D62:"N INCREAS            >F39:1250
                           >F40:1000
>E  3:" OF NAME:           >F42:5000
>E  5:"   AS OF :          >F55:/--
>E13:"  DATE               >F56:@SUM(F16...F54)
>E14:" ACQUIRED            >F57:/-=
>E15:/--                   >F59:"RRENT REP
>E16:/FI1973               >F62:/F$+J59/F56*100
>E18:/FI1976               >F63:/-*
>E19:/FI1975
>E20:/FI1977               >G  1:/F$
>E22:/FI1975               >G  4:/--
>E23:/FI1979               >G13:" USEFUL
>E24:/FI1978               >G14:" LIFE-YRS
>E26:/FI1980               >G15:/--
>E28:/FI1976               >G16:9
>E29:/FI1976               >G18:10
>E31:/FI1978               >G19:15
>E32:/FI1979               >G20:10
>E33:/FI1979               >G22:15
>E34:/FI1980               >G23:3
```

```
>G24:3
>G26:10
>G28:8
>G29:7
>G31:10
>G32:15
>G33:12
>G34:7
>G35:10
>G37:6
>G38:6
>G39:5
>G40:3
>G42:20
>G55:/--
>G59:"LACEMENT
>G62:"%

>H11:"- - ESTIM
>H12:" CURRENT
>H13:" RESALE
>H14:"  VALUE
>H15:/--
>H16:/FI(+F16)/G16*(G16-(C8-E16))
>H18:(+F18)/G18*(G18-(C8-E18))
>H19:(+F19)/G19*(G19-(C8-E19))
>H20:(+F20)/G20*(G20-(C8-E20))
>H22:(+F22)/G22*(G22-(C8-E22))
>H23:(+F23)/G23*(G23-(C8-E23))
>H24:(+F24)/G24*(G24-(C8-E24))
>H26:(+F26)/G26*(G26-(C8-E26))
>H28:(+F28)/G28*(G28-(C8-E28))
>H29:(+F29)/G29*(G29-(C8-E29))
>H31:(+F31)/G31*(G31-(C8-E31))
>H32:(+F32)/G32*(G32-(C8-E32))
>H33:(+F33)/G33*(G33-(C8-E33))
>H34:(+F34)/G34*(G34-(C8-E34))
>H35:(+F35)/G35*(G35-(C8-E35))
>H37:(+F37)/G37*(G37-(C8-E37))
>H38:(+F38)/G38*(G38-(C8-E38))
>H39:(+F39)/G39*(G39-(C8-E39))
>H40:(+F40)/G40*(G40-(C8-E40))
>H42:(+F42)/G42*(G42-(C8-E42))
>H55:/--
>H56:@SUM(H16...H54)
>H57:/-=
>H59:"VALUE DIF

>I11:"ATED - -
>I12:" REPLACE-
>I13:"  MENT
>I14:"  COST
>I15:/--
>I16:/FI+F16*(1+(N16/1)^(M16*1)
>I18:+F18*(1+(N16/1)^(M18*1)
```

```
>I19:+F19*(1+(N16/1)^(M19*1)
>I20:+F20*(1+(N16/1)^(M20*1)
>I22:+F22*(1+(N16/1)^(M22*1)
>I23:+F23*(1+(N16/1)^(M23*1)
>I24:+F24*(1+(N16/1)^(M24*1)
>I26:+F26*(1+(N16/1)^(M26*1)
>I28:+F28*(1+(N16/1)^(M28*1)
>I29:+F29*(1+(N16/1)^(M29*1)
>I31:+F31*(1+(N16/1)^(M31*1)
>I32:+F32*(1+(N16/1)^(M32*1)
>I33:+F33*(1+(N16/1)^(M33*1)
>I34:+F34*(1+(N16/1)^(M34*1)
>I35:+F35*(1+(N16/1)^(M35*1)
>I37:+F37*(1+(N16/1)^(M37*1)
>I38:+F38*(1+(N16/1)^(M38*1)
>I39:+F39*(1+(N16/1)^(M39*1)
>I40:+F40*(1+(N16/1)^(M40*1)
>I42:+F42*(1+(N16/1)^(M42*1)
>I55:/--
>I56:@SUM(I16...I54)
>I57:/-=
>I59:"ERENCE: $

>J59:+I56-F56
>J60:/-*

>K11:"        %
>K12:"INCREASE
>K13:"  SINCE
>K14:" PURCHASE
>K15:/--
>K16:/F$((+I16/F16)*100-(100))
>K18:/F$((+I18/F18)*100-(100))
>K19:/F$((+I19/F19)*100-(100))
>K20:/F$((+I20/F20)*100-(100))
>K22:/F$((+I22/F22)*100-(100))
>K23:/F$((+I23/F23)*100-(100))
>K24:/F$((+I24/F24)*100-(100))
>K26:/F$((+I26/F26)*100-(100))
>K28:/F$((+I28/F28)*100-(100))
>K29:/F$((+I29/F29)*100-(100))
>K31:/F$((+I31/F31)*100-(100))
>K32:/F$((+I32/F32)*100-(100))
>K33:/F$((+I33/F33)*100-(100))
>K34:/F$((+I34/F34)*100-(100))
>K35:/F$((+I35/F35)*100-(100))
>K37:/F$((+I37/F37)*100-(100))
>K38:/F$((+I38/F38)*100-(100))
>K39:/F$((+I39/F39)*100-(100))
>K40:/F$((+I40/F40)*100-(100))
>K42:/F$((+I42/F42)*100-(100))

>M12:"CALCULATI
>M13:/--
>M14:"YRS USED
```

```
>M15:"-----------          >M38:+C8-E38
>M16:+C8-E16             >M39:+C8-E39
>M18:+C8-E18             >M40:+C8-E40
>M19:+C8-E19             >M42:+C8-E42
>M20:+C8-E20
>M22:+C8-E22             >N12:"ON AREA
>M23:+C8-E23             >N13:"---------
>M24:+C8-E24             >N14:" DEP.RATE
>M26:+C8-E26             >N15:" -----------
>M28:+C8-E28             >N16:/FG+C9/100
>M29:+C8-E29
>M31:+C8-E31             /GC9
>M32:+C8-E32             /GFI
>M33:+C8-E33             /GOR
>M34:+C8-E34             /GRM
>M35:+C8-E35             /W1
>M37:+C8-E37
```

NET WORTH STATEMENT

This VisiCalc model can help you assess your personal net worth. It is a very practical analysis that should be performed annually. You must enter all your assets and liabilities; the model will total the assets and deduct the liabilities.

The model is designed to accommodate all categories of assets and liabilities. You can use entries from Home Inventory and Personal Possessions Evaluation in this model.
    PRINT A1...O66

Listing

```
>A 8:"CURRENT M
>A15:"CURRENT C
>A16:"LONG-TERM
>A28:"CURRENT M
>A29:"OF SECURI
>A39:"CURRENT MA
>A40:"DURABLE AS
>A56:"OTHER ASS
>A63:"TOTAL CURR

>B 6:"A  S  S  E  T
>B 7:/-=
>B 8:"ONETARY A
>B 9:"CASH ON H
>B10:"CHECKING
>B11:"SAVINGS A
>B12:"OTHER
>B15:"ASH VALUE
>B16:"  ASSETS:
>B17:"CERTIFICA
>B18:"U.S. SAVI
>B19:"ANNUITIES
>B20:"PERMANENT
>B22:"RETIREMENT
>B24:"OTHER
>B28:"ARKET VAL
>B29:"TIES:
>B30:"STOCKS
>B31:"OPTIONS
>B32:"BONDS
>B33:"MUTUAL FU
>B34:"INVESTMEN
>B35:"OTHER
>B39:"ARKET VAL
>B40:"SSETS:
>B41:"HOME, CON
>B42:"OTHER REA
>B44:"FURNITURE
>B45:"AUTOMOBIL
>B46:"RECREATIO
```

```
>B47:"CLOTHING
>B48:"HOBBY EQU
>B49:"FURS, JEW
>B50:"ANTIQUES
>B51:"STAMP, COIN
>B53:"OTHER
>B56:"ETS:
>B57:"BUSINESS
>B58:"MONEY OWE
>B59:"TAX REFUND
>B60:"OTHER
>B63:"RENT ASSE
>B65:/->

>C 2:"PERSONAL
>C 3:"NET WORTH
>C 4:/--
>C 6:"  S
>C 7:"==
>C 8:"SSETS:
>C 9:"AND
>C10:"ACCOUNTS
>C11:"CCOUNTS
>C14:"(SUB-TOTAL
>C15:"  OF
>C17:"TES OF DE
>C18:"NGS BONDS
>C20:"  LIFE INS
>C21:"POLICIES
>C22:"T AND PRO
>C23:"SHARING F
>C26:"(SUB-TOTA
>C28:"UE
>C33:"NDS
>C34:"T CLUBS
>C37:"(SUB-TOTA
>C39:"UE OF
>C41:"DO, TOWNH
>C42:"L (LAND &
>C43:"BUILDINGS
```

Model Run

```
         PERSONAL FINANCIAL        FOR: YOUR NAME              AS OF:OCTOBER 1981
           NET WORTH STATEMENT          -----------              ---------
           --------------------


        A S S E T S                      L I A B I L I T I E S
        ===========                      =====================
CURRENT MONETARY ASSETS:    $$$$$$$$$   CURRENT BILLS DUE:        $$$$$$$$$
     CASH ON HAND                500         CHARGE ACCOUNTS          1500
     CHECKING ACCOUNTS          1500              "                    250
     SAVINGS ACCOUNTS           1750         CREDIT CARD ACCOUNTS     1000
     OTHER                                   MEDICAL BILLS               0
                                             DENTAL       "
          (SUB-TOTAL).......    3750         RENT                        0
CURRENT CASH VALUE OF                        UTILITIE S
LONG-TERM ASSETS:                            HOMEOWNER'S INSURANCE     150
     CERTIFICATES OF DEPOSIT   10000         AUTO INSURANCE            650
     U.S. SAVINGS BONDS            0         LIFE INSURANCE            500
     ANNUITIES                     0         MEDICAL INSURANCE         100
     PERMANENT LIFE INSURANCE                TUITION
          POLICIES            125000         .OTHER
     RETIREMENT AND PROFIT
          SHARING FUNDS         1500              (SUB-TOTAL).......   4150
     OTHER
                                        TAXES TO DATE WHICH HAVE
          (SUB-TOTAL).......  136500    NOT BEEN WITHHELD:
                                             FEDERAL INCOME TAXES     1250
CURRENT MARKET VALUE                         STATE AND CITY TAXES        0
OF SECURITIES:                               REAL ESTATE TAXES         450
     STOCKS                     500          PERSONAL PROPERTY TAXES     0
     OPTIONS                   1250          ASSESSMENTS
     BONDS                     1000          SELF EMPLOYMENT TAXES     600
     MUTUAL FUNDS                            OTHER TAXES
     INVESTMENT CLUBS
     OTHER                                        (SUB-TOTAL).......   2300

          (SUB-TOTAL).......    2750    LOAN TO BE REPAID:
                                             MORTGAGE(S) ON HOME     37500
CURRENT MARKET VALUE OF                      MORTGAGE(S) ON OTHER
DURABLE ASSETS:                                   PROPERTY
     HOME, CONDO, TOWNHOUSE   78000          INSTALLMENT LOAN(S)      4375
     OTHER REAL (LAND &                           ON AUTO(S)
          BUILDINGS)          5000           INSTALLMENT LOAN FOR-
     FURNITURE & APPLIANCES                  FURNITURE & AND APPLIANCES  0
     AUTOMOBILE(S) AND OTHER  8250           HOME IMPROVEMENT LOAN    3000
     RECREATIONAL VEHICLES       0           EDUCATION LOAN(S)
     CLOTHING                 4500           LIFE INSURANCE LOANS     1500
     HOBBY EQUIPMENT          1500           STOCK PURCHASE ON MARGIN    0
     FURS, JEWELRY, TABLEWARE  500           SECONDARY LIABILITY (DO NOT INCLUDE)
     ANTIQUES                  750           OTHER LOANS               250
     STAMP, COIN, & OTHER     1250
          COLLECTIONS                             (SUB-TOTAL).......  46625
     OTHER
          (SUB-TOTAL).......   99750


OTHER ASSETS:
     BUSINESS INTERESTS       10000
     MONEY OWED YOU BY OTHERS  2500
     TAX REFUNDS DUE              0
     OTHER
          (SUB-TOTAL).......   12500
                             ---------                              ---------
TOTAL CURRENT ASSET VALUE   $  255250   TOTAL CURRENT LIABILITY VALUE  $   53075
                             =========                              =========
     >>>>>>>>> NET WORTH VALUE AS OF THIS DATE =$   202175<<<<<<<<<
                             =========
```

>C44:" & APPLIA
>C45:"E(S) AND
>C46:"NAL VEHIC
>C48:"IPMENT
>C49:"ELRY, TAB
>C51:"IN, & OTH
>C52:"COLLECTIO
>C54:"(SUB-TOTA
>C57:"INTERESTS
>C58:"D YOU BY
>C59:"DS DUE
>C61:"(SUB-TOTA
>C63:"T VALUE
>C65:" NET WORT

>D 2:"FINANCIAL
>D 3:" STATEMEN
>D 4:/--
>D14:"L).......
>D17:"POSIT
>D20:"URANCE
>D22:"FIT
>D23:"UNDS
>D26:"L).......
>D37:"L)........
>D41:"OUSE
>D43:")
>D44:"NCES
>D45:"OTHER
>D46:"LES
>D49:"LEWARE
>D51:"ER
>D52:"NS
>D54:"L).......
>D58:"OTHERS
>D61:"L).......
>D63:" $
>D65:"H VALUE A

>E 3:"T
>E 4:"-
>E 8:/-$
>E 9:500
>E10:1500
>E11:1750
>E14:@SUM(E8...E13)
>E17:10000
>E18:0
>E19:0
>E21:125000
>E23:1500
>E26:@SUM(E17...E25)
>E30:500
>E31:1250
>E32:1000

>E37:@SUM(E30...E36)
>E41:78000
>E43:5000
>E45:8250
>E46:0
>E47:4500
>E48:1500
>E49:500
>E50:750
>E51:1250
>E54:@SUM(E41...E52)
>E57:10000
>E58:2500
>E59:0
>E61:@SUM(E57...E60)
>E62:/--
>E63:+E14+E26+E37+E54+E61
>E64:/-=
>E65:"S OF THIS

>F 2:"   FOR:
>F65:" DATE =$

>G 2:"YOUR NAME
>G 3:/--
>G 8:"CURRENT B
>G25:"TAXES TO
>G26:"NOT BEEN
>G37:"LOAN TO B
>G63:"TOTAL CUR
>G65:+E63-K63
>G66:/-=

>H 3:/--
>H 6:"L I A B I
>H 7:/-=
>H 8:"ILLS DUE:
>H 9:"CHARGE AC
>H10:"   "
>H11:"CREDIT CA
>H12:"MEDICAL BI
>H13:"DENTAL
>H14:"RENT
>H15:"UTILITIE
>H16:"HOMEOWNER
>H17:"AUTO INSU
>H18:"LIFE INSU
>H19:"MEDICAL I
>H20:"TUITION
>H21:"OTHER
>H25:"DATE WHIC
>H26:"WITHHELD:
>H27:"FEDERAL I
>H28:"STATE AND
>H29:"REAL ESTA

```
>I48:"CHASE ON
>I49:" LIABILIT
>I50:"NS
>I52:"(SUB-TOTA
>I63:"ILITY VAL

>J 2:"   AS OF:
>J 6:"E S
>J 7:"===
>J11:"TS
>J16:"NCE
>J23:"L).......
>J27:"ES
>J28:"ES
>J30:"TAXES
>J32:"XES
>J35:"L).......
>J38:"E
>J39:"ER
>J41:")
>J42:")
>J43:"OR-
>J44:"PLIANCES
>J45:"OAN
>J47:"NS
>J48:"MARGIN
>J49:"Y (DO NOT
>J52:"L).......
>J63:"UE        $

>K 2:"OCTOBER 1
>K 3:/--
>K 8:/-$
>K 9:1500
>K10:250
>K11:1000
>K12:0
>K14:0
>K16:150
>K17:650
>K18:500
>K19:100
>K23:@SUM(K9...K22)
>K27:1250
>K28:0
>K29:450
>K30:0
>K32:600
>K35:@SUM(K27...K34)
>K38:37500
>K41:4375
>K44:0
>K45:3000
>K47:1500
>K48:0
```

```
>K49:" INCLUDE)
>K50:250
>K52:@SUM(K38...K51)
>K62:/--
>K63:+K23+K35+K52
>K64:/-=

>H30:"PERSONAL
>H31:"ASSESSMEN
>H32:"SELF EMPL
>H33:"OTHER TAX
>H37:"E REPAID:
>H38:"MORTGAGE(
>H39:"MORTGAGE(
>H41:"INSTALLME
>H43:"INSTALLMEN
>H44:"FURNITURE
>H45:"HOME IMPR
>H46:"EDUCATION
>H47:"LIFE INSU
>H48:"STOCK PUR
>H49:"SECONDARY
>H50:"OTHER LOA
>H63:"RENT LIAB
>H65:/-<

>I 6:" L I T I
>I 7:/-=
>I 9:"COUNTS
>I11:"RD ACCOUN
>I12:"ILLS
>I13:"      "
>I15:"S
>I16:"'S INSURAN
>I17:"RANCE
>I18:"RANCE
>I19:"NSURANCE
>I23:"(SUB-TOTA
>I25:"H HAVE
>I27:"NCOME TAX
>I28:" CITY TAX
>I29:"TE TAXES
>I30:"PROPERTY
>I31:"TS
>I32:"OYMENT TA
>I33:"ES
>I35:"(SUB-TOTA
>I38:"S) ON HOME
>I39:"S) ON OTH
>I40:"PROPERTY
>I41:"NT LOAN(S
>I42:"ON AUTO(S)
>I43:"NT LOAN F
>I44:" & AND AP
>I45:"OVEMENT L
```

```
>I46:" LOAN(S)
>I47:"RANCE LOA

>L 2:"981

/GC9
/GOR
/GRA
/W1
```

PERSONAL FINANCE AND BUDGET PLAN

This model will analyze your annual income and help you realistically budget your expenses and savings. By applying this model carefully, you might not ever come up short on cash again.

The entire model can be broken into three sections: Monthly Income, Expected Expenditures, and a Savings Plan. When you enter the model the first time, you might try entering savings goal percentages before looking at your income and expense levels, just to see how the totals compare. The model can easily do "what if" analysis, which will help you plan future savings and expenditures.

The model is designed to accept almost all sources of income, expenditures, and savings. You can change any row labels to fit your personal needs, but we recommend you do *not* delete or insert rows in this model. Use the Other rows to account for entries you have that cannot be accounted for elsewhere. This model might easily be adapted to business planning as well.

If you have a printer that can print longer lines of condensed print, you can print each section's totals and percentages on the same page, next to the monthly input report (B1...X24, B25...X66, B67...X98).

```
PRINT B1...024, Monthly Income
      P1...X24, Monthly Income Totals
      B25...066, Expected Expenditures
      P25...X66, Expected Expenditures
         Totals
      B67...098, Savings Plan
      P67...X98, Savings Plan Totals
```

Model Run

```
PERSONAL FINANCIAL          FOR: YOUR NAME              AS OF:MARCH 1981
   BUDGET  PLAN                   ---------------------------      ------------
-------------------
                  JAN.    FEB     MAR     APR     MAY     JUN     JUL     AUG     SEP     OCT     NOV     DEC
                  --------------------------------------------------------------------------------------------------
M O N T H L Y   I N C O M E
===============================
SOURCE            $ AMOUNT
----------------  --------

WAGES & SALARY OF:
HUSBAND  .......  2000    2100    2100
WIFE     .......  1000    1050     970
PROFIT FROM FARM,
BUSINESS,AND       100     300     500
PROFESSION .....
INTEREST &
DIVIDENDS  .....                   125

OTHER      .....
           .....
                  ----------------------------------------------------------------------------------------------------
AVAILABLE INCOME $  3100    3450    3695      0       0       0       0       0       0       0       0       0
                  ====================================================================================================
```

Monthly Income

TOTALS	% OF INCOME	
---------	---------	
0	0	WAGES & SALARY OF:
6200	60.51733	HUSBAND ....
3020	29.47779	WIFE ....
0	0	PROFIT FROM FARM,
900	8.784773	BUSINESS,AND
0	0	PROFESSION .....
0	0	INTEREST &
125	1.220107	DIVIDENDS .....
0	0	
0	0	OTHER .....
0	0	.....
---------	---------	
10245	100.	AVAILABLE INCOME $
=========	=========	

Monthly Income Totals

	JAN.	FEB	MAR	APR	MAY	JUN	JUL	AUG	SEP	OCT	NOV	DEC
E X P E C T E D												
E X P E N D I T U R E S (FIXED & VARIABLE)												
=======================												
⟨FIXED EXPENSES⟩:												
RENT, MORTGAGE	600	600	600									
INSURANCES:	0											
LIFE	45	45	45									
MEDICAL & HEALTH	95	95	95									
AUTO	0		325									
CHARGE ACT. PMTS	150	130	110									
INSTALLMENT LOANS:	200	200	200									
AUTO	0											
FURNITURE												
APPLIANCES												
HOME IMPROVEMENT												
TAX LIABILITIES			500									
OTHER												
(SUB-TOTAL F.E)...	1090	1070	1875	0	0	0	0	0	0	0	0	0
⟨VARIABLE EXPENSES⟩:												
UTILITIES:	250	250	220									
HEAT & ELECTRIC												
WATER & TELEPHONE	150	170	115									
OTHER MAINTENANCE	50	35	75									
& OPERATION	50	15	35									
FOOD	240	250	265									
TRANSPORTATION	50	55	65									
FURNITURE &	0											
APPLIANCES			325									
CLOTHING & CARE	50		225									
MEDICAL CARE												
PERSONAL NEEDS	60	60	75									
EDUCATION												
RECREATION	100	125	150									
GIFTS & DONATIONS	20	20	35									
BOOKS & JOURNALS	10	10	12									
OTHER	500	250	425									
(SUB-TOTAL V.E.)..	1530	1240	2022	0	0	0	0	0	0	0	0	0
TOTAL EXPENSES $ -	2620	2310	3897	0	0	0	0	0	0	0	0	0

Expected Expenditures

```
>B78:"AVAILABLE              >B95:"TOTALS...            >C17:"&
>B79:"SAVINGS P             >B97:"( +/-$ )             >C18:"  .....
>B80:/--                     >B98:"FOR SLUSH            >C20:"  .....
>B81:">SAVINGS                                          >C21:"  .....
>B82:"> ALLOCAT             >C 2:"PERSONAL              >C23:"  INCOME $
>B83:"HOUSE,ETC            >C 3:"   BUDGET              >C26:" E C T E D
>B84:"EDUCATION            >C 4:/--                     >C27:" D I T U
>B85:"INVST'MT             >C 7:" L Y   I N             >C28:/-=
>B86:"RETIRE'MT            >C 8:/-=                      >C29:"PENSES>:
>B87:"AUTO                 >C10:"--------                >C30:"TGAGE
>B88:"FURNITURE            >C11:"ALARY OF:               >C31:"S.
>B89:"APPLIANCE            >C12:".......                 >C33:" HEALTH
>B90:"CLOTHING             >C13:".......                 >C35:"T. PMTS
>B91:"VACATION             >C14:"OM FARM,                >C36:"NT LOANS:
>B92:"REPLC'MT             >C15:"AND                     >C39:"S
>B93:"OTHER                >C16:"N .....                 >C40:"OVEMENT
```

TOTALS	% OF EXPENSES	% OF INCOME	
0	0	0	⟨FIXED EXPENSES⟩:
1800	20.39198	17.56955	RENT, MORTGAGE
0	0	0	INSURANCES:
135	1.529398	1.317716	LIFE
285	3.228730	2.781845	MEDICAL & HEALTH
325	3.681885	3.172279	AUTO
390	4.418262	3.806735	CHARGE ACT. PMTS
600	6.797326	5.856515	INSTALLMENT LOANS:
0	0	0	AUTO
0	0	0	FURNITURE
0	0	0	APPLIANCES
0	0	0	HOME IMPROVEMENT
500	5.664439	4.880429	TAX LIABILITIES
0	0	0	OTHER
4035	45.71202	39.38507	(SUB-TOTAL F.E)...
0	0	0	⟨VARIABLE EXPENSES
720	8.156792	7.027818	UTILITIES:
0	0	0	HEAT & ELECTRIC
435	4.928062	4.245974	WATER & TELEPHONE
160	1.812620	1.561737	OTHER MAINTENANCE
100	1.132888	.9760859	& OPERATION
755	8.553302	7.369449	FOOD
170	1.925909	1.659346	TRANSPORTATION
0	0	0	FURNITURE &
325	3.681885	3.172279	APPLIANCES
275	3.115441	2.684236	CLOTHING & CARE
0	0	0	MEDICAL CARE
195	2.209131	1.903367	PERSONAL NEEDS
0	0	0	EDUCATION
375	4.248329	3.660322	RECREATION
75	.8496658	.7320644	GIFTS & DONATIONS
32	.3625241	.3123475	BOOKS & JOURNALS
1175	13.31143	11.46901	OTHER
4792	54.28798	46.77404	(SUB-TOTAL V.E.)..
		0	
8827	---------	86.15910	

Expected Expenditures Totals

>C41:"LITIES
>C43:"L F.E)...
>C44:" EXPENSES
>C45:":
>C46:"ECTRIC
>C47:"ELEPHONE
>C48:"NTENANCE
>C49:"ION
>C51:"ATION
>C52:" &
>C56:"NEEDS
>C58:"N
>C59:"ONATIONS
>C60:"OURNALS
>C62:"L V.E.)..
>C64:"ENSES $

>C76:" G S P L
>C77:/-=
>C78:" CASH FOR
>C79:"LAN: >>$
>C80:/--
>C81:" PERCENT<
>C82:"E TO: <
>C83:30
>C84:0
>C85:10
>C86:5
>C87:20
>C88:2
>C90:2.5
>C91:15
>C93:10

>C94:/--
>C95:@SUM(C83...C93)
>C97:"AVAILABLE
>C98:" FUND....

>D 2:"FINANCIAL
>D 3:" PLAN
>D 4:/--
>D 5:" JAN.
>D 6:/--
>D 7:" C O M E
>D 8:"=======
>D 9:"$ AMOUNT
>D10:/--
>D12:2000
>D13:1000
>D15:100
>D22:/--
>D23:@SUM(D11...D21)
>D24:/-=
>D26:"D
>D27:"R E S (FI
>D28:"=====
>D30:600
>D31:0
>D32:45
>D33:95
>D34:0
>D35:150
>D36:200
>D37:0
>D43:@SUM(D30...D42)
>D44:">:
>D45:250
>D47:150
>D48:50
>D49:50
>D50:240
>D51:50
>D52:0
>D54:50
>D56:60
>D58:100
>D59:20
>D60:10
>D61:500
>D62:@SUM(D45...D61)
>D63:/--
>D64:+D43+D62
>D65:/-=
>D73:"   JAN.
>D74:/--
>D76:" A N
>D77:"====
>D79:+D23-D64

```
>D80:/--                    >E36:200                    >E91:(+E79*C91)/100
>D83:(+D79*C83)/100         >E43:@SUM(E30...E42)        >E92:(+E79*C92)/100
>D84:(+D79*C84)/100         >E45:250                    >E93:(+E79*C93)/100
>D85:(+D79*C85)/100         >E47:170                    >E94:/--
>D86:(+D79*C86)/100         >E48:35                     >E95:@SUM(E83...E93)
>D87:(+D79*C87)/100         >E49:15                     >E98:+E79-E95
>D88:(+D79*C88)/100         >E50:250
>D89:(+D79*C89)/100         >E51:55                     >F 2:"    FOR:
>D90:(+D79*C90)/100         >E56:60                     >F 5:"   MAR
>D91:(+D79*C91)/100         >E58:125                    >F 6:/--
>D92:(+D79*C92)/100         >E59:20                     >F12:2100
>D93:(+D79*C93)/100         >E60:10                     >F13:970
>D94:/--                    >E61:250                    >F15:500
>D95:@SUM(D83...D93)        >E62:@SUM(E45...E61)        >F18:125
>D98:+D79-D95               >E63:/--                    >F22:/--
                            >E64:+E43+E62               >F23:@SUM(F11...F21)
                            >E65:/-=                    >F24:/-=
>E 5:"    FEB               >E73:"    FEB               >F27:"IABLE)
>E 6:/--                    >E74:/--                    >F30:600
>E12:2100                   >E79:+E23-E64               >F32:45
>E13:1050                   >E80:/--                    >F33:95
>E15:300                    >E83:(+E79*C83)/100         >F34:325
>E22:/--                    >E84:(+E79*C84)/100         >F35:110
>E23:@SUM(E11...E21         >E85:(+E79*C85)/100         >F36:200
>E24:/-=                    >E86:(+E79*C86)/100         >F41:500
>E27:"XED & VAR             >E87:(+E79*C87)/100         >F43:@SUM(F30...F42)
>E30:600                    >E88:(+E79*C88)/100         >F45:220
>E32:45                     >E89:(+E79*C89)/100         >F47:115
>E33:95                     >E90:(+E79*C90)/100         >F48:75
>E35:130
```

	JAN.	FEB	MAR	APR	MAY	JUN	JUL	AUG	SEP	OCT	NOV	DEC
SAVINGS PLAN												
AVAILABLE CASH FOR SAVINGS PLAN: >>$	480	1140	-202	0	0	0	0	0	0	0	0	0
>SAVINGS PERCENT<												
> ALLOCATE TO: <												
HOUSE,ETC	30	144	342	-60.6	0	0	0	0	0	0	0	0	0
EDUCATION	0	0	0	0	0	0	0	0	0	0	0	0
INVST'MT	10	48	114	-20.2	0	0	0	0	0	0	0	0
RETIRE'MT	5	24	57	-10.1	0	0	0	0	0	0	0	0
AUTO	20	96	228	-40.4	0	0	0	0	0	0	0	0
FURNITURE	2	9.6	22.8	-4.04	0	0	0	0	0	0	0	0
APPLIANCE		0	0	0	0	0	0	0	0	0	0	0
CLOTHING	2.5	12	28.5	-5.05	0	0	0	0	0	0	0	0
VACATION	15	72	171	-30.3	0	0	0	0	0	0	0	0
REPLC'MT		0	0	0	0	0	0	0	0	0	0	0
OTHER	10	48	114	-20.2	0	0	0	0	0	0	0	0
TOTALS...	94.5	453.6	1077.3	-190.89	0	0	0	0	0	0	0	0
(+/-$) AVAILABLE FOR SLUSH FUND....		26.4	62.7	-11.11	0	0	0	0	0	0	0	0

Savings Plan

```
>F64:+F43+F62
>F65:/-=
>F70:"D)
>F73:"    MAR
>F74:/--
>F79:+F23-F64
>F80:/--
>F83:(+F79*C83)/100
>F84:(+F79*C84)/100
>F85:(+F79*C85)/100
>F86:(+F79*C86)/100
>F87:(+F79*C87)/100
>F88:(+F79*C88)/100
>F89:(+F79*C89)/100
>F90:(+F79*C90)/100
>F91:(+F79*C91)/100
>F92:(+F79*C92)/100
>F49:35
>F50:265
>F51:65
>F53:325
>F54:225
>F56:75
>F58:150
>F59:35
>F60:12
>F61:425
>F62:@SUM(F45...F61)
>F63:/--
```

```
>F93:(+F79*C93)/100
>F94:/--
>F95:@SUM(F83...F93)
>F98:+F79-F95

>G 2:"YOUR NAME
>G 3:/--
>G 5:"    APR
>G 6:/--
>G22:/--
>G23:@SUM(G11...G21
>G24:/-=
>G43:@SUM(G30...G42)
>G62:@SUM(G45...G61)
>G63:/--
>G64:+G43+G62
>G65:/-=
>G73:"    APR
>G74:/--
>G79:+G23-G64
>G80:/--
>G83:(+G79*C83)/100
>G84:(+G79*C84)/100
>G85:(+G79*C85)/100
>G86:(+G79*C86)/100
>G87:(+G79*C87)/100
>G88:(+G79*C88)/100
>G89:(+G79*C89)/100
>G90:(+G79*C90)/100
```

```
>G91:(+G79*C91)/100
>G92:(+G79*C92)/100
>G93:(+G79*C93)/100
>G94:/--
>G95:@SUM(G83...G93)
>G98:+G79-G95

>H 3:/--
>H 5:"    MAY
>H 6:/--
>H22:/--
>H23:@SUM(H11...H21
>H24:/-=
>H43:@SUM(H30...H42)
>H62:@SUM(H45...H61)
>H63:/--
>H64:+H43+H62
>H65:/-=
>H73:"    MAY
>H74:/--
>H79:+H23-H64
>H80:/--
>H83:(+H79*C83)/100
>H84:(+H79*C84)/100
>H85:(+H79*C85)/100
>H86:(+H79*C86)/100
>H87:(+H79*C87)/100
>H88:(+H79*C88)/100
>H89:(+H79*C89)/100
>H90:(+H79*C90)/100
>H91:(+H79*C91)/100
>H92:(+H79*C92)/100
>H93:(+H79*C93)/100
>H94:/--
>H95:@SUM(H83...H93)
>H98:+H79-H95

>I 3:/--
>I 5:"    JUN
>I 6:/--
>I22:/--
>I23:@SUM(I11...I21
>I24:/-=
>I43:@SUM(I30...I42)
>I62:@SUM(I45...I61)
>I63:/--
>I64:+I43+I62
>I65:/-=
>I73:"    JUN
>I74:/--
>I79:+I23-I64
>I80:/--
>I83:(+I79*C83)/100
>I84:(+I79*C84)/100
>I85:(+I79*C85)/100
```

TOTALS	% OF INCOME	
---------	---------	
1418		

425.4	4.152269	HOUSE,ETC
0	0	EDUCATION
141.8	1.384090	INVST'MT
70.9	.6920449	RETIRE'MT
283.6	2.768180	AUTO
28.36	.2768180	FURNITURE
0	0	APPLIANCE
35.45	.3460224	CLOTHING
212.7	2.076135	VACATION
0	0	REPLC'MT
141.8	1.384090	OTHER
---------	---------	
1340.01	13.07965	
77.99	.7612494	

Savings Plan Totals

```
>I86:(+I79*C86)/100        >K74:/--                  >M62:@SUM(M45...M61)
>I87:(+I79*C87)/100        >K79:+K23-K64             >M63:/--
>I88:(+I79*C88)/100        >K80:/--                  >M64:+M43+M62
>I89:(+I79*C89)/100        >K83:(+K79*C83)/100       >M65:/-=
>I90:(+I79*C90)/100        >K84:(+K79*C84)/100       >M73:"    OCT
>I91:(+I79*C91)/100        >K85:(+K79*C85)/100       >M74:/--
>I92:(+I79*C92)/100        >K86:(+K79*C86)/100       >M79:+M23-M64
>I93:(+I79*C93)/100        >K87:(+K79*C87)/100       >M80:/--
>I94:/--                   >K88:(+K79*C88)/100       >M83:(+M79*C83)/100
>I95:@SUM(I83...I93)       >K89:(+K79*C89)/100       >M84:(+M79*C84)/100
>I98:+I79-I95              >K90:(+K79*C90)/100       >M85:(+M79*C85)/100
                           >K91:(+K79*C91)/100       >M86:(+M79*C86)/100
                           >K92:(+K79*C92)/100       >M87:(+M79*C87)/100
>J 2:"    AS OF:           >K93:(+K79*C93)/100       >M88:(+M79*C88)/100
>J 5:"    JUL              >K94:/--                  >M89:(+M79*C89)/100
>J 6:/--                   >K95:@SUM(K83...K93)      >M90:(+M79*C90)/100
>J22:/--                   >K98:+K79-K95             >M91:(+M79*C91)/100
>J23:@SUM(J11...J21)                                 >M92:(+M79*C92)/100
>J24:/-=                                             >M93:(+M79*C93)/100
>J43:@SUM(J30...J42)       >L 2:"1                   >M94:/--
>J62:@SUM(J45...J61)       >L 3:"---                 >M95:@SUM(M83...M93)
>J63:/--                   >L 5:"    SEP             >M98:+M79-M95
>J64:+J43+J62              >L 6:/--
>J65:/-=                   >L22:/--
>J73:"    JUL              >L23:@SUM(L11...L21)      >N 5:"    NOV
>J74:/--                   >L24:/-=                  >N 6:/--
>J79:+J23-J64              >L43:@SUM(L30...L42)      >N22:/--
>J80:/--                   >L62:@SUM(L45...L61)      >N23:@SUM(N11...N21)
>J83:(+J79*C83)/100        >L63:/--                  >N24:/-=
>J84:(+J79*C84)/100        >L64:+L43+L62             >N43:@SUM(N30...N42)
>J85:(+J79*C85)/100        >L65:/-=                  >N62:@SUM(N45...N61)
>J86:(+J79*C86)/100        >L73:"    SEP             >N63:/--
>J87:(+J79*C87)/100        >L74:/--                  >N64:+N43+N62
>J88:(+J79*C88)/100        >L79:+L23-L64             >N65:/-=
>J89:(+J79*C89)/100        >L80:/--                  >N73:"    NOV
>J90:(+J79*C90)/100        >L83:(+L79*C83)/100       >N74:/--
>J91:(+J79*C91)/100        >L84:(+L79*C84)/100       >N79:+N23-N64
>J92:(+J79*C92)/100        >L85:(+L79*C85)/100       >N80:/--
>J93:(+J79*C93)/100        >L86:(+L79*C86)/100       >N83:(+N79*C83)/100
>J94:/--                   >L87:(+L79*C87)/100       >N84:(+N79*C84)/100
>J95:@SUM(J83...J93)       >L88:(+L79*C88)/100       >N85:(+N79*C85)/100
>J98:+J79-J95              >L89:(+L79*C89)/100       >N86:(+N79*C86)/100
                           >L90:(+L79*C90)/100       >N87:(+N79*C87)/100
                           >L91:(+L79*C91)/100       >N88:(+N79*C88)/100
>K 2:"MARCH 198            >L92:(+L79*C92)/100       >N89:(+N79*C89)/100
>K 3:/---                  >L93:(+L79*C93)/100       >N90:(+N79*C90)/100
>K 5:"    AUG              >L94:/--                  >N91:(+N79*C91)/100
>K 6:/--                   >L95:@SUM(L83...L93)      >N92:(+N79*C92)/100
>K22:/--                   >L98:+L79-L95             >N93:(+N79*C93)/100
>K23:@SUM(K11...K21                                  >N94:/--
>K24:/-=                                             >N95:@SUM(N83...N93)
>K43:@SUM(K30...K42)       >M 5:"    OCT             >N98:+N79-N95
>K62:@SUM(K45...K61)       >M 6:/--
>K63:/---                  >M22:/--
>K64:+K43+K62              >M23:@SUM(M11...M21       >O 5:"    DEC
>K65:/-=                   >M24:/-=                  >O 6:/--
>K73:"    AUG              >M43:@SUM(M30...M42)      >O22:/---
```

```
>O23:@SUM(O11...O21             >Q40:@SUM(D40...O40)          >S18:(+O18/O23)*100
>O24:/-=                        >Q41:@SUM(D41...O41)          >S19:(+O19/O23)*100
>O43:@SUM(O30...O42)            >Q42:@SUM(D42...O42)          >S20:(+O20/O23)*100
>O62:@SUM(O45...O61)            >Q43:@SUM(D43...O43)          >S21:(+O21/O23)*100
>O63:/--                        >Q44:@SUM(D44...O44)          >S22:/--
>O64:+O43+O62                   >Q45:@SUM(D45...O45)          >S23:@SUM(S11...S21)
>O65:/-=                        >Q46:@SUM(D46...O46)          >S24:/-=
>O73:"    DEC                   >Q47:@SUM(D47...O47)          >S26:"   % OF
>O74:/--                        >Q48:@SUM(D48...O48)          >S27:"EXPENSES
>O79:+O23-O64                   >Q49:@SUM(D49...O49)          >S28:/--
>O80:/--                        >Q50:@SUM(D50...O50)          >S29:(+O29/O64)*100
>O83:(+O79*C83)/100             >Q51:@SUM(D51...O51)          >S30:(+O30/O64)*100
>O84:(+O79*C84)/100             >Q52:@SUM(D52...O52)          >S31:(+O31/O64)*100
>O85:(+O79*C85)/100             >Q53:@SUM(D53...O53)          >S32:(+O32/O64)*100
>O86:(+O79*C86)/100             >Q54:@SUM(D54...O54)          >S33:(+O33/O64)*100
>O87:(+O79*C87)/100             >Q55:@SUM(D55...O55)          >S34:(+O34/O64)*100
>O88:(+O79*C88)/100             >Q56:@SUM(D56...O56)          >S35:(+O35/O64)*100
>O89:(+O79*C89)/100             >Q57:@SUM(D57...O57)          >S36:(+O36/O64)*100
>O90:(+O79*C90)/100             >Q58:@SUM(D58...O58)          >S37:(+O37/O64)*100
>O91:(+O79*C91)/100             >Q59:@SUM(D59...O59)          >S38:(+O38/O64)*100
>O92:(+O79*C92)/100             >Q60:@SUM(D60...O60)          >S39:(+O39/O64)*100
>O93:(+O79*C93)/100             >Q61:@SUM(D61...O61)          >S40:(+O40/O64)*100
>O94:/--                        >Q62:@SUM(D62...O62)          >S41:(+O41/O64)*100
>O95:@SUM(O83...O93)            >O63:/--                      >S42:(+O42/O64)*100
>O98:+O79-O95                   >O64:@SUM(D64...O64)          >S43:(+O43/O64)*100
                               >O65:/-=                      >S44:(+O44/O64)*100
                               >O73:"   TOTALS               >S45:(+O45/O64)*100
>Q 5:"  TOTALS                 >O74:/--                      >S46:(+O46/O64)*100
>Q 6:/--                       >O79:+O23-O64                 >S47:(+O47/O64)*100
>O11:@SUM(D11...O11)            >O80:/--                      >S48:(+O48/O64)*100
>O12:@SUM(D12...O12)            >O83:@SUM(D83...O83)          >S49:(+O49/O64)*100
>O13:@SUM(D13...O13)            >O84:@SUM(D84...O84)          >S50:(+O50/O64)*100
>O14:@SUM(D14...O14)            >O85:@SUM(D85...O85)          >S51:(+O51/O64)*100
>O15:@SUM(D15...O15)            >O86:@SUM(D86...O86)          >S52:(+O52/O64)*100
>O16:@SUM(D16...O16)            >O87:@SUM(D87...O87)          >S53:(+O53/O64)*100
>O17:@SUM(D17...O17)            >O88:@SUM(D88...O88)          >S54:(+O54/O64)*100
>O18:@SUM(D18...O18)            >O89:@SUM(D89...O89)          >S55:(+O55/O64)*100
>O19:@SUM(D19...O19)            >O90:@SUM(D90...O90)          >S56:(+O56/O64)*100
>O20:@SUM(D20...O20)            >O91:@SUM(D91...O91)          >S57:(+O57/O64)*100
>O21:@SUM(D21...O21)            >O92:@SUM(D92...O92)          >S58:(+O58/O64)*100
>O22:/--                        >O93:@SUM(D93...O93)          >S59:(+O59/O64)*100
>O23:@SUM(D23...O23)            >O94:/--                      >S60:(+O60/O64)*100
>O24:/-=                        >O95:@SUM(O83...O93)          >S61:(+O61/O64)*100
>O27:"TOTALS                    >O98:+O79-O95                 >S62:(+O62/O64)*100
>O28:/--                                                     >S63:/--
>O29:@SUM(D29...O29)                                         >S64:/--
>O30:@SUM(D30...O30)            >S 4:"   % OF                 >S65:/--
>O31:@SUM(D31...O31)            >S 5:"  INCOME                >S72:"   % OF
>O32:@SUM(D32...O32)            >S 6:/--                      >S73:"  INCOME
>O33:@SUM(D33...O33)            >S11:(+O11/O23)*100           >S74:/--
>O34:@SUM(D34...O34)            >S12:(+O12/O23)*100           >S83:(+O83/O23)*100
>O35:@SUM(D35...O35)            >S13:(+O13/O23)*100           >S84:(+O84/O23)*100
>O36:@SUM(D36...O36)            >S14:(+O14/O23)*100           >S85:(+O85/O23)*100
>O37:@SUM(D37...O37)            >S15:(+O15/O23)*100           >S86:(+O86/O23)*100
>O38:@SUM(D38...O38)            >S16:(+O16/O23)*100           >S87:(+O87/O23)*100
>O39:@SUM(D39...O39)            >S17:(+O17/O23)*100
```

```
>S88:(+Q88/Q23)*100          >W11:"WAGES & S          >W89:"APPLIANCE
>S89:(+Q89/Q23)*100          >W12:"HUSBAND           >W90:"CLOTHING
>S90:(+Q90/Q23)*100          >W13:"WIFE              >W91:"VACATION
>S91:(+Q91/Q23)*100          >W14:"PROFIT FR         >W92:"REPLC'MT
>S92:(+Q92/Q23)*100          >W15:"BUSINESS,         >W93:"OTHER
>S93:(+Q93/Q23)*100          >W16:"PROFESSIO
>S94:/--                     >W17:"INTEREST
>S95:(+Q95/Q23)*100          >W18:"DIVIDENDS
>S98:(+Q98/Q23)*100          >W20:"OTHER             >X11:"ALARY OF:
                             >W23:"AVAILABLE         >X12:"......
>U26:"  % OF                 >W29:"<FIXED EX         >X13:".......
>U27:" INCOME                >W30:"RENT, MORT        >X14:"OM FARM,
>U28:/--                     >W31:"INSURANCE         >X15:"AND
>U29:(+Q29/Q23)*100          >W32:"LIFE             >X16:"N .....
>U30:(+Q30/Q23)*100          >W33:"MEDICAL &         >X17:"&
>U31:(+Q31/Q23)*100          >W34:"AUTO              >X18:"  .....
>U32:(+Q32/Q23)*100          >W35:"CHARGE AC         >X20:"  .....
>U33:(+Q33/Q23)*100          >W36:"INSTALLME         >X21:"  .....
>U34:(+Q34/Q23)*100          >W37:"AUTO              >X23:"  INCOME $
>U35:(+Q35/Q23)*100          >W38:"FURNITURE         >X29:"PENSES>:
>U36:(+Q36/Q23)*100          >W39:"APPLIANCE         >X30:"TGAGE
>U37:(+Q37/Q23)*100          >W40:"HOME IMPR         >X31:"S:
>U38:(+Q38/Q23)*100          >W41:"TAX LIABI         >X33:" HEALTH
>U39:(+Q39/Q23)*100          >W42:"OTHER             >X35:"T. PMTS
>U40:(+Q40/Q23)*100          >W43:"(SUB-TOTA         >X36:"NT LOANS:
>U41:(+Q41/Q23)*100          >W44:"<VARIABLE         >X39:"S
>U42:(+Q42/Q23)*100          >W45:"UTILITIES         >X40:"OVEMENT
>U43:(+Q43/Q23)*100          >W46:"HEAT & ELE        >X41:"LITIES
>U44:(+Q44/Q23)*100          >W47:"WATER & T         >X43:"L F.E)...
>U45:(+Q45/Q23)*100          >W48:"OTHER MAI         >X44:" EXPENSES
>U46:(+Q46/Q23)*100          >W49:" & OPERAT         >X45:":
>U47:(+Q47/Q23)*100          >W50:"FOOD              >X46:"ECTRIC
>U48:(+Q48/Q23)*100          >W51:"TRANSPORT         >X47:"ELEPHONE
>U49:(+Q49/Q23)*100          >W52:"FURNITURE         >X48:"NTENANCE
>U50:(+Q50/Q23)*100          >W53:" APPLIANCES       >X49:"ION
>U51:(+Q51/Q23)*100          >W54:"CLOTHING          >X51:"ATION
>U52:(+Q52/Q23)*100          >W55:"MEDICAL C         >X52:" &
>U53:(+Q53/Q23)*100          >W56:"PERSONAL          >X53:"ES
>U54:(+Q54/Q23)*100          >W57:"EDUCATION         >X54:" & CARE
>U55:(+Q55/Q23)*100          >W58:"RECREATIO         >X55:"ARE
>U56:(+Q56/Q23)*100          >W59:"GIFTS & D         >X56:"NEEDS
>U57:(+Q57/Q23)*100          >W60:"BOOKS & J         >X58:"N
>U58:(+Q58/Q23)*100          >W61:" OTHER            >X59:"ONATIONS
>U59:(+Q59/Q23)*100          >W62:"(SUB-TOTA         >X60:"OURNALS
>U60:(+Q60/Q23)*100          >W83:"HOUSE,ETC         >X62:"L V.E.)..
>U61:(+Q61/Q23)*100          >W84:"EDUCATION
>U62:(+Q62/Q23)*100          >W85:"INVST'MT
>U63:(+Q63/Q23)*100          >W86:"RETIRE'MT         /GC9
>U64:(+Q64/Q23)*100          >W87:"AUTO              /GOC
>U65:/-=                     >W88:"FURNITURE         /GRA
                                                      /W1
```

COLLECTOR'S VALUES

If you're a collector of rare books, coins, stamps, wines, antiques, or just about anything, try organizing the value of your collection on a model like this.

Basically, each item in the collection is given a rating. Wines, for instance, have ratings published by recognized connoisseurs. The example shown here for coins uses ratings devised by the model maker for the condition of the coin. With this data, along with the cost of the item, a cost-per-point figure can be obtained. The current value of the item determines its standing in the collection. Summary figures for points, cost per point, total value, and gain or loss reflect the value of your collection.

As the collection increases or decreases, the dollar amounts will change, giving you a current assessment of the worth of your holdings.

PRINT A1...G17

Model Run

```
                 COLLECTOR'S VALUES

                         POINTS                     GAIN/
     DESCRIPTION    COST  RATING  COST/PT CURR VAL   LOSS
     HOLDEN PENNY   3.50   10.00    0.35     3.50    0.00
     BUFFALO NICKLE 6.75   12.00    0.56     7.00    0.25
     INDIAN CENT    8.00    5.00    1.60    10.00    2.00
     JEFFERSON QUARTER 10.00 6.00   1.67     9.00   -1.00
     CONFEDERATE NOTE  2.50  3.00   0.83     3.00    0.50
     1925 LB NOTE  13.50    5.50    2.45    12.00   -1.50
     LOUIS HALF/DOLLAR 45.00 8.75   5.14    44.00   -1.00
     1938 FRANC    12.00   10.00    1.20    11.00   -1.00
     CARRIER DIME  34.00   15.00    2.27    37.50    3.50

                  AVERAGE   AVG    TOTAL   TOTAL
                   POINTS  COST/PT VALUE    G/L
                     8.36   1.79  137.00    1.75
```

Listing

```
>A  4:"DESCRIPTI            >B  5:"NNY
>A  5:"HOLDEN PE            >B  6:"ICKLE
>A  6:"BUFFALO N            >B  7:"NT
>A  7:"INDIAN CE            >B  8:" QUARTER
>A  8:"JEFFERSON            >B  9:"TE NOTE
>A  9:"CONFEDERA            >B10:"OTE
>A10:"1925 LB N             >B11:"F/DOLLAR
>A11:"LOUIS HAL             >B12:"C
>A12:"1938 FRAN             >B13:"IME
>A13:"CARRIER D
                           >C  1:"HOBBY COL
>B  4:"ON                   >C  4:/FR"COST
```

```
>C  5:3.5                          >E12:+C12/D12
>C  6:6.75                         >E13:+C13/D13
>C  7:8                            >E15:/FR"TOTAL
>C  8:10                           >E16:/FR"VALUE
>C  9:2.5                          >E17:@SUM(F5...F13)
>C10:13.5
>C11:45                            >F  4:/FR"CURR VAL
>C12:12                            >F  5:3.5
>C13:34                            >F  6:7
>C15:"AVERAGE                      >F  7:10
>C16:"POINTS                       >F  8:9
>C17:@AVERAGE(D5...D13)            >F  9:3
                                   >F10:12
>D  1:"LECTION                     >F11:44
>D  3:/FR"POINTS                   >F12:11
>D  4:/FR"RATING                   >F13:37.5
>D  5:10                           >F15:/FR"TOTAL
>D  6:12                           >F16:/FR"G/L
>D  7:5                            >F17:@SUM(G5...G13)
>D  8:6
>D  9:3                            >G  3:/FR"GAIN/
>D10:5.5                           >G  4:/FR"LOSS
>D11:8.75                          >G  5:+F5-C5
>D12:10                            >G  6:+F6-C6
>D13:15                            >G  7:+F7-C7
>D15:/FR"AVG                       >G  8:+F8-C8
>D16:/FR"COST/PT                   >G  9:+F9-C9
>D17:@AVERAGE(E5...E13)            >G10:+F10-C10
                                   >G11:+F11-C11
>E  4:/FR"COST/PT                  >G12:+F12-C12
>E  5:+C5/D5                       >G13:+F13-C13
>E  6:+C6/D6
>E  7:+C7/D7                       /GC9
>E  8:+C8/D8                       /GF$
>E  9:+C9/D9                       /GOC
>E10:+C10/D10                      /GRA
>E11:+C11/D11                      /W1
```

PERSONAL CHECK REGISTER

As a check register, this model is designed to record each check amount in its appropriate category; as a printout, it is an itemized record of expenses that you can use in calculating tax deductions when the year ends.

The last column lists the Balance, which is derived by a formula that adds the Deposit column to the previous Balance and subtracts the @SUM of the columns for checks written. Since a money amount will appear only in its proper column, the @SUM represents the correct amount for that check. By using such a formula, it

can be created once and replicated down the Balance column for as many lines as are needed to complete a check entry session.

The Totals are created with @SUM. The first coordinate in the @SUM is the first line entry; the last is the dashed line. By including the dashed line (which has a value of 0) in @SUM, the formula grows automatically as new lines are inserted (/IR) to add checks in the register. This minimizes the need to reenter the necessary formulas.

PRINT A1...N24

Model Run

```
                PERSONAL CHECK REGISTER

                ISSUE/DEPOSIT    CHECK AMOUNT OF CHECK - - - BY CATEGORY
  CHECK #  DATE  DESCRIPTION     RENT    MEDICAL  ENTERTAIN   FOOD  UTILITY   OTHER   DEPOSIT  BALANCE
                                                                                               850.00 <BALANCE FORWARD>
    101   MAY 1   ELECTRIC                                          10.00                       840.00
    102   MAY 7   GAS                                               12.00                       828.00
          MAY 15  PAY CHECK                                                          2000.00   2828.00
    103   MAY 17  RENT          450.00                                                         2378.00
    104   MAY 18  GROCERY                                   45.00                              2333.00
    105   MAY 18  SUBSCRIPTION                                               18.50             2314.50
    106   MAY 19  DENTIST                 45.00                                                2269.50
    107   MAY 20  DOCTOR                  37.60                                                2231.90
    108   MAY 20  DRUG STORE              14.56                                                2217.34
    109   MAY 21  D. HENDRICKS                                               79.00             2138.34
    110   MAY 23  INSURANCE               55.00                                                2083.34
    111   MAY 25  TELEPHONE                                         109.45                     1973.89
    112   MAY 29  MASTER CHARGE                                              57.00             1916.89
    113   JUNE 1  VISA                                                       34.00             1882.89
    114   JUNE 3  WARDS                                                      23.00             1859.89
    115   JUNE 4  P.SCOTT DEPT STORE                                         40.00             1819.89
    116   JUNE 10 AMERICAN EXPRESS                                          110.00             1709.89
  ------------------------------------------------------------------------------------------------------
                TOTALS:        450.00   152.16    0.00     45.00  131.45   361.50  2000.00
```

Listing

```
>A  4:"CHECK #          >A12:/FL106
>A  5:/FI              >A13:/FL107
>A  6:/FL101           >A14:/FL108
>A  7:/FL102           >A15:/FL109
>A  8:/FL              >A16:/FL110
>A  9:/FL103           >A17:/FL111
>A10:/FL104            >A18:/FL112
>A11:/FL105            >A19:/FL113
```

>A20:/FL114
>A21:/FL115
>A22:/FL116
>A23:/--

>B 4:"DATE
>B 6:"MAY 1
>B 7:"MAY 7
>B 8:"MAY 15
>B 9:"MAY 17
>B10:"MAY 18
>B11:"MAY 18
>B12:"MAY 19
>B13:"MAY 20
>B14:"MAY 20
>B15:"MAY 21
>B16:"MAY 23
>B17:"MAY 25
>B18:"MAY 29
>B19:"JUNE 1
>B20:"JUNE 3
>B21:"JUNE 4
>B22:"JUNE 10
>B23:/--

>C 1:"PERSONAL
>C 3:"ISSUE/DEP
>C 4:"DESCRIPTI
>C 6:"ELECTRIC
>C 7:"GAS
>C 8:"PAY CHECK
>C 9:"RENT
>C10:"GROCERY
>C11:"SUBSCRIPT
>C12:"DENTIST
>C13:"DOCTOR
>C14:"DRUG STOR
>C15:"D. HENDRI
>C16:"INSURANCE
>C17:"TELEPHONE
>C18:"MASTER CH
>C19:"VISA
>C20:"WARDS
>C21:"P.SCOTT D
>C22:"AMERICAN
>C23:/--

>D 1:"CHECK REG
>D 3:"OSIT
>D 4:"ON
>D11:"ION
>D14:"E
>D15:"CKS
>D18:"ARGE
>D21:"EPT STORE

>D22:"EXPRESS
>D23:/--
>D24:"TOTALS:

>E 1:"ISTER
>E 3:"CHECK AMO
>E 4:"RENT
>E 9:450
>E23:/--
>E24:@SUM(E6...E23)

>F 3:"UNT OF CH
>F 4:"MEDICAL
>F12:45
>F13:37.6
>F14:14.56
>F16:55
>F23:/--
>F24:@SUM(F6...F23)

>G 3:"ECK - - -
>G 4:"ENTERTAIN
>G23:/--
>G24:@SUM(G6...G23)

>H 3:" BY CATEG
>H 4:/FR"FOOD
>H10:45
>H23:/--
>H24:@SUM(H6...H23)

>I 3:"ORY
>I 4:/FR"UTILITY
>I 6:10
>I 7:12
>I17:109.45
>I23:/--
>I24:@SUM(I6...I23)

>J 4:/FR"OTHER
>J11:18.5
>J15:79
>J18:57
>J19:34
>J20:23
>J21:40
>J22:110
>J23:/--
>J24:@SUM(J6...J23)

>K 4:/FR"DEPOSIT
>K 8:2000
>K23:/--
>K24:@SUM(K6...K23)

```
>L  4:/FR"BALANCE
>L  5:850
>L  6:+L5+K6-@SUM(E6...J6)
>L  7:+L6+K7-@SUM(E7...J7)
>L  8:+L7+K8-@SUM(E8...J8)
>L  9:+L8+K9-@SUM(E9...J9)
>L10:+L9+K10-@SUM(E10...J10)
>L11:+L10+K11-@SUM(E11...J11)
>L12:+L11+K12-@SUM(E12...J12)
>L13:+L12+K13-@SUM(E13...J13)
>L14:+L13+K14-@SUM(E14...J14)
>L15:+L14+K15-@SUM(E15...J15)
>L16:+L15+K16-@SUM(E16...J16)
>L17:+L16+K17-@SUM(E17...J17)
>L18:+L17+K18-@SUM(E18...J18)
```

```
>L19:+L18+K19-@SUM(E19...J19)
>L20:+L19+K20-@SUM(E20...J20)
>L21:+L20+K21-@SUM(E21...J21)
>L22:+L21+K22-@SUM(E22...J22)
>L23:/--

>M  5:" <BALANCE

>N  5:" FORWARD>

/GC9
/GF$
/GOC
/GRA
/W1
```

168

PERSONAL INSURANCE REQUIREMENTS

This model will help estimate how much insurance coverage is required to provide financial security for a family. It is limited to life insurance only. Because incomes, numbers of dependents, and lifestyles change continually, any calculations performed in this model should be regarded solely as estimates.

The three main concerns of family insurance planning are coverage for dependent children, coverage for a spouse (both before and after social security benefits), and coverage when social security benefits are not available. This lapse in social security payments is defined at the Blackout area in this model.

You can use some of the totals from the Net Worth Statement model to estimate the Clean-Up and Debt Payoff amount; you should include probate costs and last illness and death expenses, if possible. Also, be sure to include group and association life insurance benefits in your Less Current Insurance amount.

This model uses the net present value of money to assist you in evaluating actual current insurance needs against future financial requirements. You can easily perform "what if" analysis by changing any of the numbers you enter.

PRINT A1...J45

Listing

```
>A  6:"INTEREST
>A  8:/--
>A10:"PERIOD OF
>A11:"COVERAGE
>A13:/--
>A15:"CHILD
>A16:"REARING
>A17:/--
>A18:"SOCIAL
>A19:"SECURITY
>A20:"BLACKOUT
>A21:/--
>A22:"AFTER
>A23:"AGE
>A24:"    60
>A25:/--
>A27:"TOTALS

>B  3:"INSURANCE
>B  4:/--
>B  6:"INVESTMEN
>B  8:/--
>B  9:"! INCOME
>B10:"! NEEDED
>B11:"!PER MNTH
>B12:"!
>B13:/--
>B15:1250
```

```
>B17:/--
>B19:750
>B21:/--
>B23:850
>B25:/--
>B27:@SUM(B14...B24)
>B28:/-=

>C  3:" REQUIREM
>C  4:/--
>C  6:"T RATE %:
>C  8:/--
>C  9:"!SOCIAL
>C10:"!SECURITY
>C11:"! $/MNTH
>C12:"!
>C13:/--
>C15:550
>C17:/--
>C19:"    NONE
>C21:/--
>C23:250
>C25:/--
>C27:@SUM(C14...C24)
>C28:/-=

>D  3:"ENTS
>D  4:"------
```

Model Run

```
         INSURANCE REQUIREMENTS    PREPARED FOR: JOHN SMITH
         ----------------------    DATE: 10-15-81


  INTEREST INVESTMENT RATE %:        6.5                              WORK AREA
                                                                      ---------
                                                                          %
  !-----------------------------------------------------------------!
  !          ! INCOME !SOCIAL  !(+ OR -)! NUMBER ! TOTAL  ! PRESENT! AMOUNT  !
  !PERIOD OF ! NEEDED !SECURITY! PER     ! OF YRS !   $    ! VALUE  !COVERAGE !
  !COVERAGE  !PER MNTH! $/MNTH ! MONTH   ! NEEDED ! NEEDED !  OF    ! NEEDED  !
  !          !        !        !         !        !        !COVERAGE!         !
  !-----------------------------------------------------------------!


  CHILD
  REARING     1250     550      700        10     84000 70205.42 70205.42       .065
            ----------------------------------------------------


  SOCIAL
  SECURITY    750     NONE      750        30    270000 224249.9 224249.9
  BLACKOUT
            ----------------------------------------------------


  AFTER
  AGE         850      250      600      LIFE      96000 80036.89 80036.89
    60
            ----------------------------------------------------


                            TOTAL AMOUNT OF INSURANCE
  TOTALS     2850     800          NEEDED FOR INCOME    $ 374492.2
           ==================       REPLACEMENT         ---------


                            CLEAN-UP & DEBT PAYOFF       25000
                                                       ---------


                            MORTGAGE REDEMPTION          12500
                                                       ---------


                            TOTAL INSURANCE COVERAGE
                                 REQUIRED             $ 411992.2
                                                       =========


                            LESS CURRENT INSURANCE     150000
                                                       ---------


                            ADDITIONAL INSURANCE
                                 REQUIRED             $ 261992.2
                                                       =========
```

```
>D 6:6.5                    >D15:+B15-C15
>D 8:/--                    >D17:/--
>D 9:"!(+ OR -)             >D19:+B19-C19
>D10:"! PER                 >D21:/--
>D11:"! MONTH               >D23:+B23-C23
>D12:"!                     >D25:/--
>D13:/--
```

```
>E  3:"PREPARED                    >G15:@NPV(J15,D15...F15)
>E  4:"DATE: 10--                  >G17:/---
>E  8:/---                         >G19:@NPV(J15,D19...F19)
>E  9:"! NUMBER                    >G21:/---
>E10:"! OF YRS                     >G23:@NPV(J15,D23...F23)
>E11:"! NEEDED                     >G25:/---
>E12:"!                            >G26:"SURANCE
>E13:/---                          >G27:"COME        $
>E15:10                            >G30:"YOFF
>E17:/---                          >G33:"N
>E19:30                            >G36:"VERAGE
>E21:/---                          >G37:"           $
>E23:"  LIFE                       >G40:"ANCE
>E25:/---                          >G43:"CE
>E26:"TOTAL AMOU                   >G44:"           $
>E27:"     NEED
>E28:"     REPL                    >H  8:/---
>E30:"CLEAN-UP                     >H  9:"! AMOUNT
>E33:"MORTGAGE                     >H10:"!COVERAGE
>E36:"TOTAL INS                    >H11:"! NEEDED)
>E37:"     REQU                    >H12:"!
>E40:"LESS CURR                    >H13:/---
>E43:"ADDITIONA                    >H15:+G15
>E44:"     REQU                    >H17:/---
                                   >H19:+G19
>F  3:"FOR: JOHN                   >H21:/---
>F  4:"15-81                       >H23:+G23
>F  8:/---                         >H25:/---
>F  9:"! TOTAL                     >H27:@SUM(H15...H24)
>F10:"!    $                       >H28:/---
>F11:"! NEEDED                     >H30:25000
>F12:"!                            >H31:/---
>F13:/---                          >H33:12500
>F15:+D15*E15*12                   >H34:/---
>F17:/---                          >H37:@SUM(H27...H33)
>F19:+D19*E19*12                   >H38:/-=
>F21:/---                          >H40:150000
>F23:+D23*160                      >H41:/---
>F25:/---                          >H44:+H37-H40
>F26:"UNT OF IN                    >H45:/-=
>F27:"ED FOR IN
>F28:"ACEMENT                      >I  8:"!
>F30:"& DEBT PA                    >I  9:"!
>F33:"REDEMPTIO                    >I10:"!
>F36:"URANCE CO                    >I11:"!
>F37:"IRED                         >I12:"!
>F40:"ENT INSUR                    >I13:"!
>F43:"L INSURAN
>F44:"IRED                         >J  6:"WORK AREA
                                   >J  7:/---
>G  3:" SMITH                      >J  8:"       %
>G  8:/---                         >J15:+D6/100
>G  9:"! PRESENT
>G10:"! VALUE                      /GC9
>G11:"!    OF                      /GOC
>G12:"!COVERAGE                    /GRA
>G13:/---                          /W1
```

HOUSEHOLD AIDS

EVENTS SCHEDULING

This model will help you schedule events for any evening's entertainment. You can use it to plan talent shows, dinners, convention seminars, or musical accompaniment. With the data entered here, the model is being used to schedule starting times for records to be played at a party.

To begin, you are required to enter a Time Chart for the elapsed time of your event. Depending on how precisely you must plan the components of the evening, you can segment the chart into any increments of time — seconds, minutes, quarter hours, and so forth. In the model we use five-minute increments. Starting with 0 minutes at 7 o'clock, we add 5 to the previous line and replicate down both columns. This creates a chart with 100 minutes to the hour, so we simply change the time where necessary to make the chart reflect the clock. For instance, where the chart should show 760, we change it to 800. The formula causes all succeeding times to change accordingly. At 860, we enter 900, and so on.

Once you have set the Time Chart, you must enter the elapsed time for each component of the evening or event. The model will schedule its starting time.

PRINT A1. . .J51

Listing

```
>A  6:"RECORD NA        >A18:"   NUMBER        >A30:"   NUMBER
>A  7:"   NUMBER        >A19:"   NUMBER        >A31:"   NUMBER
>A  8:"   NUMBER        >A20:"   NUMBER
>A  9:"   NUMBER        >A21:"   NUMBER        >B  6:"ME
>A10:"   NUMBER         >A22:"   NUMBER        >B  7:/FL1+B6
>A11:"   NUMBER         >A23:"   NUMBER        >B  8:/FL1+B7
>A12:"   NUMBER         >A24:"   NUMBER        >B  9:/FL1+B8
>A13:"   NUMBER         >A25:"   NUMBER        >B10:/FL1+B9
>A14:"   NUMBER         >A26:"   NUMBER        >B11:/FL1+B10
>A15:"   NUMBER         >A27:"   NUMBER        >B12:/FL1+B11
>A16:"   NUMBER         >A28:"   NUMBER        >B13:/FL1+B12
>A17:"   NUMBER         >A29:"   NUMBER        >B14:/FL1+B13
```

Model Run

```
                      EVENTS SCHEDULING
                      ====== ==========                    TIME CHART
                                                            0        7
                              TOTAL  APPROX.                5      705
                      RUNNING ELAPSED START    PERSON      10      710
                      TIME    MINUTES TIME     ASSIGNED    15      715
    RECORD NAME                                            20      720
      NUMBER   1      5          5      7      JOHN         25      725
      NUMBER   2      4          9    705                   30      730
      NUMBER   3      5         14    710                   35      735
      NUMBER   4      8         22    715                   40      740
      NUMBER   5      3.5       25.5  720                   45      745
      NUMBER   6      4.5       30    725                   50      750
      NUMBER   7      6         36    730                   55      755
      NUMBER   8      8.25      44.25 735                   60      800
      NUMBER   9      2         46.25 745                   65      805
      NUMBER  10      3         49.25 745                   70      810
      NUMBER  11      5.5       54.75 750                   75      815
      NUMBER  12      8         62.75 755                   80      820
      NUMBER  13      1.5       64.25 800      AL           85      825
      NUMBER  14      2         66.25 805                   90      830
      NUMBER  15      3.5       69.75 805                   95      835
      NUMBER  16      6.5       76.25 810                  100      840
      NUMBER  17      3         79.25 815                  105      845
      NUMBER  18      1         80.25 820                  110      850
      NUMBER  19      3.5       83.75 820                  115      855
      NUMBER  20      8.5       92.25 820                  120      900
      NUMBER  21      4.5       96.75 830                  125      905
      NUMBER  22      4        100.75 835                  130      910
      NUMBER  23      7        107.75 840                  135      915
      NUMBER  24     10        117.75 845                  140      920
      NUMBER  25      4.5      122.25 855                  145      925
                                                          150      930
                                                          155      935
                                                          160      940
                                                          165      945
                                                          170      950
                                                          175      955
                                                          180     1000
                                                          185     1005
                                                          190     1010
                                                          195     1015
                                                          200     1020
                                                          205     1025
                                                          210     1030
                                                          215     1035
                                                          220     1040
                                                          225     1045
                                                          230     1050
                                                          235     1055
                                                          240     1100
```

```
>B15:/FL1+B14          >E 9:+E8+D9
>B16:/FL1+B15          >E10:+E9+D10
>B17:/FL1+B16          >E11:+E10+D11
>B18:/FL1+B17          >E12:+E11+D12
>B19:/FL1+B18          >E13:+E12+D13
>B20:/FL1+B19          >E14:+E13+D14
>B21:/FL1+B20          >E15:+E14+D15
>B22:/FL1+B21          >E16:+E15+D16
>B23:/FL1+B22          >E17:+E16+D17
>B24:/FL1+B23          >E18:+E17+D18
>B25:/FL1+B24          >E19:+E18+D19
>B26:/FL1+B25          >E20:+E19+D20
>B27:/FL1+B26          >E21:+E20+D21
>B28:/FL1+B27          >E22:+E21+D22
>B29:/FL1+B28          >E23:+E22+D23
>B30:/FL1+B29          >E24:+E23+D24
>B31:/FL1+B30          >E25:+E24+D25
                       >E26:+E25+D26
>D 1:"EVENTS SC        >E27:+E26+D27
>D 2:"====== ==        >E28:+E27+D28
>D 5:"RUNNING          >E29:+E28+D29
>D 6:"TIME             >E30:+E29+D30
>D 7:/FL5              >E31:+E30+D31
>D 8:/FL4
>D 9:/FL5              >F 4:/FR"APPROX.
>D10:/FL8              >F 5:/FR"START
>D11:/FL3.5            >F 6:/FR"TIME
>D12:/FL4.5            >F 7:@LOOKUP(E7-D7+1,I3...I36)
>D13:/FL6              >F 8:@LOOKUP(E8-D8+1,I3...I36)
>D14:/FL8.25           >F 9:@LOOKUP(E9-D9+1,I3...I36)
>D15:/FL2              >F10:@LOOKUP(E10-D10+1,I3...I36)
>D16:/FL3              >F11:@LOOKUP(E11-D11+1,I3...I36)
>D17:/FL5.5            >F12:@LOOKUP(E12-D12+1,I3...I36)
>D18:/FL8              >F13:@LOOKUP(E13-D13+1,I3...I36)
>D19:/FL1.5            >F14:@LOOKUP(E14-D14+1,I3...I36)
>D20:/FL2              >F15:@LOOKUP(E15-D15+1,I3...I36)
>D21:/FL3.5            >F16:@LOOKUP(E16-D16+1,I3...I36)
>D22:/FL6.5            >F17:@LOOKUP(E17-D17+1,I3...I36)
>D23:/FL3              >F18:@LOOKUP(E18-D18+1,I3...I36)
>D24:/FL1              >F19:@LOOKUP(E19-D19+1,I3...I36)
>D25:/FL3.5            >F20:@LOOKUP(E20-D20+1,I3...I36)
>D26:/FL8.5            >F21:@LOOKUP(E21-D21+1,I3...I36)
>D27:/FL4.5            >F22:@LOOKUP(E22-D22+1,I3...I36)
>D28:/FL4              >F23:@LOOKUP(E23-D23+1,I3...I36)
>D29:/FL7              >F24:@LOOKUP(E24-D24+1,I3...I36)
>D30:/FL10             >F25:@LOOKUP(E25-D25+1,I3...I36)
>D31:/FL4.5            >F26:@LOOKUP(E26-D26+1,I3...I36)
                       >F27:@LOOKUP(E27-D27+1,I3...I36)
>E 1:"HEDULING         >F28:@LOOKUP(E28-D28+1,I3...I36)
>E 2:"========         >F29:@LOOKUP(E29-D29+1,I3...I36)
>E 4:/FR"TOTAL         >F30:@LOOKUP(E30-D30+1,I3...I36)
>E 5:/FR"ELAPSED       >F31:@LOOKUP(E31-D31+1,I3...I36)
>E 6:/FR"MINUTES
>E 7:+E6+D7            >H 5:"PERSON
>E 8:+E7+D8            >H 6:"ASSIGNED
```

>H 7:"JOHN
>H19:"AL

>I 2:"   T
>I 3:0
>I 4:+I3+5
>I 5:+I4+5
>I 6:+I5+5
>I 7:+I6+5
>I 8:+I7+5
>I 9:+I8+5
>I10:+I9+5
>I11:+I10+5
>I12:+I11+5
>I13:+I12+5
>I14:+I13+5
>I15:+I14+5
>I16:+I15+5
>I17:+I16+5
>I18:+I17+5
>I19:+I18+5
>I20:+I19+5
>I21:+I20+5
>I22:+I21+5
>I23:+I22+5
>I24:+I23+5
>I25:+I24+5
>I26:+I25+5
>I27:+I26+5
>I28:+I27+5
>I29:+I28+5
>I30:+I29+5
>I31:+I30+5
>I32:+I31+5
>I33:+I32+5
>I34:+I33+5
>I35:+I34+5
>I36:+I35+5
>I37:+I36+5
>I38:+I37+5
>I39:+I38+5
>I40:+I39+5
>I41:+I40+5
>I42:+I41+5
>I43:+I42+5
>I44:+I43+5
>I45:+I44+5
>I46:+I45+5
>I47:+I46+5
>I48:+I47+5
>I49:+I48+5
>I50:+I49+5
>I51:+I50+5

>J 2:"IME CHART

>J 3:/FR7
>J 4:/FR705
>J 5:/FR710
>J 6:/FR715
>J 7:/FR720
>J 8:/FR725
>J 9:/FR730
>J10:/FR735
>J11:/FR740
>J12:/FR745
>J13:/FR750
>J14:/FR755
>J15:/FR800
>J16:/FR805
>J17:/FR810
>J18:/FR815
>J19:/FR820
>J20:/FR825
>J21:/FR830
>J22:/FR835
>J23:/FR840
>J24:/FR845
>J25:/FR850
>J26:/FR855
>J27:/FR900
>J28:/FR905
>J29:/FR910
>J30:/FR915
>J31:/FR920
>J32:925
>J33:930
>J34:935
>J35:940
>J36:945
>J37:950
>J38:955
>J39:1000
>J40:1005
>J41:1010
>J42:1015
>J43:1020
>J44:1025
>J45:1030
>J46:1035
>J47:1040
>J48:1045
>J49:1050
>J50:1055
>J51:1100

/GC9
/GOC
/GRA
/W1

VACATION TOUR PLANNER

This VisiCalc model is ideal for planning a trip by car. With this model, you can route your tour in advance and estimate how much that vacation will cost.

The mileage between cities can be obtained from any map. As the model shows, the starting point was Chicago. From there to Cincinnati (the first stop on the tour), there is a distance of 293 miles. From Cincinnati to Pittsburgh the distance is 284 miles. Further down the list, from Washington to Springfield, Illinois, the distance is 758 miles. Between cities expenses are entered for traveling.

The Lodging, Food, and Fun Costs are totaled from your estimates. By totaling the mileage entries, and averaging in the price of gasoline and the gas mileage of your car, you can calculate the approximate costs for gasoline.

PRINT A1...G43

Listing

```
>A  3:"STARTING
>A  7:"DAY #
>A  8:/-=
>A  9:/FL+A7+1
>A10:/FL+A9+1
>A11:/FL+A10+1
>A12:/FL+A11+1
>A13:/FL+A12+1
>A14:/FL+A13+1
>A15:/FL+A14+1
>A16:/FL+A15+1
>A17:/FL+A16+1
>A18:/FL+A17+1
>A19:/FL+A18+1
>A20:/FL+A19+1
>A21:/FL+A20+1
>A22:/FL+A21+1
>A23:/FL+A22+1
>A24:/FL+A23+1
>A25:/FL+A24+1
>A26:/--
>A29:"TOTL DAYS
>A30:"TOTL MLS
>A32:"HYWAY MIL
>A33:"AVG COST/

>B  3:"POINT:
>B  7:"DATE
>B  8:/-=
>B  9:"OCT 1
>B10:"OCT 2
>B11:"OCT 3
>B12:"OCT 4
>B13:"OCT 5
>B14:"OCT 6
```

```
>B15:"OCT 7
>B16:"OCT 7
>B17:"OCT 8
>B18:"OCT 9
>B19:"OCT 10
>B20:"OCT 11
>B21:"OCT 12
>B22:"OCT 13
>B23:"OCT 14
>B24:"OCT 15
>B25:"OCT 16
>B26:/--
>B29:@COUNT(A9...A25)
>B30:@SUM(D9...D25)
>B32:"ES/GALLON
>B33:"GALLON
>B36:"PROJECTED

>C  1:/FR"VACATION
>C  3:"CHICAGO
>C  7:"DESTINATN
>C  8:/-=
>C  9:"CINCINAT
>C10:"PITTSBUR
>C11:"PHILA
>C12:"PHILA
>C13:"PHILA
>C14:"NEW YORK
>C15:"NEW YORK
>C16:"NEW YORK
>C17:"NEW YORK
>C18:"BOSTON
>C19:"BOSTON
>C20:"TRAVEL'G
>C21:"WASHINGTN
```

Model Run

```
                  VACATION TOUR PLANNER

    STARTING POINT:   CHICAGO

                                  ROAD
                                  MILES    <COST ESTIMATES>
    DAY # - DATE     DESTINATN  BETWEEN  LODGING    FOOD     FUN
    ==============================================================
    1      OCT 1     CINCINAT      293    60.00    25.00    50.00
    2      OCT 2     PITTSBUR      284    60.00    30.00    50.00
    3      OCT 3     PHILA         305    75.00    35.00   100.00
    4      OCT 4     PHILA                75.00    35.00   100.00
    5      OCT 5     PHILA                75.00    35.00   100.00
    6      OCT 6     NEW YORK       93    75.00    60.00   150.00
    7      OCT 7     NEW YORK             75.00    60.00   150.00
    8      OCT 7     NEW YORK             75.00    60.00   150.00
    9      OCT 8     NEW YORK             75.00    60.00   150.00
    10     OCT 9     BOSTON        216    75.00    50.00   100.00
    11     OCT 10    BOSTON               75.00    50.00   100.00
    12     OCT 11    TRAVEL'G             60.00    50.00   100.00
    13     OCT 12    WASHINGTN     437    75.00    50.00   100.00
    14     OCT 13    TRAVEL'G             60.00    25.00    50.00
    15     OCT 14    TRAVEL'G             60.00    25.00    50.00
    16     OCT 15    SPRNGFLD      758     0.00     0.00    50.00
    17     OCT 16    CHICAGO       193     0.00    25.00     0.00

    --------------------------------------------------------------


    TOTL DAYS       17
    TOTL MLS      2579

    HYWAY MILES/GALLON    22.5
    AVG COST/GALLON       1.34


         PROJECTED COSTS:

                    GAS    153.59
                   FOOD    675.00
                LODGING   1050.00
                    FUN   1550.00
                         ---------
                  TOTAL   3428.59
```

>C22:"TRAVEL'G   >C36:" COSTS:
>C23:"TRAVEL'G   >C38:/FR"GAS
>C24:"SPRNGFLD   >C39:/FR"FOOD
>C25:"CHICAGO   >C40:/FR"LODGING
>C26:/--   >C41:/FR"FUN
>C32:22.5   >C43:/FR"TOTAL
>C33:1.34

```
>D  1:"  TOUR PLA              >F17:/F$60
>D  5:/FR"ROAD                 >F18:/F$50
>D  6:/FR"MILES                >F19:/F$50
>D  7:/FR"BETWEEN              >F20:/F$50
>D  8:/-=                      >F21:/F$50
>D  9:293                      >F22:/F$25
>D10:284                       >F23:/F$25
>D11:305                       >F24:/F$0
>D14:93                        >F25:/F$25
>D18:216                       >F26:/--
>D21:437
>D24:758                       >G  6:"S>
>D25:193                       >G  7:/FR"FUN
>D26:/--                       >G  8:/-=
>D38:/F$(B30/C32)*C33          >G  9:/F$50
>D39:/F$@SUM(F9...F25)         >G10:/F$50
>D40:/F$@SUM(E9...E25)         >G11:/F$100
>D41:/F$@SUM(G9...G25)         >G12:/F$100
>D42:/--                       >G13:/F$100
>D43:/F$@SUM(D38...D41)        >G14:/F$150
                               >G15:/F$150
                               >G16:/F$150
>E  1:"NNER                    >G17:/F$150
>E  6:"     <COST              >G18:/F$100
>E  7:/FR"LODGING              >G19:/F$100
>E  8:/-=                      >G20:/F$100
>E  9:/F$60                    >G21:/F$100
>E10:/F$60                     >G22:/F$50
>E11:/F$75                     >G23:/F$50
>E12:/F$75                     >G24:/F$50
>E13:/F$75                     >G25:/F$0
>E14:/F$75                     >G26:/--
>E15:/F$75
>E16:/F$75
>E17:/F$75                     >H  9:/F$
>E18:/F$75                     >H10:/F$
>E19:/F$75                     >H11:/F$
>E20:/F$60                     >H12:/F$
>E21:/F$75                     >H13:/F$
>E22:/F$60                     >H14:/F$
>E23:/F$60                     >H15:/F$
>E24:/F$0                      >H16:/F$
>E25:/F$0                      >H17:/F$
>E26:/--                       >H18:/F$
                               >H19:/F$
                               >H20:/F$
>F  6:"  ESTIMATE              >H21:/F$
>F  7:/FR"FOOD                 >H22:/F$
>F  8:/-=                      >H23:/F$
>F  9:/F$25                    >H24:/F$
>F10:/F$30
>F11:/F$35
>F12:/F$35                     /GC9
>F13:/F$35                     /GOC
>F14:/F$60                     /GRA
>F15:/F$60                     /W1
>F16:/F$60
```

PAINT A ROOM

This model estimates the cost of painting a single room. The height, width, and length of the room provide the overall area to be painted. Windows, archways, doors, and trim, are then listed as exclusions. The ceiling is calculated on width and height. Trim consists of door jambs, window frames, and other areas to be painted separately.

Costs for each area are calculated on the area's measurements (less exclusions for the room itself), the number of coats to be applied, the cost per gallon of paint, and the square footage covered by one gallon (which is usually listed on the can by the manufacturer).

The result is the number of gallons needed and the cost of the paint. Added to this is the amount to be spent on supplies. The final result is a cost estimate for the room.

The model could be augmented with time estimates and the value of your time per hour. This would allow you to compare the cost of contracting for the job with the cost of doing it yourself.

PRINT A1...H42

Listing

```
>A  4:"ROOM DIME
>A  7:"WINDOWS/A
>A  8:"AND OTHER
>A  9:"EXCLUSION
>A13:"CEILING:
>A15:"DOORS:
>A17:"TRIM:
>A23:/--
>A25:"SUPPLIES:
>A34:"ROOM:
>A35:"CEILING:
>A36:"TRIM:
>A37:"DOORS:

>B  4:"NSIONS:
>B  7:"RCHWAYS
>B  9:"S:
>B23:/--
>B25:/FR"BRUSHES
>B26:18.5
>B32:/FR"AREA
>B34:/F$+F5-@SUM(F8...F11)
>B35:+F13
>B36:@SUM(F18...F21)
>B37:@SUM(F15...F16)

>C  1:"PAINT A RE
>C  4:"HEIGHT
>C  5:/FL8
>C  8:/FL5
>C  9:/FL6
>C10:/FL4
>C11:/FL6.5
```

Model Run

```
                    PAINT A ROOM


ROOM DIMENSIONS:  HEIGHT   WIDTH    LENGTH        AREA
                    8        15       25        640.00


WINDOWS/ARCHWAYS
AND OTHER           5        3.5                 17.50
EXCLUSIONS:         6        3                   18.00
                    4        2                    8.00
                    6.5      3.75                24.38


CEILING:                                        375.00


DOORS:              6        3                   18.00
                    5        3.5                 17.50

TRIM:
                             .25      18          4.50
                             .25      17          4.25
                             .3       17          5.10
                             .3       18          5.40


----------------------------------------------------------


SUPPLIES:  BRUSHES    PANS  ROLLERS   OTHER    TOTAL
            18.50    22.00   45.00    35.00    85.50




                                  SQ FEET    COST
                                  COVERED     PER  GALLONS    AREA
           AREA     COLOR   COATS  (1 GAL)  GALLON  NEEDED    COST


ROOM:      572.13   WHITE      3   140.00   18.50   13.76   254.56
CEILING:   375.00   BLUE #2    2   120.00   24.00    7.25   174.00
TRIM:       19.25   BLUE #4    3   145.00   25.00    1.90    47.46
DOORS:      35.50   BLUE #3    3   150.00   20.00    2.21    44.20
                                                   --------------
                                  SUB-TOTALS:       22.91   476.01

                  TOTAL COST INCLUDING SUPPLIES:            561.51
```

```
>C15:/FL6                      >C36:/FR"BLUE #4
>C16:/FL5                      >C37:/FR"BLUE #3
>C18:/FL
>C23:/--                       >D 1:"OOM
>C25:/FR"PANS                  >D 4:"WIDTH
>C26:22                        >D 5:/FL15
>C32:/FR"COLOR                 >D 8:/FL3.5
>C34:/FR"WHITE                 >D 9:/FL3
>C35:/FR"BLUE #2               >D10:/FL2
```

```
>D11:/FL3.75              >F16:+C16*D16
>D13:/FR                  >F18:+D18*E18
>D15:/FL3                 >F19:+D19*E19
>D16:/FL3.5               >F20:+D20*E20
>D17:/FL                  >F21:+D21*E21
>D18:/FL.25               >F23:/--
>D19:/FL.25               >F25:/FR"TOTAL
>D20:/FL.3                >F26:@SUM(B26...D26)
>D21:/FL.3                >F30:/FR"COST
>D23:/--                  >F31:/FR"PER
>D25:/FR"ROLLERS          >F32:/FR"GALLON
>D26:45                   >F34:18.5
>D32:/FR"COATS            >F35:24
>D34:/FI3                 >F36:25
>D35:/FI2                 >F37:20
>D36:/FI3                 >F39:"TOTALS:
>D37:/FI3                 >F41:"NG SUPPLI
>D41:"TOTAL COST
                          >G13:/FR
>E 4:"LENGTH              >G15:/FR
>E 5:/FL25                >G19:/FR
>E13:/FR                  >G23:/--
>E18:/FL18                >G31:/FR"GALLONS
>E19:/FL17                >G32:/FR"NEEDED
>E20:/FL17                >G34:+D34*((B34/E34)+.5)
>E21:/FL18                >G35:+D35*((B35/E35)+.5)
>E23:/--                  >G36:+D36*((B36/E36)+.5)
>E25:/FR"OTHER            >G37:+D37*((B37/E37)+.5)
>E26:35                   >G38:/--
>E30:/FR"SQ FEET          >G39:@SUM(G34...G36)
>E31:/FR"COVERED          >G41:"ES:
>E32:/FR" <1 GAL>
>E34:140                  >H31:/FR"AREA
>E35:120                  >H32:/FR"COST
>E36:145                  >H34:+G34*F34
>E37:150                  >H35:+G35*F35
>E39:/FR"SUB-             >H36:+G36*F36
>E41:"T INCLUDI           >H37:+G37*F37
                          >H38:/--
>F 4:/FR"AREA             >H39:@SUM(H34...H36)
>F 5:(2*D5*C5)+(2*E5*C5)  >H41:+F26+H39
>F 8:+C8*D8
>F 9:+C9*D9               /GC9
>F10:+C10*D10             /GF$
>F11:+C11*D11             /GOC
>F13:+D5*E5               /GRA
>F15:+C15*D15             /W1
```

About the Authors

David M. Castlewitz and **Lawrence J. Chisausky** together manage a company called 20th Century Business Systems, a Chicago-based systems house that develops "turnkey" applications software for Apple II and Apple III computers. They aim to make the computers friendly and easy to use, and to dispel the mystique that often surrounds computers for the novice or infrequent user. This, they believe, gives their company an advantage over competitors who swamp the user with computer buzz words. These authors also claim to manage their company using some of the VisiCalc models presented here.

Mr. Castlewitz is also a co-author of *Some Common Basic Programs, Apple II Edition* (Berkeley: Osborne/ McGraw-Hill, 1981), having converted the book's original BASIC programs to Applesoft.

Patricia Kronberg has experience in retail management, marketing support, and editorial work. She has at times been responsible for sales merchandising, product promotion and display, and inventory control.

L.D. Chukman specializes in the fine arts, and works as an illustrator and journalist. He received his Bachelor of Fine Arts degree from the Art Institute of Chicago.